CONCILIUM

THEOLOGY IN THE AGE OF RENEWAL

CONCILIUM

CONCILIUM/VOL. 10

SCRIPTURE

THE
HUMAN
REALITY
OF
SACRED
SCRIPTURE

Volume 10

CONCILIUM
theology in the age of renewal

PAULIST PRESS
NEW YORK, N.Y. / GLEN ROCK, N.J.

Library of Congress Catalogue Card Number: 65-28869

Suggested Decimal Classification: 291.8

BOOK DESIGN: Claude Ponsot

Paulist Press assumes responsibility for the accuracy of the English translations in this Volume.

PAULIST PRESS
EXECUTIVE OFFICES: 304 W. 58th Street, New York, N.Y. and 21 Harristown Road, Glen Rock, N.J.
Executive Publisher: John A. Carr, C.S.P.
Executive Manager: Alvin A. Illig, C.S.P.
Asst. Executive Manager: Thomas E. Comber, C.S.P.

EDITORIAL OFFICES: 304 W. 58th Street, New York, N.Y.
Editor: Kevin A. Lynch, C.S.P.
Managing Editor: Urban P. Intondi

Printed and bound in the United States of America by
The Colonial Press Inc., Clinton, Mass.

CONTENTS

PREFACE 1
Pierre Benoit, O.P./Jerusalem, Jordan
Roland E. Murphy, O. Carm./Washington, D.C.
Bastiaan van Iersel, S.M.M./Nijmegen, Netherlands

PART I

ARTICLES

INSPIRATION AND REVELATION 6
Pierre Benoit, O.P./Jerusalem, Jordan
Translated by
David H. Connor

THE BOOK OF THE PEOPLE OF GOD 25
Bastiaan van Iersel, S.M.M./Nijmegen, Netherlands
Translated by
Theodore L. Westow

THE PERICOPE AND PREACHING 39
Heinrich Kahlefeld/Munich, W. Germany
Translated by
Tarcisius Rattler, O.S.A.

THE TORAH OF MOSES AND
CHRIST AS SAVIOR 52
Henri Cazelles, S.S./Paris, France
Translated by
Robert J. Bolanos, S.J.

GOD'S FIRST AND LAST WORD: JESUS
(MARK 1, 1-13 and JOHN 1, 1-18) 75
Johannes Willemse, O.P./Nijmegen, Netherlands
Translated by
David T. LeFort

THE PEOPLE OF GOD
ACCORDING TO EPH. 1, 3-14 96
Franz Mussner/Trier, W. Germany
Translated by
Eileen O'Gorman, R.S.C.J.

PART II

BIBLIOGRAPHICAL SURVEY

RECENT LITERATURE ON THE PROPHETS 112
Bruce Vawter, C.M./St. Louis, Mo.
THE WISDOM LITERATURE
OF THE OLD TESTAMENT 126
Roland E. Murphy, O. Carm./Washington, D.C.

PART III

DO-C: DOCUMENTATION CONCILIUM

FAMILY PLANNING AND LATIN-AMERICAN
PROBLEMS: PERSPECTIVES IN 1965 142
Gustavo Pérez Ramírez/Bogotá, Colombia
Translated by
Paul Burns

PART IV

CHRONICLE OF THE LIVING CHURCH

AGGIORNAMENTO IN THE MISSION FIELD 165
BIOGRAPHICAL NOTES 171
SUBJECT INDEX (CONCILIUM: Vol. 1–Vol. 10) 173

PREFACE

Pierre Benoit, O.P./*Jerusalem, Jordan*
Roland E. Murphy, O.Carm./*Washington, D. C.*
Bastiaan van Iersel, S.M.M./*Nijmegen, Netherlands*

The whirlwind development of Catholic biblical science can be attributed only partly to the discovery of new extra-biblical documents for comparative study, to the far-reaching improvement in methods of scientific research and to intensive contacts with other Christian exegetes. Just as important as all these factors is the change of climate that has taken place in contemporary thought. In many sciences, one notices a heightened concern for concrete reality and, especially, for man and his world. Theology, too, has felt the results of this change of climate and more than ever before has turned to involvement with the concrete realities of man and world, strongly supporting further developments, begun long before, in scientific exegesis of the Bible.

For several decades now, the human aspects of the Scriptures have demanded attention. The interest of exegetes tends more clearly than ever before toward the intentions of the various authors of the books of the Bible. Before asking questions on a theological level, they examine painstakingly the texts of Sacred Scripture with the help of classical and modern methods of literary analysis. This means, in fact, that the human reality of Sacred Scripture is taken quite seriously. Behind this lies the conviction that it is only through the human dimensions of the Scriptures that we can gain access to the meaning of God's Word

1

which has taken shape in the Bible. It may be considered obvious, therefore, that a tension has arisen between the accepted conclusions of classical theology on the one hand and, on the other, the newer textual interpretations which seemingly disagree with classical positions. We cannot avoid the questions arising out of this tension.

More recently, still another aspect of this human reality has become clearer than ever before: by reason of advances in the study of man, we take more account now of the fact that each individual is bound in many ways to his environment. Every person can be considered to a certain degree representative of the community to which he belongs. This insight influences exegesis. Apparently the authors of the Bible generally express less of their personal outlook than of the traditions of the community of believers in which they have taken root. In this way the accent has shifted: both the *formgeschichtliche* and the *traditionsgeschichtliche Methode* take particular interest in that community of believers where the texts have originated and in the then current traditions worked into those texts. For this very reason, the Bible becomes recognizable as the book of the People of God in its literary-historical aspect as well. And although the *redaktionsgeschichtliche Methode*—with its questions concerning the private views and intentions of the actual authors or final editors—has restored the balance, many questions are still raised with regard to the collective features so deeply involved in the origin of the Sacred Scriptures. We may not bypass these questions either, especially when they have consequences for pastoral theology.

Still, in those volumes of CONCILIUM allotted to it, it cannot be the only function of the section on Sacred Scripture to present such questions. For they resemble the tops of icebergs rising visibly above the water; to approach them without danger, one must know what lies beneath. Thus, attention must be given in equal measure to the dynamic evolution of basic traditions within the Scriptures themselves. For it is just this dynamism within the Bible that exemplifies the modern *aggiornamento*.

Finally, there must be special concern for whatever may be fruitful in the area of pastoral theology, in the broadest sense of the term. In particular, the exegesis already employed in the Scriptures for making past facts present ("re-presentation" or "actualization"), would seem to be of great value in proclaiming the Gospel today. Perhaps in this way the somewhat isolated movement in biblical circles can be better integrated into the life of the Church, which may thereby receive new impulses for the effective use of the Bible as the book of the People of God for this day and age.

The CONCILIUM volume on Scripture raises matters of fundamental importance. The first article deals with inspiration and revelation; in these two words are summed up everything that the Bible has always meant to the Church. The ideas associated with these terms are studied in depth and modified in the light of contemporary insights. The second article develops one of the conclusions of the foregoing study and emphasizes that Sacred Scripture is the book of the People of God. Recent literary-historical research has made it impossible to sketch a history of how the Bible came to be a history showing clearly that the Bible arose as the book of the People of God. The Church did not acknowledge the traditions of her belief merely after the fact—in a book produced outside of herself—but rather she recognized her traditions there because it was in the Bible that the Israel of old and the primitive Church had expressed themselves in the written word.

So it is that theological and literary-historical investigations are converging lines that meet at one point: The Bible is the book of the People of God. This implies, however, that the Scriptures must continue their role in the Church of today and tomorrow and, indeed, especially where the Church is actually assembled as the People of God, i.e., in the celebration of the liturgy. Of course, only a very small part of the whole Bible can be read and made actual through preaching at any given liturgical service. H. Kahlefeld's article takes up this very point and deals with bible-text and sermon.

In the next three articles, this basic information is illustrated with several scriptural passages in which the same factors are present: the Word of God addressed to the People of God. H. Gazelles sheds light on the figure of Moses. J. Willemse offers a commentary on the prologue of St. John's Gospel, which expresses clearly that God personally has spoken and continues to speak of Jesus. F. Mussner's study of Ephesians 1, 3–14 shows how the People of God is called and kept together by God's Word and Spirit.

The two articles concerning the prophetical books and the wisdom writings are not unrelated to the general topic of this volume. In a certain sense, they represent two extremes in Sacred Scripture. In the prophetical books, countless sayings present themselves as the express and actual Word of God; inspiration and revelation are recognizable here in the highest degree. The wisdom writings, on the other hand, contain Israel's own reflections on questions about man and the world. They do not claim, as the prophetical corpus does, to be revelation, yet they form part of the Word of God.

The treatment of these basic problems clears the ground for a discussion of the manifold and difficult questions arising from contemporary scriptural investigations, and lays the foundation for an acquaintance with modern methods of research and their conclusions insofar as they affect systematic and pastoral theology.

PART I

ARTICLES

Pierre Benoit, O.P./*Jerusalem, Jordan*

Inspiration and Revelation

I

INSPIRATION

1. *The Faith of the Church and the Teachings of the Magisterium*

The Church has always had the conviction that she was the possessor of sacred writings wherein she heard the Word of God, the guide of her faith and conduct. She has made progress, however, in the formulation and explanation of this divine gift.

In the beginning, the Church received from the synagogue, through the mediation of Jesus and the apostles, the "Holy Scriptures" (Matt. 22, 29; Rom. 1, 2), where the "Word of God" was to be found, the Word which could not be broken (John 10, 35) but rather had to be fulfilled (Matt. 26, 54; John 13, 18). It is God who speaks through the mouth of Moses (Mark 12, 26) or of the Prophets (Luke 1, 70). Making use of Jewish formulas, the New Testament cites the Old in expressions such as "God has spoken" (2 Cor. 6, 16), "he says" (2 Cor. 6, 2) or "the Scripture says" (Rom. 4, 3), "it is written" (Matt. 4, 4). At times a reference to the Holy Spirit is explicit (Matt. 22, 43; Acts 1, 16; 28, 25), especially in 2 Peter 1, 20ff. and in 2 Timothy 3, 16; the latter text even uses the technical term *theopneustos:* "inspired by God".

In the New Testament and in the Fathers of the Church, the "Scripture" refers to the Old Testament. But soon the Church noted that she had received from Christ's followers new writings which have no less authority than the older writings, and which

6

in fact fulfill the older writings and provide the definitive statement of revelation. This conviction is expressed as early as 2
Peter 3, 16 where St. Paul's letters are compared to "the rest of
the Scriptures". This assertion is made from the beginning of
the 2nd century with the establishment of a "Canon" of sacred
books over which the Church is considered the authority and
norm.

And yet, though the new writings crown the old, they do not
suppress them, as the Gnostics and Manichaeans contended,
attributing the Jewish writings to an inferior, even evil, God. The
Church rejected their view in maintaining the unity of the two
Testaments; it is in answer to their theories, moreover, that there
appears in the documents of the magisterium, in the 5th and 6th
centuries, the notion of God as the "author" of the Old as well
as the New Testament.[1]

Taking up this statement in its Decree on the Jacobites
(1441), the Council of Florence further justified it in declaring
that the same Spirit has inspired the authors of the two Testaments.[2] The term "inspiration" which appears here for the first
time in the documents of the magisterium is far from new. We
have already come upon its equivalent in the New Testament.
It is traditional in the Fathers as well, and was to be used by the
Council of Trent in an analogous phrase: *Spiritu Sancto dictante.*

But it is not until the 19th century that the teaching authority
went any further in explaining the *nature* of inspiration. At that
time certain errors were threatening the doctrine. The rise of the
physical and historical sciences had drawn attention to the limitations and deficiencies of certain matters that fell within the
province of the Bible; it became urgent to present a better definition of the human activity responsible for the Bible, while at the
same time protecting the efficaciousness of the divine influence
directing the human work. Some tended to minimize the one and

[1] Cf. Augustine Cardinal Bea, "Deus Auctor Sacrae Scripturae: Her-
kunft und Bedeutung der Formel," in *Angelicum* 20 (1943), pp. 16–31.
[2] *Enchiridion Biblicum* (^{3}1956), 47: "quoniam eodem Spiritu Sancto
inspirante utriusque Testamenti sancti locuti sunt".

exaggerate the other. Vatican Council I reacted to the controversy by rejecting certain faulty concepts of inspiration which reduced it to a subsequent approbation by God of a previous human work, or to a simple preservation from error. The Council reaffirmed the traditional teaching of an inspiration of the Holy Spirit which caused the sacred books to be written and made God their author.[3]

The encyclical *Providentissimus* went further. It was intent on analyzing the activity of the divine influence on the faculties of the human author, an influence so encompassing that the author could clearly conceive, faithfully envision and surely execute a work of which God was truly the author and which expressed his infallible truth. According to a theory already elaborated by the Fathers and the scholastic theologians, the author acts like an "instrument" manipulated by the principal author, God.[4]

To see this teaching from another aspect, we may look at the encyclical *Spiritus Paraclitus*. It emphasizes, following St. Jerome, the way in which the divine influence, preventing the human interpreter from teaching any error, still does not hinder him in any way from expressing himself in a manner consonant with his own talents and cultural background.[5]

Following up this argument, the encyclical *Divino afflante Spiritu* insists upon the need for understanding, through competent literary criticism, the Eastern modes of speech in ancient (biblical) times (so different from our own); only in this way is it possible to understand what the author intended to say and to teach. This is the primary norm of interpretation. Thus many groundless misgivings about error in the Bible would fade away.[6]

Vatican Council II has impressed this upon us anew in the Schema for the Constitution: *De Divina Revelatione,* discussing and confirming the assertions of previous documents which had

[3] *Ibid.,* 77.
[4] *Ibid.,* 125.
[5] *Ibid.,* 448.
[6] *Ibid.,* 556–60.

come to be cited.[7] The Council reaffirmed that the inspiration of the sacred books means that God is their author,[8] that the two Testaments are unified,[9] that there is a sovereign action of the divine influence upon all the faculties of the human interpreter,[10] that the inspiration of Scripture is integral and that an infallible teaching flows from it,[11] and that it is necessary to examine closely the human language that God has seen fit to be used in his service. Thus we may see his intentions better through those of the sacred writer, and refrain from calling something erroneous when it is only a manner of speaking peculiar to some time and place.[12]

The official declarations of the teaching authority of the Church establish the essential principles of the Christian faith. They do not presume to invalidate the speculations of theologians, who remain free. Such speculations have, in fact, been borne out upon two major topics. One deals with the manner of conceiving or understanding the concurrence of the two causes of Scripture, the divine and the human. Some envision this concurrence in a rather anthropomorphic manner as though it were a collaboration in which God has his role (the ideas) and man his (the words); others adopt a more theological viewpoint in speaking of a kind of subordination where the human instrument is controlled entirely by the divine agent in such a way that the effect produced, the book, is entirely the work both of God and of the human author, each in different respects. According to this second theory, the author has truly furnished, knowingly and freely, all that is in the book, the thoughts as well as their literary expression; but the divine influence has gripped him in a manner so supremely efficacious that these thoughts and this expression are definitely from God himself, the first author.[13]

[7] References are to the Schema of the Constitution presented at the third session of Vatican Council II (1964).
[8] Chap. 3, §11.
[9] Chap. 4, §16.
[10] Chap. 3, §11.
[11] Ibid.
[12] Chap. 3, §12.
[13] Cf. P. Synave and P. Benoit, La Prophétie (Paris: Editions de la

Another more pressing area where research is being carried on touches upon a more precise distinction between inspiration (a charism of guidance and practical execution) and revelation (a charism of illumination and understanding).[14] Instead of considering all inspiration as a perception of divine truth, some judge it fitting to reserve this to "revelation"—then the concomitant charism of "inspiration" would be traced to that impulse which is responsible for the discovery, formulation and communication of the message which transmits the content of revelation. This last viewpoint takes note of the fact that St. Thomas (whose genius has provided many guiding principles in this area) had formally analyzed only the specific instance of prophetic revelation and not scriptural inspiration in general. His treatment employed the distinction between "speculative judgment" and "practical judgment". But rather than push this scholastic discussion any further (for it is not in keeping with this study), it seems more desirable to address ourselves to the data of the Bible itself, data much neglected, which seem of their nature better able to situate the question in a new light.

2. *Varied Richness of Inspiration, according to Biblical Data*[15]

The Scriptures do, indeed, speak profusely of the divine gift of inspiration, but in a manner sufficiently flexible and subtle as to deserve further study.

First it is true to say that the technical term "inspiration" is used sparingly in the Scriptures and not at all in the Old Testament. In its place it makes use of various other formulas: the

---

Revue des Jeunes, 1947). American edition: *Prophecy and Inspiration* (New York, 1961).

[14] Cf. P. Benoit, "Révélation et Inspiration selon la Bible, chez saint Thomas et dans les discussions modernes," in *Revue Biblique* 70 (1963), pp. 321–70. English translation: *Inspiration and the Bible* (London, 1965).

[15] Cf. P. Benoit, "Les analogies de l'Inspiration," in *Sacra Pagina, Miscellanea Biblica Congressus Internationalis Catholici de Re Biblica* I (Paris: Gembloux, 1959), pp. 86–99; cf. the article cited in the previous note, pp. 343–6.

INSPIRATION AND REVELATION 11

Spirit is "in" the one inspired, or "upon" him; it "dwells upon" him, "rests upon" him, "comes into" him, "covers" him, etc. The idea underlying these various images is that of an appropriation, a divine power taking possession of a man and driving him irresistibly to do something in God's behalf.

But the action that so elevates a man is not at first an impulse to write a book. It is important to remember this second fact. The writing will come, but later on; and in the Old Testament it is never directly attributed to the influence of the Holy Spirit. The Spirit moves a man first of all to act and also to speak.

Often the Spirit takes hold of a man to have him perform certain acts from which the history of the chosen people takes shape. It is the Spirit who gives Moses and the men of old the mandate of leading the people during the exodus (Num. 11, 17 and 25; cf. Is. 63, 11 and 13); he dwells in Joshua conquering the Promised Land (Num. 27, 18); he pours life into a Gideon (Judg. 6, 34), a Jephthah (Judg. 11, 29), a Samson (Judg. 14, 6 and 19; 15, 14), all of whom delivered the oppressed people of Israel by their courageous deeds. It is he who, after having aroused Saul (1 Sam. 10, 6–10; 11, 6) and then having departed from him (1 Sam. 16, 14), "rests upon" David at the time he is anointed King (1 Sam. 16, 13); he waits to settle in all his fullness upon the offspring of the root of Jesse (the Messiah-King), who will rule over the People of God in justice and peace (Is. 11, 1ff.; cf. 42, 1ff.; 61, 1ff.). It is quite fitting to speak in all of these instances of a kind of "pastoral" inspiration, which guides the "shepherds" of the chosen people, and through them shapes the sacred history which prepares for the salvation of the Messiah.

The Spirit also makes a man speak out. The people must hear the Word which unravels the meaning of the works of God,[16]

[16] Vatican Council II, Schema for the Constitution: *De Revelatione*, Chap. 1, §2: "The economy of revelation is brought about by deeds and words which are intrinsically related in such a way that the works (performed by God in the history of salvation) show forth and support the teaching and the reality signified by the words; the words, however, proclaim the works and throw light upon the mystery contained in them."

reveals to them the purpose and the appeal of God's inmost thoughts, sets forth his commandments for them and implants in their hearts the call to follow him. The prophets are the messengers who carry the Word to the ears of the people; to effect this, the Spirit pours his life into them. He rests upon Ezekiel and makes him speak (Ez. 11, 5), puts the words of God into the mouth of Isaiah and those who followed him (Is. 59, 21), fills Micah with strength, justice and courage (Mic. 3, 8). Hosea is a "man of the Spirit" (Hos. 9, 7). The ministry of the prophets is the work of the Spirit (Zech. 7, 12; Neh. 9, 30). Through gifts of this sort the Messianic era is prepared, the era when the Holy Spirit will pour himself out upon all men (Joel 3, 1–2), an outpouring which St. Peter saw realized on Pentecost (Acts 2, 16ff.). This gift of the Word, which accompanies and explains the gift of action, might be said to represent another aspect of inspiration (which could be called "oral") accompanying and completing "pastoral" inspiration.

In addition, one follows upon the other, and they find their flowering at the time of the fullness of revelation in Christ. Jesus commissioned his apostles to preach the Gospel and to found the Church, not to write books. It is once more the Holy Spirit who directs these new shepherds and prophets who are Christ's apostles. The Holy Spirit guides the missionary activity of Philip (Acts 8, 29 and 39), of Peter (Acts 10, 19ff.; 11, 12), of Paul (Acts 13, 2 and 4; 16, 6ff.), and "has placed them as bishops to rule the Church of God" (Acts 20, 28). It is he who, according to the promise of Jesus (Matt. 10, 19ff.), inspires in the apostles the words of conquest and of defense of the faith (Acts 2, 4; 4, 8; 13, 9). It is he who, through his "charisms", bestows different gifts upon Christians, gifts of action and of speech, and he who builds up the community (1 Cor. 12, 4–11). In the new economy as well as in the old (but now in all its fullness), the Spirit inspires the deeds and living words which illuminate and direct the People of God in their journey toward salvation.

Furthermore, in the new economy and the old, the writings appear later in order to establish a remembrance of those things

that were said and done. God had once given the command to
Moses (Ex. 17, 14; 34, 27), to Joshua (Josh. 24, 26), to
Samuel (1 Sam. 10, 25), to Isaiah (Is. 30, 8), to Jeremiah
(Jer. 30, 2), to Habakkuk (Hab. 2, 2), and to Daniel (Dan. 12,
4) and in this way there was set up the canonical collection of
the "Law of Moses, the Prophets and the Psalms" which constituted "the Scriptures" (Luke 24, 44ff.). The apostolic message
is to arise from this very source: after having preached and having founded the Church, the apostles and their followers will set
in writing the essential elements of the message in order to safe-
guard it, preserve it and pass it on to future generations. In this
way a new collection of writings will soon take its place beside
the old; and with the old law it will confer a "changeless character" upon the "highest rule of faith", a character that will always
inhere in it.[17]

But it is remarkable that, in the New Testament (Apoc. 1, 11
and 19ff.) as well as in the Old, the divine mandate to write is
never explicitly connected with the Holy Spirit. This is a fact
which demands consideration. There is no question here of cast-
ing doubt upon "scriptural" inspiration; this teaching, established by Judaism, formally summarized in 2 Timothy 3, 16,[18]
has already been accepted by the Church, insured by her teaching authority and spelled out by her theologians. It is, as it were,
the crown and necessary consequence of all the activity of inspiration which preceded it. And precisely for this reason it is
important to connect inspiration to its antecedents and to retain,
so to speak, its historic setting. To isolate the inspiration of the
Bible from its inspired preparation in Action and Word is to run
the risk of sterilizing the Bible by reifying it, to make it as barren
as an abstract textbook, a collection of terse, private "truths"

---

[17] Chap. 6, §21: "The Church has always maintained that these sacred
writings, together with tradition, are the highest rule of her faith. For
they are not only inspired by God (thus setting forth the very Word of
God), but they also bring before her eyes that changeless character of
the rule of faith."
[18] It should be noted that 2 Peter 1, 20ff. still looks upon Scripture in
the context of prophetic speech.

which, torn from the soil that nourished them, can only deceive; again, it is to reify the Bible as though it were a preexistent Torah derived from a branch of Judaism, or an Islamic Koran, a book fallen from the sky, whose human origins and appointments have been lost.

"Scriptural" inspiration has nothing to fear from seeing itself put back into the great pattern of "biblical" inspiration of which it is a part, next to and following "pastoral" and "oral" inspiration. On the contrary, it can only stand to gain by benefiting from a realism which completes it. Before being written, the message was first lived and spoken: this experience of life and this concrete speaking still reverberate in the text. They are concentrated there, by God's will, in an astonishing terseness; but they precede the text, accompany it, follow it, overflow it and explain it. For all this richness comes from the same Spirit.

The problem of tradition[19] can be usefully illuminated in three ways. First we may look at the confrontation of the Catholic argument by the Protestant problematic. The Reformers reified the Scriptures as the sole source of revelation, at the same time rejecting tradition. From the beginning, the Council of Trent answered them by establishing that both the Scripture and tradition were inspired.[20] But when, in the 19th century, this view was in turn attacked (tradition no longer being an issue), it was to defend and to explain the inspiration of Scripture that the declarations of the magisterium and the efforts of theologians were directed; they did not, however, address themselves directly

---

[19] It should be clearly understood that we are speaking here of the *apostolic* tradition which begins with the teaching of the apostles and rises toward the era of Revelation not yet closed.

[20] *Enchiridion Biblicum* ([3]1956), 57: "(And we perceive) that this truth and teaching (the Gospel of Jesus Christ) is contained in written books and in unwritten traditions. They have come to us either as received by the apostles from the mouth of Christ, or from the apostles themselves under the prompting (*dictante*) of the Holy Spirit." The Council of Trent decreed that the Church received the writings of the Old and New Testaments, and "also those traditions dealing with faith and morals either from the mouth of Christ, so to speak, or through the promptings of the Holy Spirit. These traditions are preserved in an unending continuity in the Catholic Church."

to the question of the inspiration of tradition. Though tradition was not abandoned, still the explanation of its nature did not much benefit from these new and more precise explanations.

To reinstate in emphasis the inspiration of tradition side-by-side with the inspiration of the Scriptures will surely be of great value in delineating more sharply the subtle interchange (*échange*) that marks their relationship; they are not two sources from which parallel streams, different "truths", emanate, but rather two ways of talking about the same inspired current of truth—part of it lived and spoken, the other written. This one truth controls the faith and practice of the Church in a rich, two-fold manner, the Word guaranteed by the text, and the text animated by the ever-living Word.[21]

The Schema for the Constitution *De Divina Revelatione* of Vatican Council II seems to stress this orientation of meaning when it rightly associates (in many places, especially in chapter 2) the preaching of the apostles, nourished by the teachings of Christ and by the promptings of the Holy Spirit, with the inspired writing which followed the preaching.[22] It is a clear invitation to hear, confronted by the "splendid witness" (*testimonium eximium*) of Scripture, the "evangelical preaching" which is the life of the Scriptures and which was itself directed by the Holy Spirit.[23]

---

[21] Vatican Council II, Schema for the Constitution: *De Revelatione,* Chap. 2, §9: "Tradition and Sacred Scripture are closely connected, and mutually correspondent. For both, proceeding from the same divine source, somehow coalesce and are directed toward the same goal. Sacred Scripture is the Word of God put in writing under the influence of the Holy Spirit. Tradition, however, is made up of the ideas (*mens*) and teaching and example and commands of Christ faithfully passed down, with the help of the Holy Spirit, through the apostles and their followers." The Council insistently associates tradition and Scripture: Chap. 2, §7; §8; §10; Chap. 6, §21; §24.

[22] Chap. 2, §7: The Gospel of Christ is passed down "both by the apostles who, in their preaching, by their example and their works (*institutionibus*) pass down what they received from the mouth, conduct and works of Christ; and also by apostolic men who, endowed with a certain charism, and inspired by the same Holy Spirit, put in writing the message of salvation". Cf. also Chap. 5, §18; Chap. 6, §21.

[23] Chap. 6, §21; Chap. 5, §20.

3. *Inspiration is not "collective", but it is for the "Assembly" of the Faithful: The Scripture is the Book of the People of God.*

Understood in the fullness that we have outlined in behalf of biblical data, inspiration has assumed a social significance (*valeur*) rising from the concept of "Church". This is another consequence that deserves attention.

Sometimes reference is made to a "collective" inspiration, but the expression is not apt. It brings to mind a charism given to the assembly as such; or it arises from a rather questionable, even false, philosophy of sociology which would impart to a group an autonomous, overriding existence which submerges the individual. This is contrary to the facts: the community does not exist by itself, it is not of itself the source of creative activity; on the contrary, it relies upon and benefits from the gifted individuals who guide its destiny. What is true of the entire human community is, *a fortiori,* true of a people elevated and guided by God. Thus the Schema for the Constitution *De Divina Revelatione* rejects the notion of "a creative power emanating from a primitive community";[24] and it reasserts that, in order to compose the holy books, "God chose men" whom he directed, etc.[25] In fact, those who would be pastors, prophets, apostles and writers, are always privileged individuals whom the Spirit has seized and made use of. Carrying the argument a bit further, we could show that these individuals were numerous, more numerous than we might ever guess: a good many hands contributed to the actual shaping of the Pentateuch or the Gospels. But the number and anonymity of these biblical workers does not gainsay the fact that they were individuals, moved by the Spirit to carry their stone, big or small, and contribute it to building up the monument of revelation. They were all "charismatics". Seen in this light, inspiration cannot be called "collective".

Once this is certainly established, it remains no less true that inspiration is destined for the good of the assembly. It is to

[24] Chap. 5, §19: ". . . proceeding from the creative potency of the primeval community."
[25] Chap. 3, §11.

instruct and to inform his people that God has entrusted a mission to some of its members. Salvation is collective; men are grouped together in sin and in grace. All men died in the spiritual death of the First Adam, and they must rediscover life in the New Adam, Christ, whose body they form. Doubtless each man has his own destiny for which he is personally responsible. He does not, however, go to God by himself; he goes there with a group of men from whom he benefits and to whom he gives. That is why God formed for himself a people in order to save the individual members of this people, and through them all, of humankind.[26] He reveals his name to them, makes them understand his plan of salvation, gives them laws and institutions, chastises them and raises them up in order to bring them up in his love; and he does all this through his chosen intermediaries, men whom he elevates and to whom he imparts his Spirit. His inspired pastors help him to form sacred history; his inspired prophets form the spirit and conscience of his people; his inspired writers gather up all that is essential and entrust it to books that are passed on to succeeding generations.

Seen in this light, scriptural inspiration ceases to be the charism of one isolated individual working in a vacuum and taking down on paper "truths" wafted to his ears. It is the last moment of a long thrust of the Spirit which, after having forged a divine-human exploit which reaches its peak in the coming of the Son and, after having announced in diverse manners the message of the Father up to the time of the last appeals of his Son (Heb. 1, 1), places all this in sacred writings which are to reach men of all times and all places. The Scriptures cease to be a collection of more or less timeless truths like those which so many religions offer; instead it becomes the book of a people, a people ageless and holy; it becomes a "family record", a chronicle always fresh that records God's actions and the challenges he presents to his children. The Bible is truly the book of a chosen People, the Church.

[26] Chap. 4, §14: "God, in his great love and concern for the salvation of the human race, by a singular dispensation chose for himself a people to whom he entrusted certain promises."

II

REVELATION

Revelation is the immediate corollary of inspiration, its end and effect, a different aspect of, but connected with, the same charism. It is different, because it is the manifestation of an inscrutable mystery, while inspiration is a practical impulse to live, speak and write with a view to searching out this mystery. Revelation is related to the charism of inspiration because this same search, stimulated and guided by inspiration, ends in the knowledge of revelation. They are rightly associated because there exist in God both Spirit and Word; it is through the dynamic and creative breath of his Spirit that God causes his Word to be heard and realized (2 Sam. 23, 2; Is. 59, 21; Matt. 10, 20; John 14, 24–6; 16, 13). What we have already said about inspiration will enable us to understand better the nature of revelation.[27]

1. *Revelation is an active discovery by the human spirit illuminated by the Holy Spirit.*

To begin with, revelation should not be understood as the divine truth breaking into a purely passive mind like a prediction uttered by the Pythian oracle in a frenetic state, deprived of clear conceptual powers; nor should it be regarded as a preexisting Torah or a prefabricated Koran falling from the sky into a man's hands. Biblical revelation is, rather, the living perception of the Word, the flowering that comes from the intense reaction of a man's mind raised up by the Spirit of God and transported by this Spirit to the very limits of its powers.

Undoubtedly, the initiative is to be found in God. To him, and to him alone, belongs the discovery of the mystery when and how he wishes. His light is most important, and it will happen that its burning brilliance will dismay and terrify the human being it strikes. Isaiah felt "doomed" when he saw the thrice-holy

[27] Cf. P. Benoit, *loc. cit., Revue Biblique* 70 (1963), pp. 336–43, 347–49, 367–70.

God in the temple (Is. 6, 1–5); Jeremiah, called by God, appealed to his own weakness (Jer. 1, 4–6); Daniel and Paul fell to the earth, senseless (Dan. 8, 17–18) or blinded (Acts 9, 3–9). But even in these extreme cases when the divine broke in on man's life, the man, inspired, understood and obeyed: Isaiah offers himself as the divine messenger (Is. 6, 8); Jeremiah declares himself mastered and conquered by God (Jer. 20, 7–9); Paul rises and starts out to win the world (Acts 9, 18–20).

More often it happens in another way. Sweetly and slowly the divine light brings the human spirit to maturity in understanding the divine teaching. Hagiographers have drawn out at great length from the pages of history the great rules of justice and love which have motivated the conduct of God toward his people.[28] The theologian who takes up the wonderful story of the creation and the fall has to meditate profoundly on human suffering and evil in the world, before understanding, enlightened by the Holy Spirit, the revealed solution to this tragic puzzle.

2. *Revealed truth in the Bible is concrete, personal,
   complete, a truth of life.*

What God opens up to man in this way is not an abstract truth, purely speculative, the conclusion of a kind of Greek philosophy. It is a truth of life, more existential than essential, if one understands these terms correctly. The hebrew word *emeth* that we translate "truth" means primarily, *solidity, fidelity.* This divine attribute evokes in the heart of man the basic response of faith and love.[29] Yet, *understanding* surely plays an important role here, too, an understanding desired not just for its own sake, shutting itself off to savor its own pleasures; rather, it is an understanding of life, directed toward the salvation of all men. "To know" God, in its biblical usage, is to love him and to walk

---

[28] Schema for the Constitution: *De Revelatione*, Chap. 4, §15: (The books of the Old Testament) "make it clear to all men how the just and merciful God dealt with mankind."
[29] Chap. 1, §5.

holily in his paths. To know Jesus is "to follow him", for he is "the way and the truth and the life" (John 14, 5).

God does not reveal himself in the dictation of abstract truths; it is through "words and deeds" that he reveals himself as the "one God, living and true", permitting his people to "experience the ways of God with men".[30] If Christ the Lord is the consummation of all divine revelation,[31] it is due not only to his teachings, but also and above all to his life, death and resurrection:[32] from "his mouth, his conversation, his works", the apostles grasp those things that they pass on "in preaching, in examples and in institutions".[33]

In a word, biblical revelation is not merely the manifestation of this or that divine secret, dreamed up by authors of apocalypses, but a personal encounter with a living God, an encounter which reaches its peak in the union of faith and love with the incarnate Word. "Philip, he who sees me sees also the Father" (John 14, 9).

This is why the biblical message is in a language so simple; not employing complicated speculation, it is universal, accessible to men of all cultures. It is not limited (like the "revelations" of so many non-Christian religions) to certain social or political directives, to wise maxims or narrations of pious legends or spiritual favors, touching only upon superficial questions of life on this earth; it enlightens man about the fundamental problem of his salvation, offering him not only light from on high but also the strength to make up his mind. Hence biblical revelation

[30] Chap. 4, §14: "He revealed himself in words and actions as the one, true, living God, so that Israel might understand the ways of God with man."

[31] Chap. 2, §7: "Christ the Lord, in whom the complete revelation of the most high God is perfected. . . ."

[32] Chap. 1, §4: "Wherefore he completed and perfected revelation by his words and his works, by signs and miracles (especially his death and his glorious resurrection from the dead), and by sending the Spirit of Truth, and by his own person." Cf. Chap. 5, §17.

[33] Chap. 2, §7; cf. Chap. 5, §§19, 20: In the apostolic writings of the New Testament "the saving strength of Christ's divine work is preached, and an account of the founding and wonderful spread of the Church is given."

is the zenith of truth and power,[34] touching man in its entirety, bringing him true and sure consolation from a divine hand which stretches forth to gather him into the bosom of the Father in union with the Son.

3. *Biblical revelation is progressive, leading man away from ignorance and sin to the fullness of truth and salvation.*

This discovery of the truth, this personal encounter with God the creator and Savior, is not brought about by the Spirit in a trice, by a sudden, magical transformation which would be in-human. Speaking to man in his darkness and in the weakness of his sin, God speaks in man's own language and adopts his own slow ways. The fathers of the Council express this wonderfully: the divine "condescension" employs a painstaking "pedagogy".[35]

Down through the vicissitudes of sacred history, after so many words tirelessly repeated and finished, until the remembrance of himself is finally established in the Scriptures, God adapts him-self to the lowly capacities of his rebellious children, uncovering to them the secrets of his heart a little at a time, setting them right gradually, steadily. He does not overwhelm them from the outset with a light so brilliant that they cannot look upon it; he does not show them all of his truth immediately. He does not even tell them of certain "truths" to believe. Instead he invites them, questions them, draws them out, coaxes them, allows them to be involved in sublime and in tragic experiences. In stages seemingly out of joint but, in God's exalted wisdom, really wonderfully rhythmical, he leads them step-by-step up to the day when they will be capable of hearing his incarnate Word and of receiving his spirit in its fullness.

Thus the astonishing variety of the Bible is explained, and explained, too, are its apparent deficiencies and its obvious splendors. Everything in the Bible is inspired, but not everything is revealed. Or, to be more precise, the entire work builds up to

[34] Chap. 1, §4: "The Christian economy therefore does not point to a passing phase in religious history; it is the very last and definitive period."
[35] Chap. 3, §13; Chap. 4, §15.

a full revelation which disengages itself from the whole; but each detail, though it be inspired, does not contain in addition a revelation commanding the assent of faith. To maintain otherwise would only lead to scandal and would harm the wise discretion of God. Vatican Council II sums up the matter concisely: The Books of the Old Testament contain a great many things that are "imperfect and provisional", yet still teach Christians the meaning of "the true pedagogy of God".[36] The Council also teaches this golden rule of hermeneutics: to gain a proper understanding of the meaning of the sacred texts one must continually survey the entire content of Scripture, in the living tradition of the Church and under the analogy of faith.[37] This is the key law of context, and of the larger context. What is said in one place in the Bible will be said elsewhere in another manner. To lead men toward the perception of his mystery, God proceeds dialectically, by a succession of indirect moves, in the face of apparent discord; the synthesis, once made, reveals beneath the superficial, trivial obstacles the basic permanent unity of the truth that is taught. It is the difficult but admirable task of exegesis (crowned by biblical theology) to realize this synthesis.[38]

It is along these lines that we must situate the explicitation of the revealed notions supplied by Scripture and tradition; theologians down through the centuries have devoted themselves to this pursuit and, guided by the teaching authority of the Church, have expressed themselves in new formulations of the dogma. There is no question here of adding substantially new truths to revelation (which was completed at the close of the apostolic era),[39] but rather of perceiving more distinctly and expressing more sharply what was once given in the definitive encounter

[36] Chap. 4, §15: "The books of the Old Testament, even though they contain much that is imperfect and provisional, are of importance even to Christ's faithful in setting down the divine teaching."
[37] Chap. 3, §12: "In order to derive the real meaning from the sacred texts, it is necessary to look at the content of the entire Sacred Scriptures, as it is found in the living tradition of the Church, under the analogy of faith."
[38] Chap. 6, §23.
[39] Chap. 2, §10: "The magisterium of the Church is not above the Word of God; it serves that Word, and teaches only what is passed down."

with the incarnate God. As we noted previously, this was not merely a collection of teachings to be received and preserved as such; it was also, and above all, a contact with life achieved through deeds, examples and institutions as well as through teachings.[40] The apostolic tradition living in the Church is based upon this "intimate experience of spiritual things".[41]

When tradition comments upon and explains Scripture, it is not by adding to it this or that particular truth which would be transmitted only orally; it is by employing this "sense of faith" given to the Church by the Spirit, which authorizes the Church and moves her, over the course of centuries, to contemplate and to express—in new ways adapted to changing times, places and diverse cultures—the eternal, inexhaustible treasure entrusted to her. Many centuries have been necessary to understand with more clarity the mystery of Christ, in his person and in his two natures of God and man. Subsequently, the Church directed her attention toward other mysteries—that of Mary, for example; when she proclaimed new dogmas on this subject, she was really only forming a better expression of what she had always believed, not perhaps in clear notions, but in that unsettling experience that the Church has always had of the role of Mary in the work of her Son.

The Church can and should do this, because she still possesses that same Spirit who inspired revelation.[42] This holy People has lived, spoken the Word, and written the Scriptures. Established by Christ to keep and present the faith to all men till the end of time, the Church has the authority of the magisterium whose teaching is ensured against error.[43] Under her maternal and unerring guidance, the inspired book (nourished by the lived and

---

[40] Chap. 2, §9: Cf. the texts cited in footnotes 22, 32 and 33.

[41] Chap. 2, §8: "This living tradition in the Church progresses with the help of the Holy Spirit. For it grows by reason of its understanding of the realities and of the words handed down; it grows because of the contemplation of the faithful who bear these things in their hearts (cf. Luke 2, 19 and 51), and it grows through its intimate experience of spiritual realities."

[42] Chap. 2, §8: "The Holy Spirit, who makes the living voice of the Gospel resound in the Church, and (through the Church) in the world."

[43] Chap. 2, §10; cf. Chap. 3, §12.

living Word which it bears, and which, in turn, supports it) will never cease offering to men of goodwill the revelation from which forever flows their life, their light and their holiness.[44]

"Chap. 2, §8: "That which is passed down by the apostles includes all those things which bring holiness of life and an increase of faith to the People of God; thus the Church, in her teaching, her life, and her liturgy perpetuates all these things and passes them down to each generation. For this is all that she possesses and all that she believes." Chap. 6, 21: "There is such strength and force in the Word of God that it provides, for all the Church's sons, energy for their faith, food for their spirits, and a fountain of living water for the life of their souls."

Bastiaan van Iersel, S.M.M./*Nijmegen, Netherlands*

The Book of the People of God

The reality of Sacred Scripture, like any other reality, can be approached from different angles. Each angle of approach will obviously show a new aspect and so lead to a different view. These different and diverging views sometimes appear to be contradictory, but we know that they are actually complementary and that the true and complete image of the reality can only be apprehended at the point where they converge.

Christian tradition has always regarded the Scriptures principally as Sacred Scripture, the sacred books, the inspired writings, God's Word. These expressions contain essential aspects of the Scriptures that cannot be ignored without loss. They express the aspect of faith that sees the Scriptures as coming from God.

But one can also approach the Bible from its empirical aspects, that is, those aspects that are accessible to positive science, and this may lead to a "faithful" interpretation of what the Scriptures mean to us. In this case the Bible may be described as "The Book of the People of God". And while this description can never claim a monopoly, it is, nevertheless, an important complement to the description of the Bible as "The Word of God". As "The Book of the People of God", the Bible has a place among other books. It also allows us to distinguish it from

25

those other books and will tell us something about the way in which it came into being. Lastly, it also shows the function of the book once it has come to be completed.

The Bible as Book

However much the Bible may be beyond our grasp as the Word of God, it is very much within our grasp as the book with a place, alone or among other books, on the shelves of millions of Christian homes of all denominations, and which has its place in all churches where Christians meet. It is there for anyone who can read, and, as such, it is a book like any other book. This aspect is by no means theologically irrelevant. It is just as important as the fact that Jesus of Nazareth is truly man among other men. It means, among other things, that the Bible exists as a book also for those who do *not* look on it as the Word of God. And this implies that those who *do* look on it as such should not overlook this aspect. They cannot look on the Bible, whether in theory or in practice, as a writing that has come down straight from heaven as the Mormons look on the Book of Mormon. Unfortunately, this is done occasionally as demonstrated by the legend that the seventy translators of the Greek Septuagint managed to provide independently seventy identical translations. Such legends are far from harmless, even in theology, because such views would completely sever the revelation contained in the Bible from the living reality of this human world, and God's revelation in the Bible would lose its essential connection with God's revelation in creation and incarnation.

The fact that the Bible is a book among others has various consequences. Two of these must be mentioned here because they are connected with factors that will appear elsewhere in this article. Because the Bible is a book among other books, it can be approached in the same way as other books are approached. This means that the Bible can be the object of literary criticism and literary analysis. This very approach gives us an insight in the way the Bible grew historically and so shows us

the Bible as "The Book of the People of God". The other consequence concerns the reading of the Bible. Once it is clearly
understood that the Bible is in no sense a book that dropped
miraculously out of the sky, one will reply more carefully to the
question whether any Christian ought to read the Bible indis-
criminately. The conviction that the Spirit will assist the reader
does not alter the fact that one can only read the Bible fruitfully
when one has acquired the art of reading with a certain maturity.
Normally such maturity can only be taken for granted with
people who read other books as well as the Bible. This does not
mean, of course, that professional literary training is required,
but it *does* imply that one recognize the Bible as a book among
other books. It is, therefore, not very intelligent to counsel
personal reading of the Bible in the case of people who never
open another book. Experience has shown that these people
simply lose their way in the Bible.

On the other hand, the Bible must be clearly distinguished
from all other books. On the bookshelves it has its place next to
other books, but there are also situations where the Bible occu-
pies an exclusive or at least a very special place. This is the case
wherever people assemble as the Church of Christ. Whether
such a gathering is that of an ecumenical council or that of a
local celebration of the eucharist, the book of the Bible is treated
with exceptional reverence and has a special place in the celebration. In many reformed churches the open Bible is given a
permanent place. This exceptional reverence shows that this one
book is a very special book. It is *the* book of the Church.

In itself it would have been quite possible for the Church of
Christ to have found a ready-made guidebook for her faith and
practice. This would have been the case if Jesus himself had
written a book to serve as a guide in these matters for his followers. This is precisely what the Bible is not. The Bible originated
in the Church herself, or, more accurately, within the People
of God.

In this history of its growth one can distinguish various
phases that equally deserve our attention. First of all, we have

to deal with the origin of the various writings that make up the Bible. And at this stage we have to distinguish the books of the Old Testament from those of the New for more than one reason. But the fact that all these books came to be written does not yet constitute them as Sacred Scripture in the way in which it functions actually as the book of the Church. This constitutes the second phase that we usually describe as the period during which the Canon was fixed, but which might better be described as the period during which these several writings, selected from many others, grew together into the one Bible.

Growth of Old Testament Writings

Whoever studies the literary "prehistory" and growth of the books of the Old Testament is confronted with a confusing multiplicity of data and hypotheses that make the reconstruction of this growth a precarious business. There is, however, a large measure of agreement insofar as the main lines of development are concerned. And then we see first of all that the number of "authors" is immediately multiplied. There is practically not a single book that does not show a long prehistory. This does not only concern the Pentateuch, whose roots stretch back far into the age of the patriarchs and whose final redaction was not achieved until after the exile, that is, after many generations of Israelites from various societies and regions had made their own contribution. It also concerns the books of the prophets. The most striking illustration of this is perhaps the book attributed to the prophet Isaiah, who lived in the second half of the 8th century B.C. There is general agreement that chapters 40–55 were written by another prophet who appeared during the exile, that is, about two hundred years later. Chapters 56, 58 and 66 (and perhaps also 57) were written after the exile, and the same can be said of the so-called apocalypse of Isaiah (24–27) and the strongly apocalyptic chapters 63–65. Even in the other chapters (1–39), for the greater part the work of Isaiah himself, there are many fragments of a later date. We do not know for certain when the Hebrew text was finally established, but one can estimate that this happened before the 2nd century B.C. For the rest, the various parts show so much in common that they may justly be attributed to Isaiah and a tradition that lived on his inspiration. All this means that the book seems to have been composed by a whole school of prophets and authors.

This situation is typical. What I have tried to illustrate in a few words in the case of Isaiah applies by far to the greater number of the books of the Old Testament, although not always in the same manner. Many persons were involved in this history of the origins of each book, though the vast majority of them have remained unknown to us. This does not mean, of course, that the many collaborators are not real persons. Moreover, Israel does not trace its traditions back to Moses and the prophets without reason. It may be true that what is attributed to Moses is not all his own work and that the books attributed to the prophets contain many later additions. But there is no reason to doubt that the fact that, at certain decisive moments, men like Moses and the prophets molded the traditions of their people. However, the great figures that spoke and wrote from their special religious experience are far more numerous than we might think from the usual list of authors, and most of these can no longer be identified. This implies at least that far more members of the Old Testament People of God were concerned in the origin of the Old Testament than we once thought.

To this we must add that the material used by many authors for their text is frequently borrowed from traditions which show all the features of popular stories, popular poetry and popular wisdom. It is enough to refer here to the stories about the period of the patriarchs and the judges with their many references to popular etymology, and to various pieces in the Book of Proverbs and the other wisdom literature. Those that made a direct contribution to the writing of the various biblical books stood with both feet firmly planted in the traditions of their own people to which they meant, above all, to be loyal.

Even more important is the fact that the composers of the various traditions and biblical books aimed deliberately at the actual wants and needs of the old Israel. The Elohist traditions of the Pentateuch, which set out to provide definite religious teaching, reminded Israel of the fact that it was chosen by God to be his own people. Deuteronomy and the Deuteronomic history (Joshua, Judges, Samuel and Kings) depict Israel's faithlessness, show that this was bound to lead to catastrophe, and in this way exhort the rest of God's People to conversion and penance. The particular tradition of the Pentateuch, which is designated by the letter *P,* means to set out a program of spiritual restoration after the exile, based on the old traditions. The prophets attribute Israel's lack of loyalty to its old traditions and summon the people to a searching of heart and penance. It is true that the psalms did not originate as popular songs, but they were certainly intended for participation by all the people in the form of one chorus or alternating choruses. The wisdom literature, particularly Proverbs and Sirach (Ecclesiasticus), is again more deeply rooted in popular tradition. It is less directly concerned with a definite religious message for Israel, but shows very clearly that the world and the ordinary reality of everyday life have a definite place in the religious experience of Israel.

Growth of New Testament Books

The ecclesial origin and purpose of the different New Testament books is even more evident. This holds also for the Gospels. The Instruction on the Historical Truth of the Gospels, issued by the Biblical Commission, describes three phases of the tradition within which the text material of the Gospels took shape. It mentions, first of all, the words and actions of Jesus, then the witness of the apostles and lastly the evangelists. Yet, something is missing here. The use of the form-criticism method has shown that the authors of the Gospels did not draw directly on the oral and written traditions which derived directly from the apostles, but that these traditions were active in the life of the Church before the evangelists made use of them. This is implicitly recognized in the last paragraph of the relevant section of the Instruction in which biblical scholars are advised to bear in mind the

various ways in which the tradition found expression: catechetics, stories, witnesses, hymns, doxologies, prayers, etc. For
it is obvious that a number of these forms of expression, such
as hymns, doxologies and prayers, have an ecclesial rather than
an immediately apostolic origin.

There were various ways in which the witness of the apostles
was integrated in the traditions of the early Church. And this
stage, too, deserves attention because it is precisely here that the
Church as such set her seal on the tradition. Of course the evangelists drew from the tradition (and this holds also for the letters
of the New Testament) that was apostolic in origin. But the
present state of the text shows, even now, how these traditions
were used by the diverse communities of the original Church
for preaching, catechizing, praying and singing. The evangelists,
therefore, did indeed use the apostolic witness in writing their
respective Gospels, but this witness operated first in the Church
where it was given the shape in which the evangelists used it.

The fact that the final authors drew mainly on ecclesial tradition is not the only factor enabling us to look on the books of
the New Testament as, above all, the embodiment of this tradition. There is another essential point, namely, the authors whose
names these books bear did not write merely for the sake of
writing. They wrote almost always for a definite community or
group of communities and attuned their writing to actual problems which were experienced in these communities or which
they diagnosed in the life of these communities. This is most
evident in the letters. For example, in 1 Corinthians, Paul refers
to various abuses in the community of Corinth, replies to several
questions and lays down certain rules for the smooth running of
the community. In 2 Thessalonians he deals with the strained
mood in which a number of Christians of that community expected the parousia. In the Gospels this connection with a particular community or group of communities is not always clear.
It is still a matter for debate where and for which communities
the several Gospels were written, but there is general agreement
that the distinct character of the four Gospels is not caused

exclusively by the personal temperament of the evangelists but is also determined in a large measure by whatever community they were writing for. And this feature, too, shows that the Gospels were preeminently ecclesial documents.

Origin of the Canon

The final redaction of the various books of the Old and New Testaments may be considered to be the end of their growing stage in history. But it is not the end of the whole growing process of the Bible as such, for this includes the assembling of these texts in the Canon. Strictly speaking, the Canon is merely the list of biblical books, fixed by the Church as containing the norms for our faith and our life. But in actual fact it also means that these books, so different among themselves, are collected under the one name of "Holy Scriptures", and that the Church treats them as one book of which the various parts clarify and complement one another. The Canon was finally established by the doctrinal authority of the Church and as such the Canon is the business of the Church. But it is curious that this formal and final establishment of the Canon for the whole Church only took place at the Councils of Florence (1441) and Trent (1546).

Two points, however, must be mentioned here. First of all, although these formal decisions concerned the Canon as a whole, in fact, they concerned each time a relatively small number of biblical writings or fragments, the canonicity of which had been queried. This does not mean that until that time the Church had had to manage without the Canon. It was rather a matter of lack of precision resulting in a possible doubt about a few of the writings. Secondly, these decisions brought nothing new. They confirmed formally what had already been accepted virtually by the whole Church. It is, therefore, not correct, as is often done, to make the history of the Canon coincide with the post-biblical history of doubts, controversies and declarations. The history of the origin of the Canon can only be formally distinguished from that of the origin of the biblical books; in fact, the two run parallel, although it usually took some time before a biblical book was considered to be authoritative and binding.

The "prehistory" of the Canon coincides with that of the biblical books. The oral formulation and transmission of apodictic law and case law, ritual formulas, oracles and other similar elements were no doubt considered authoritative before they were written down and gathered into collections. They counted as divine utterances. It is understandable that prophetic utterances, though presented as coming from Yahweh, had more difficulty in obtaining recognition. They exposed Israel's failures in the light of the old traditions and threatened punishment. Thus, they were usually preserved (and supplemented) for some time by the prophet's followers and only later obtained universal authority, particularly after the fall of Jerusalem in 587 B.C.

The real history of the Canon began when the traditions were put in writing and collected. One may take it as a fact that the various traditions of the Pentateuch were already considered canonical before they were put together in one book. It seems also likely that the final redaction of the Deuteronomic history during the exile and that of the Pentateuch after the exile were decisive moments in the growth of the Canon. By the beginning of the 2nd century B.C. the collection of prophetic writings was also universally admitted as appears from, among other texts, Sirach (Ecclesiasticus) 48, 22–49, 12. Insofar as the remaining books which belong to the sacred writings are concerned, the situation still remained in a state of flux for some centuries. It is also clear that in the diaspora more books were considered canonical than in Palestine itself. The differences of opinion, however, never bore on the Law and the Prophets but only on a limited number of books and fragments belonging to the more vague category of "writings". The synod of Jamnia (ca. 100 A.D.), as it is called, was unable to solve the problems. There remained differences of opinion about, for example, the Song of Songs and Ecclesiastes. And although this Jewish synod is no doubt important in the history of the Canon, it must be emphasized that here, too, it was a question of marking off the boundaries. The canonicity of the vast majority of biblical books had already been established for a long time. It is, however, not clear at all how it came to be established. There is no evidence at all that points to some official declaration. The People of God of the Old Testament probably recognized the normative authority of these books as they came to take shape, while the other books were not considered to have the same authority. We remain completely in the dark as to what criteria may have guided this process.

Although all the evidence shows that Jesus and the apostles treated the Old Testament (probably covering the same contents as the Greek Septuagint) as canonical, it is not necessary, so it seems to me, to refer to this fact in order to explain why the Church recognized the canonicity of the Old Testament from the beginning. The People of God of the New Testament took over this conviction from the old Israel. On the other hand, the early Church had to start without books of her own in which God's work of salvation in Jesus Christ had been put in writing. There is, however, no doubt that the words of the Lord Jesus were credited with special authority already in the earliest communities (1 Cor. 7, 10; cf. 7, 11.25 and also 23).

The same may be said about the apostolic tradition (1 Cor. 15, 1.3 and 11). Obviously, this same authority was also attributed to the writings in which these traditions were fixed, and this was transferred to the Gospels which were composed on this basis. On the other hand, the writings of the apostles themselves were accepted as normative. On what basis these writings were selected is not certain, although it seems certain that their apostolic character played a decisive part. This implies, moreover, that these writings were uniquely bound up with the facts of salvation, the life, death and resurrection of Jesus, of which the apostles were witnesses. But here again, nowhere is there an official declaration that fixed this normative character of the writings in an authoritative manner until we come to the Councils of Hippo, Carthage and Florence. Here, too, it must be pointed out that these conciliar declarations were important mainly for marking off the Canon that was already established in its main features. This leads almost inevitably to the conclusion that the essential phase of the growth of the Canon—and, therefore, of Holy Scripture as the one book of the Church— preceded all official declarations and lies hidden in the darkness that veils the origin of the Church, the People of God.

It would of course be wrong to think of the Hebrews, the old Israel, the Jewish people or the earliest Church as a shapeless crowd without spiritual leaders. Apart from tribal chiefs, judges and kings, the People of God was also led by prophets, priests, wise men, scribes, apostles, *episkopoi* and teachers, and the latter no doubt exercised a certain form of doctrinal authority. It is, therefore, obvious that they greatly influenced the way in which the authority of the holy books was established (*see*, for example, 2 Kgs. 23 and Neh. 8). But the actual acceptance of the Scriptures remained nevertheless a matter of the People of God, who had no formal and generally valid decisions to fall back on, as is clearly shown in the difference between the Canon of Palestine and that of Alexandria.

The Book of the Church

The historical growth of the books of both the Old and New Testaments as well as that of the Canon clearly shows that Scripture can only be understood by approaching it from the reality of the People of God, *i.e.*, from the ecclesial traditions out of which it grew. Scripture then appears to be a book of the Church. If we want to understand what Sacred Scripture is and what function it has in the present-day Church, we must obviously not forget that the authors of these books were inspired by the Spirit of God and, among other things, the consequences of this fact for their authority. But this is not all. This writing has been preceded by so much of essential importance and so much has followed it afterward that it is not enough to concentrate exclusively on this divine inspiration, the inspired author and the various elements in the process of this inspiration. The history of the origin of the Bible comprises three stages, the most accessible of which is the middle one, the actual composition of the biblical writings. The first and last stages are surrounded by question marks. However, one thing is clear: whatever happened in these two stages was preeminently something ecclesial, something that happened within the community of the People of God. The driving force, particularly in these two stages, is the faith of Israel and of the early Church.

This faith did not come about by itself. It is a response to God's saving deeds and words. Many texts of the Scriptures have preserved not only the witness of this faith in God's action, but also the divine utterances insofar as they were understood by the men of the old Israel and by the witnesses of the life of Jesus. The Scriptures confront the People of God with these utterances spoken by God. But this does not allow us to think that this statement implies that we can apply it to the whole of the Scriptures or that this can only be found in the words of the Bible. On the one hand, there are many passages in the Bible that present themselves in no sense as the words of God (one has but to think of the psalms and the wisdom literature in the Old Testament and of the letters in the New Testament). On the other hand, other books were written at the same time as some biblical books, and large sections of these were meant to be understood as "words of God" (for example, the Book of Jubilees and the Apocalypse of Baruch). Yet, some books became part of Sacred Scripture while the apocrypha did not—whatever authority they may have had. Why? Because the People of God, guided by God's Spirit, saw the first as conforming to their own authentic faith and did not recognize this quality in the others. The Bible may be called "Holy Scripture", not only because it contains God's Word, but also because it contains in an authentic manner the religious traditions of the chosen "holy" People of God out of which the Bible grew.

Since the Bible originated as a book of the Church, it is clear that it can only truly fulfill its purpose within the Church. But there, it can only do this fully if today's People of God are aware, in their faith, of their continuity with the People of God of the

Old Testament and of the earliest Church. In other words, a Christian awareness, which is limited to contemporary Christians and the contemporary world, is too narrow an approach to the understanding of the Scriptures. This horizontal approach demands a corresponding vertical approach, *i.e.,* a sense of union with the Church of the centuries and with the People of God of the Old Testament. Only when we realize that we are the spiritual descendants of Israel and the earliest Church, can we experience the continuity of the faith sufficiently to believe that their history is our prehistory and that God's Word to them contains a message for us. Only then can we understand God's Word and carry forward that response in faith which the Scriptures give us. This is one of the principal reasons, though not the only one, why the Scriptures can only achieve their full purpose within Christ's Church. Here alone can we read the history of God's dealings with Israel, in the way it is expressed in the books of the whole Bible, as the prehistory of the Church and even see our own history in the salvation history of the Old Testament. It is only on the basis of this continuity that we can recognize the core of our own approach to the faith in the confessions of faith of the old Israel and the earliest Church; that we can join in the prayer of the psalms which seem so alien to us in imagery, in poetic style and in their view of the world; and that the prophetic utterances, however conditioned by the age of the prophets, can still touch us.

Because Sacred Scripture has its full and proper meaning only when read and heard within the Church, the most appropriate place for this reading and understanding is there, where the Church is assembled in the celebration of her liturgy, and where the unity and continuity of the People of God find expression. There, in the sacrament, God's salvation is again fulfilled in us. There, too, the Word of the Scriptures is not only read and heard but proclaimed and made actual. And the purpose of this proclamation is none other than to make this Word, congealed in the Scriptures, flow and live again, and to transfer it from distant antiquity to the present-day Church. Because the Church

cannot be simply identified with the People of God in the
Old Testament or with that of the earliest Church, but is a
continuation of both, the proclamation cannot be sheer repe-
tition. Following the line of tradition, this Word of the Scriptures must be adapted to the present, and, where necessary, be
corrected and complemented. That personal reading of the Scriptures can be fruitful here, whether done individually or in a
group, seems obvious. It is equally obvious that such "individual" reading must never be "individualistic". The ecclesial
bearing of the scriptural text itself demands that it be read in
conscious continuity with the People of God.

This is not all that can be said. Other approaches to the Bible
will bring to light other dimensions which may well be more important, such as God's self-revelation. But whatever approach
we choose, it will always be enriched if we remember the fact
that the Bible originated within the People of God and that it
embraces the People of God's traditions of faith.

Heinrich Kahlefeld/*Munich, W. Germany*

The Pericope and Preaching

T he great accomplishment of theology—lifting divine truth out of
the flowing stream of the kerygma,
defining it and offering it as its highest subject to the human
mind for systematic elaboration—has been paid for by a lessen-
ing of interest in the methodology of scriptural exegesis. It was
easy for the opinion to gain ground that we now knew what
Scripture revealed, and that we could confine our use of it to
prove the truths derived from it. It was possible to think that
no new theological questions could arise from listening to Scripture and that the main purpose of Scripture was that of edifica-
tion. Clearly there was no need for such a condition to arise,
but it is an historical fact. It seems to be the task of our generation to initiate a change.

Preaching in the New Testament

The greater part of Sacred Scripture consists of documents
which, as written or spoken addresses, were originally directed
to the assembly of the faithful. There is mention of "witnesses"
who could have said as St. Paul did: "I have seen the Lord"
(1 Cor. 9, 1), or of those who, compelled by a charisma, had
to communicate their insight to the meaning of, and the reason
for, what happened to Christ, and to interpret their spiritual
experience to those who were baptized. This original proclama-

tion, which communicated the Word of God to the hearing Church and served as a tool for the kingdom of God and the salvation of souls, must be carried through the length and breadth of the nations of the earth and through the chain of succeeding generations. What is proclaimed must always be the Word which was spoken before and must remain always the same, but it must be translated into the language of another space and another time.

Great care must be taken lest the entrusted Word be "made void" (1 Cor. 1, 17) or be lost in the swirl of opinions prevailing at any time (2 Tim. 4, 3–5). There is likewise the need to be attuned to the way of thought, the cares, the longings and the particular receptiveness of one's contemporaries. Such preaching gives to the hearer more than a "truth of the faith". Even the theologian learns something new, for the truth of God "comes toward him"; the Word speaks to him and challenges him. Even today it is possible that hearers, if the Scriptures are truly "opened up to them", may exclaim: "Was not our heart burning within us?" (Luke 24, 32) It may happen that some of those who follow the Gospel for a long time will ask themselves anew: "What are we to do, brethren?" (Acts 2, 37)

This is true especially of preaching in which Christ's very words are used, *i.e.,* of the Gospel in the strict sense. His words cannot be replaced, surpassed or imitated, not only because of the respect we owe to him who speaks, but because of their very substance. No charismatic person was or is ever entitled to make statements about God's thoughts such as we find in the parable of the pharisee and publican (Luke 18, 9ff.); or to assure the poor, the hungry and the weeping in this world that God in the eschatological event will change their fate and give them whatever they lacked (Luke 6, 20–21. 24–25); or to show to the poorest of the poor, the despised sinners, that God has not rejected them but is seeking after them with a love that can be spoken of only under the veil of a parable (Luke 15, 1ff. 11ff.). Such words must be handed on exactly as they have been spoken. Of course, they could be expanded through commentary, or adapted to the internal and external situation of the hearers, or, again, used thematically in the composition of an extended speech. But it was always clearly understood that the Word of the Lord could not be invented. This shows us the nature and purpose of the sermon: its task is (1) to present the apostolic proclamation, including the original words of Jesus, to the hearing congregation, and (2) to endeavor, in humble and loving service, to convey its message to the hearts of those hearing the Word. Because the proclamation offers not only God's truth but the very Word in which it was spoken, the biblical homily is without peer among the possible kinds of spiritual speech.[1]

An Example

In the large composition known as the "Sermon on the Mount", Matthew presents a didactic poem consisting of three stanzas in chapter 6, 1–18. This becomes clear when one excludes verses 7–8, 9–13, 14–15, which have been inserted as part of the composition. The theme reads: "Take heed not to do your good before men in order to be seen by them; otherwise, you shall have no reward with your Father in heaven" (Matt. 6, 1). There follow three examples, *i.e.*, the works of piety, beneficence, prayer and fasting, used in the instruction to the Jews, by which the warning of the theme is being illustrated. Those who like to be praised as benefactors or to be seen at their prayers and in their fasts may indeed find their own glory, but God is not interested in their deeds. God claims the whole service for himself and does not share it even with the pious. Here it is also true that no one can serve two masters (Matt. 7, 24). People must be urged to shun such self-deception. The benefactor should remain unnamed; he that prays should do so

[1] In the program of instructions for the faithful there is, no doubt, a place for the "dogmatic sermon"; there is room also for the "moral sermon". It would be rewarding to show, especially from New Testament writings, under what conditions they would be appropriate. Apologetical sermons, which offer a Christian interpretation of practical situations in life, have their just place. All types of instruction, admonition and kerygmatic proclamation should be heard in the course of the pastoral program of the parish, without prejudice to the high esteem for the biblical homily.

in the privacy of his room, while those who fast should appear like those who go to a banquet. In all this we are assured that God sees whatever is done for his sake.

The seriousness of this doctrine is shown by other words which also refer to good deeds: "When thou givest a dinner or a supper, do not invite thy friends, or thy brethren, or thy relatives, or thy rich neighbors, lest perhaps they also invite thee in return, and a recompense be made to thee. But when thou givest a feast, invite the poor, the crippled, the lame, the blind; and blessed shalt thou be, because they have nothing to repay thee with; for thou shalt be repaid at the resurrection of the just" (Luke 14, 12–14).

The point is that good deeds must not find their terminus within the world. Their goodness and sincerity must be such that they come from God. Their God-directedness must be preserved by hiding them, *i.e.*, by a manner of acting which is not plausible and hence appears as foolishness. What sort of language is this! It reveals God's saving jealousy demanding that nothing and no one be worshipped except him; it also points up man's weakness, constantly troubled whether or not the deeds that go beyond his own interest really pay. He is held in a state of openness toward God which the Gospel calls "faith". Faith in the biblical sense is the result of a therapeutic process; in fact, it is a process that fundamentally never stops. As long as the believer is on the way, he is in need of the physician; he must make use of the medicine of the Gospel until his last moment on earth.

When we realize that neither of the pericopes (Matt. 6, 1–18 nor Luke 14, 12–14) are being utilized in the Sunday eucharistic celebration, we begin to understand why the Council decided to introduce an *Ordo Lectionum* extending over several years. We can no longer in good conscience allow the great majority of the baptized, who come to holy Mass on Sunday but do not "read the Bible", to be ignorant of the fact that the Lord offers them healing by these words.

This example incidentally shows also that it cannot be a question of merely carving out pericopes but also of freeing texts, such as this poem, from compositional insertions in order to bring out their full effect. At other times, both the composition and the evangelical kerygma embedded in it may have to be stressed. All this illustrates the magnitude of the task involved in compiling the future *Ordo Lectionum.*

The Value of the Early Formulas of Faith

Among the texts more troublesome for the modern preacher are those early formulas that attempt to summarize and express the heart of Christian belief. There, insight into the faith appears strangely undeveloped and, in comparison to what is now official doctrine, quite primitive.[2] Should preaching take notice of these texts at all? Should they be treated with condescending indulgence, and marginally, as outgrown relics of former ages? Or can both the preacher and the hearer learn something from them?

Let us consider Romans 10, 9 as an example. It is beautifully interwoven with the context of verses 8–11a; and yet it remains recognizable: "If you confess . . . that Jesus is the Lord and believe . . . that God has raised him from the dead, you shall be saved."

The lesson intended in the short main clause is the essential condition for salvation, the border over which one has to cross in order to be a Christian. The parallel conditional clauses express one truth: God has raised Jesus from the dead and given him the power of the *Kyrios* (Lord). The formula certainly could be enriched; it might combine the confession of faith in Christ with that of faith in God, as in 1 Thessalonians 1, 9f: ". . . to serve the living and true God, and to await from heaven Jesus, his Son, whom he raised from the dead, who has delivered us from the wrath to come."

[2] It is evident that these texts are eminently precious to biblical theology since they are part of the oldest literary stratum of the New Testament, *i.e.,* the more important letters of St. Paul; furthermore, they are pre-Pauline formulations of the professed faith, *e.g.,* 1 Corinthians 15, 3–5, or again, cultic poems such as the Kyrios Psalm in Philippians 2, 6–11.

The Christian content appears here in the manner of speech used by the early Christian community; the formula reminds us of the cultic acclamation "marana ta". Yet it is also a confession of the work that God accomplished in Jesus who had been put to death, thus making it an act of faith. We again find the same expressed somewhat differently in the concluding sentence of St. Peter's address on Pentecost (Acts 2, 36): "God has made both Lord and Christ, this Jesus whom you crucified."

If we could theologically characterize such statements, we would speak of a Christology of exaltation. It comes close to what is found in St. Luke's Gospel, and yet it differs clearly and seems to be more original in time. Thus, we ask: What is the value of such formulas?

People of Western mentality have, more or less, a developed sense of history. We must assume that they are capable of understanding when they learn that New Testament revelation, as every other genuine revelation, is given in large acts and must be appropriated through long-range endeavors of vision and thought and varied attempts at linguistic expression. Such a lesson learned from the above example should indeed strengthen many people's faith in Sacred Scripture; it should be understandable to those whose cast of mind is biblical; it should increase the enjoyment of the vitality of its words as well as increase the reverence for the many human speakers involved, whose personalities may be recognized by the tone of their language. There should also be an increase of respect for tradition under the guidance of the Holy Spirit as well as a deeper understanding of the Church.

According to the formulas mentioned above, faith in Christ is based on events that took place, to be precise, on the work that God accomplished through and in Jesus. Fundamentally and primarily, faith is directed to him who "has raised up the Lord" (1 Cor. 6, 14; 2 Cor. 4, 14; Rom. 8, 11). From the divine deed of raising from the dead, the witnessing of which is the task of the apostles, faith turns to the death of Jesus and realizes that this death was more than the martyrdom of a prophet, but rather the work of atonement and redemption. What is the meaning of the old formula which states that God, when he raised up Christ from Hades and transferred him into his own realm, "made him Lord and Messiah" (Acts 2, 36)? This statement could dispose of a problem. The Jews are indeed right when, in Jesus, they miss the majesty and power, the victory and supremacy of the saving king.

What they do not understand is the explication of the phases by which history and its laws are kept intact. In history there are no unbroken forces, and yet it proceeds with supreme power. Thus, God made no use of force in behalf of his Chosen One. This was not understood by the Jews and became for them a stumbling block. Christ's disciples shared this misunderstanding, an instance of which is the rebuke which Peter, out of love but yet foolishly, administers to the Master (Mark 8, 32). But it is through the grace of the disciples that in the dark hour of Christ's defeat they remain blindly on the road even though they stumble. They do not understand, but they persevere. Then they see the work of God and they begin to realize that Jesus against all expectation has obtained the power which is the due of the Messiah. Is this not the ever recurring mistake of men: they cannot keep apart the ages of creation and thus try to mingle the age of glory with that of lowliness. Is the triumphalism stigmatized by the Council anything else?

At this point we should make plain to ourselves the process of insight into the faith. It always begins with a perceptive gaze (*Anschauung*) and then turns into perception of the meaning: first perception of an event, followed by progressive yet groping insight into its "being". Anyone who realizes this will not begin a dialogue with a discussion of the external existence of Christ, but will wisely show the way into the mystery of faith along the road the apostles have already taken. It should also be clearly understood that the seeker after truth does cross the threshold to the inner sphere of faith not before he comes to believe that the Incomparable One, whose dignity he is not yet able to describe, is alive and at the throne of God as the Shepherd of mankind and of all creation. Such prudently cautious language might open the door to many who otherwise feel as if they were facing a solid wall.

Another Example

We wish to present here, for the purpose of illustrating the rise and growth of insight into faith, a difficult text of St. Paul that anyone hardly ever dares to use as a text for a sermon. The difficulty does not seem to lie in the thought expressed but in the situation of the time as the background for a discussion of the Christian faith in contrast to the Jews who refuse to believe. This discussion is, furthermore, conducted in the form of Rabbinical Midrash and hence intelligible only to those acquainted with that sort of exegesis. But as an example of charismatic speech, this text is so grandiose that it should not be ignored.

We first present the pericope as an interrupted text containing that which can be announced to the community. In the explanation, a more comprehensive use of the text and context must be made so as to assure clarity and depth of understanding.

2 Corinthians 3, 15–18; 4, 3–4.6

(15) Down to this very day, when Moses is read, the veil covers their hearts [of the sons of Israel (v. 13)]

(16) "When, however, 'one' turns to the Lord, the veil is taken away" (Ex. 34, 34).

(17) The Lord is the spirit; and where the Spirit of the Lord is, there is freedom.

(18) We all, with faces unveiled, reflecting as in a mirror, the glory of the Lord, are being transformed into his very image from glory to glory as [it is wrought] through the Spirit of the Lord.

(4, 3) And if our gospel also is "veiled", it is "veiled" only for those who are on the way to destruction.

(4)   Their unbelieving minds have been blinded by the god of this age so that they do not see the shining light of

the gospel of the glory of Christ, who is the image of God [5].

(6)   For God, who said: "Let light shine from darkness", has shone in our hearts that we might make known the glory of God shining on the face of Christ.

This pericope is the last section of a larger context (2 Cor. 3, 1—4, 6). St. Paul demonstrates the legitimacy of his apostolate because it is based on a called from God. He first draws attention to the community itself. Its very living existence is "a letter of commendation" for him; a letter written by the Spirit of God and legible to all men (2 Cor. 3, 3). The community is the work of God; St. Paul is the instrument. It is absurd that anyone can work as an apostle without being called and empowered by God (2 Cor. 3, 4). Here comes the main thought. What a task! He serves another, a new covenant which far surpasses the one of Sinai. It is the eschatological covenant of which Jeremiah spoke (31, 31) and which has already begun and is at work through the death and exaltation of Christ (2 Cor. 3, 6–11). The only thing befitting this situation is openness and boldness of the Word of God in which the undiminished glory of God shines before men, quite differently than when Moses had the reflection of God's glory on his countenance, but had to veil his face because no one was able to bear its splendor (2 Cor. 3, 13).

At this point there comes the secondary theme of the blindness of the Jews to whom the prophetic writings brought no understanding. The veil that originally covered the head of Moses, and in turn the books of Moses when they were read in the synagogues, really now covers the hearts of the hearers. The Scriptures are not locked, but the minds of men are locked. They are not free, for they are not able to grasp the work of God (2 Cor. 3, 13–15). The account of this situation is contrasted with the discussion of the grace of the faithful. Here the text of the pericope begins.

The removal by Moses (15f.) of the veil from his head when he appears before God is interpreted typologically, *viz.*, the very same thing happens to anyone who, by an act of faith, turns to God by subjecting himself to the representative of God, the *Kyrios,* Jesus. The separating veil is removed, and there arises what St. Paul calls freedom.

That part of the argument—not expressly stated, because it is evident for St. Paul, namely, that the *Kyrios* quoted from Exodus 34, 34 refers to Christ, through whom we come to God —must be stated explicitly for modern hearers. For St. Paul there exists not only the Scriptures but also the preaching of the apostles. This latter occasioned the whole discussion contained in 2 Corinthians 3, 1–2. 4–5. Verse 12 was about himself, and so also the sentence omitted here, *i.e.,* "We preach not ourselves, but Jesus Christ as Lord (2 Cor. 4, 5). This, then, is the reason why the Jews do not understand the prophecy about Christ in the Old Testament: they reject the Gospel of the new Easter.

But St. Paul intends something else. He is concerned with the internal process of turning to Christ. In the inner sanctum of the soul there is only one activity: the Lord himself must open up the way to himself and create the immediacy of the personal encounter. The power, which is at work in the depths of the human being and which creates freedom, is the Spirit of God who is at the disposal of the heavenly Christ. The power of the exalted Christ manifests itself in the sweeping force of the Pneuma. Both the Lord, on the right hand of God, who encounters the believer, and the Spirit of God by which he draws the believers unto himself, are so much one that St. Paul ventures the bold and, even for St. Paul, unique formula: "The Lord is the Spirit" (2 Cor. 3, 17).

Now it is possible (2 Cor. 3, 18) to explain what it means to believe in Christ, *viz.,* seeing the manifestation made by the Spirit of the glory of the heavenly Lord. He who contemplates it has this vision imprinted upon himself to the extent of the intensity and length of his gaze. He becomes a living mirror reflecting the original image. As he grows through his intimacy with the Lord, so he becomes also like him; he is being transformed in a process that inchoatively initiates the eschatological transfiguration. These are indeed bold statements, apt to embarrass anyone who, in his concern for the majesty of God, insists that no such changes through grace are possible in man. But this is precisely the way in which the Gospel lights up the darkness of our minds. Hence, it is so much more important that this truth be made known in our preaching.

The realism of the new beginning of the pericope (2 Cor. 4, 3) may appear as a disturbance. But St. Paul is compelled to struggle. There are objections to his high insight. One may ask the question: Why are not all men compelled to embrace the faith by their own personal conviction, if the truth of Christ shines forth so brightly? It is with such questions that St. Paul deals. He feels that another one is at work, one who works for bondage and finds easy entrance into a heart that is not open to the Lord (*Kyrios*). This part could be left aside, making for a good conclusion of the pericope with verse 6. But it is intriguing to see the proclamation of the faith and its sacral speech arising out of St. Paul's daily vexations caused by small opponents whom he must answer and silence. The proclaimed truth is strong enough to remain integrally preserved in such critical reflections.

In the very same sentence in which we are told that "the god of this age" could prevent that understanding whereby men escape Christ's grasp only by blinding their minds, we are also told what that understanding is. It is the perception of the splendor issuing forth from the glory of the exalted Christ, which shines forth from the Gospel as soon as it is preached and heard. This thought is gratefully professed in the last sentence of the pericope (2 Cor. 4, 6) serenely unencumbered by argumentation. The baptized profess here the great things God has done to them. The same God who in the morning of creation commanded light to shine out of darkness has now made bright with light[3] also the hearts of men. He has enabled them to perceive

[3] The word *lampein* is commonly used intransitively in the sense of being resplendent, shining forth. But there are also texts warranting its transitive use which is actually suggested here by the context. Cf. Liddell-Scott, 1028.

the light shining over the whole of creation: the face of Jesus Christ resplendent with the glory of God.

A Further Reflection

We shall first consider questions connected with the last pericope discussed and then broaden our subject.

1. The text clearly indicates that St. Paul speaks from experience. He makes explicit mention of it in other places: "And last of all . . . he was seen also by me" (1 Cor. 15, 8); "But it pleased him . . . to reveal his Son to me" (Gal. 1, 15f.); "Have I not seen the Lord?" (1 Cor. 9, 1). We are in need of such testimony. It is not only a foundation of belief, but it also encourages its clear profession as well as the expectation that the personal experience of the realities to which one is a witness is possible. If the exaltation of Jesus is true and real, and if he is Lord of all over whom his name has been invoked, then it is to be expected that he—through the word of evangelical proclamation—will turn to the believer and shine in his believing mind. This is the burden of the whole pericope, namely, that "the veil has been taken away" and an immediate encounter established.

2. The sentences under discussion assume several times the character of language used in cultic celebrations; also its ideas and imagery are cultic in character. In the last sentence (2 Cor. 4, 6) we hear the "We" of the community and the praise and thanksgiving of the faithful to God for his work of grace. Their gaze is focused on the face of the heavenly Lord whence the glory of God shines upon the whole being of the believer, and the Spirit of God performs the work of transformation.

These things need to be made known to us if we are to understand what takes place in liturgical worship and how to partake of its proper reality. Thus we cannot afford to miss the beginning of St. John's Apocalypse as part of the liturgy. St. John sees and hears these things on "the day of the Lord", the day of the holy assembly, and communicates them to the communities. Again, one sees the figure of the heavenly Lord who, as judge and shepherd, knows the communities and is anxious to lead them to salvation.

I wish to point out again that neither the text of St. Paul discussed above nor the opening vision of the Apocalypse are being used as pericopes. This situation must be remedied by the new *Ordo Lectionum*. We see a great need for it. We understand also that its content and comprehensiveness—whether it be spread over three or four years—should not be decided under such a formal aspect but rather from the point of view of the material made available to the faithful.

3. These considerations should provide another important suggestion in the various deliberations about the training of our theologians and continued education of priests working for the care of souls. First of all, it seems that biblical subjects should be accorded a higher priority in the scheme of the theological disciplines. In return for this demand, biblical scholars should go more beyond the philological work than is done in many places and provide more of the content of Sacred Scripture. If theological questions and answers are also given in classes of exegesis, if a beginning of biblical theology is made by way of corollaries or such biblical theology is developed in formal lecture courses, then it would seem that the other systematic departments could allot some time to scriptural training of preachers. We know that this problem is entwined with others and somewhat complicated. But it seems to be time to attempt its solution.

This leads to a discussion of the nature of homiletics. Its subject is not primarily sacred "oratory", but is closely related to the systematic theological and biblical disciplines, the development of kerygmatic material. We must seek a practical theory of what must and can be preached, always keeping in mind the congregations to be addressed and their concrete situations. Homiletics is doubtlessly a theological discipline which, under the impulse given to us by the Council to reflect upon the kerygma, might become one of the major subjects for study.

Henri Cazelles, S.S./*Paris, France*

The Torah of Moses and Christ as Savior

In the fourth Gospel Christ explicitly says to the Samaritan woman: "Salvation is from the Jews" (John 4, 22). It is the only use of the word "salvation" in this Gospel, although in other places the terms "savior" and "to save" are used. Now, this same Gospel closely connects the mission of the incarnate Word and the message of Moses: "If you believed Moses, you would believe me also, for he wrote of me" (John 5, 46). In the same truly apostolic vein, the Council has been able to approve the text, not yet promulgated, concerning the relationships between Judaism and Christianity. The "Twelve" and the group which was gathered in the cenacle with Mary at the time of Pentecost form the hinge, as it were, from Judaism to Christianity. No one of the apostles or disciples would have believed that he was abandoning the knowledge of God, which he had received from the Judaism of his time, when he accepted Jesus of Nazareth as the fulfillment of the Torah.

It remains to be seen how they conceived of what we call the Law and they called the Torah, as do the Jews of today. How, too, did they conceive of salvation and the connection between the Law and the salvation about which Christ spoke to the Samaritan woman? Is this salvation an earthly force of grace from a living God, strengthening man against the seeds of death? Is it merit acquired for a life hereafter by fidelity to a divine order? Or must we view both aspects at the same time? These questions already set us on the path of exegesis and history. This history is not only the recording of documents or writings of the past, but, thanks to the methodical study of the texts we possess, the vivid recollection of the real life and thought of Jews and Christians.

The biblical notion of salvation is at once very simple and very full; it is coexistent with human life. Christ "saves" in curing a sick man (Mark 3, 4; 5, 23; Matt. 9, 22). But in many cases it is purely and simply a question of saving a man's life or the entire person (Matt. 16, 25 et par.). The adversaries of Christ on the cross asked him if he was going to save himself by coming down from his cross (Mark 15, 30f. et par). On the other hand, in a more limited and temporal sense, we see the disciples calculating the riches necessary to save themselves (Matt. 19, 25) before Jesus dissuades them from such ideas by assuring them that what is radically impossible for man, rich or poor, is possible for God.

Besides these individual meanings, there are collective meanings. Christ is defined in the apparition to Joseph as he who "shall save his people" (Matt. 1, 21). Again, in the fourth Gospel (John 3, 17; 12, 47), it is the world which he will save. So, too, Paul, in Romans 1, 16, sees in salvation an act of the power of God; it is the work of Christ (Acts 4, 12) for he, by his resurrection, has been established in power (Rom. 1, 6). Throughout this same Epistle to the Romans Paul considers himself "saved" from manifestations of the divine wrath by this same life of Christ (5, 9–10; cf. 1 Cor. 5, 18). Especially throughout his life as a believer Paul encounters this power of salvation that gives life through the Spirit, particularly when there is a question of threats against his life.[1]

It is not our intention here to study the various nuances taken by the theology of salvation, depending upon the bent of the different authors of the New Testament. We must take into

---

[1] This is developed in L. Cerfaux, Le chrétien dans la Théologie paulinienne (Paris, 1962), pp. 198ff., 300ff.

consideration, however, the fact that this intuition, so rich and
so profound, of a power of God in the heart of the world renewing the life of his creatures, was prepared for by the Law of
Moses and by Moses himself in his Torah. A difficulty arises
with such a subject because nowadays it must be approached
by taking into account the works of biblical criticism[2] and the
contribution of Eastern archaeology since Champoilion and
Layard. The historical method has proven itself and it has been
illustrated by Père Lagrange. It allows us to determine the exact
thought of an author who is fully aware of the problem of salvation at any given period of time. Like all human sciences, the
historical method has its lights and shadows. While taking account of both, the following pages will have as their framework
the Torah and its redactional strata without, however, always
being able to distinguish clearly what is due to Moses or only
stems from him through his successors.

I

SALVATION THROUGH THE DIVINE CHOICE OF THE KING

Salvation and the Life in Structured Institutions

It is, indeed, a well-known fact that in the ancient East and
in the Bible the notion of salvation in primitive times was tied
in with the monarchy as an institution. Everyone knows that the
name of Jesus is connected with the Hebrew word "to save",
yasha. It is less well-known that this word is rare in the Torah.
It appears in Exodus 2, 17 referring to Moses who "delivers" the
daughters of Raguel from the evil shepherds. Again, it is also
said that, at the time of the crossing of the Red Sea, the Lord
saved Israel from the hands of the Egyptians (Ex. 14, 30; cf. 14,
13). So, too, in a rather military context, we find in the canticle
of Moses: "The Lord saved me" (Ex. 15, 2). After this the

---

[2] For a presentation of the opinions of biblical criticism concerning
Moses, cf. R. Smend, *Das Mosebild von Heinrich Ewald bis Martin Noth*
(Tübingen, 1959); H. Cazelles, "Moise," in *Suppl. Dict. Bibl.* V (Paris,
1957), 1308–1337.

word is found only in a half dozen passages of Deuteronomy, influenced in very great measure by monarchical institutions. It is the Lord who comes or does not come to help Israel in war (Deut. 20, 4; 28, 29. 31; 32, 15; 33, 29). By way of exception, it is used in the case of an individual bringing help to a young woman who is being attacked (Deut. 22, 27).

The idea, however, is as old in the East as war and human misery. It is at the time of the great Philistine danger, with respect to the institution of monarchy, that the question of "salvation" is quite pronounced in the Book of Samuel (1 Sam. 10, 19; 11, 3f.). The savior par excellence is the king (2 Kings 12, 5). If the Torah or Pentateuch say little about the salvation of the people or their savior it is because the notion of salvation was attached to the royal institution; the Torah, however, is centered about other institutions and gives monarchy only a limited place (in Deuteronomy, to be exact).

In the Torah the dominant institution is that of the priesthood,[3] but it is not only the priesthood; more precisely, it is the priesthood of Aaron. Ethnology in general and Eastern archaeology in particular have made us very aware of the varieties of sacerdotal institutions. There is the patriarchal (and royal) priesthood of the chief who offers sacrifice and presides at the sacred banquet;[4] there is the priesthood of the guardian of the sanctuary[5] where he receives offerings in the name of the divinity (and thereby consecrates them) and where he ensures the regulation of the right of refuge when it exists. There is, finally, the oracular priesthood, depositary and revealer of the divine will.[6]

[3] R. de Vaux, *Les Institutions de l'Ancien Testament* I–II (Paris, 1958–1960), deals with the institution of the priesthood in II, pp. 195–279.

[4] This was the reason for the altars built by Abraham, Isaac and Jacob before the establishment of the Levitical priesthood. The priest is not necessarily bound to the service of the altar and even in Leviticus 1, 5 it is not the priest who immolates the victim.

[5] This was the case with Achimelech at the sanctuary of Nobe (1 Sam. 21, 7). The right of refuge was regulated in the Torah (Ex. 21, 13–14; Deut. 19 and Num. 33).

[6] This was the case with the Levite Micah (Judg. 17, 5), of Abiathar and of Sadoc, guardians of the Ark of the Covenant (2 Sam. 15, 24–25)

The Aaronic priesthood, as it appears in the Torah, cannot be reduced to any of these three functions, even though an historical process made it depend on all three functions and even on other functions such as those of judge and king.

Alongside the Aaronic institution there was the prophetic institution which rose up under the patriarchs and under Moses (Deut. 18, 18; Num. 11, 25–29). But the Moses of the Torah is no more reducible to the prophetic function than to the priestly. In relation to Aaron it is Moses who is the mediator and consecrator (Lev. 8, 5ff.), and it is he who has the power to "invest" Eleazar at the death of Aaron (Num. 20, 28). Moses is more than a prophet (Num. 12, 7) for God reveals himself to the prophets in dreams and visions while he spoke to Moses face to face, plainly and not in riddles. Not only does he see the "form" (*temunah*) of the Lord (Num. 12, 8), but he is, if anything, the guardian of the sanctuary since he "is faithful in the whole house" of the Lord.

Finally, in the entire Pentateuch it is Moses alone, save God, who may be called "savior" in Israel (apropos of the daughters of Raguel) and who may be presented as the minister of the "salvation" of God. This fact shows that, outside of Deuteronomy where the royal function is explicitly defined[7] (whence the frequent occurrence of the notion of salvation), there are some traces of the royal function with respect to Moses.[8] We should expect as much, for, in the rich pagan culture that surrounded him, the royal function was considered mediatory and salvific. Because of this pagan and foreign origin of monarchy we can see that its admission in Israel would face resistance. This is clearly noted in the Books of Samuel (1 Sam. 8, 5–19). It was, nonetheless, accepted in the name of the God of Israel and considered as salvific from the reign of Saul (1 Sam. 10, 1; 11, 1–11)

---

in which were deposited the tables of the Law, and even more true of the tribe of Levi (Deut. 33, 8–10).

[7] Deuteronomy 17, 14–20; see *infra*, p. 68.

[8] Many features of this have been noted by J. Porter, *Moses and Monarchy* (Oxford, 1963). Cf. also H. Cazelles, *Suppl. Dict. Bibl.* VII, 767–768, 798–800.

even in the differing accounts of inspiration, favorable or un-
favorable.

The Savior-King in the Ancient East

The salvific function of the monarchy in the ancient East is
one aspect of the sacred and religious character of that institution. R. Labat, in his book *Caractère religieux de la monarchie
assyro-babylonienne* (Paris, 1939),[9] devotes an entire chapter
to "the holy war" which the king leads with divine help and with
the favor of divine intervention. Another chapter of the book is
entitled "Le roi est celui qui maintient la vie de son pays, par
les rites, les prières et les travaux". ("The king is he who sustains
the life of his country through ritual, prayer, and work.") Designated by the divinity, often before his birth, the king builds the
temples and exercises by right the sovereign priesthood.

In Egypt, the sacred character of the pharaoh has been recognized since the classic work of A. Moret in 1902.[10] The Egyptians did not have a very metaphysical or very defined notion[11]
of the divine, but the pharaoh and his function were not only
sacred but divine. H. Frankfort has reopened the question in his
book, *Kingship and the Gods*,[12] with all the facts gathered from
Egyptology over the last half century, detailing the different vital
functions of the monarchy with regard to his subjects. The
pharaoh has one particular power, an intense spirit-power, a
concept difficult to elucidate but certainly suggesting a principle
of vital energy.[13]

The pharaoh as the image of Re, the great sun god who orders
the rhythm of the year and the seasons, participates in his crea-

[9] R. Labat, *Le caractère religieux de la monarchie assyro-babylonienne*
(Paris, 1939).
[10] A. Moret, *Rituel du culte divin journalier en Egypt* (Paris, 1902).
[11] This explains the reservations of G. Posener, *De la divinité du
Pharaon* (Paris, 1960).
[12] H. Frankfort, *Kingship and the Gods* (Chicago, 1948).
[13] S. Sauneron, in *Dictionnaire de la civilisation égyptienne* (Paris,
1959), H. Bonnet, *Wörterbuch der aegyptischen Religionsgeschichte*
(Berlin, 1952), pp. 358f.; S. Morenz, *Aegyptische Religion* (Stuttgart,
1960), p. 179.

tive power. Inasmuch as he is the image of "the mighty bull", the son of Hathor, the pharaoh shares in his reproductive power in animal and trees. As the likeness of Horus, the son of Osiris and god of the grain, the pharaoh has power over the harvests. "I was the one who made barley, the beloved of the grain-god. The Nile honored me on every broad expanse. No one hungered in my years; no one thirsted therein." Thus spoke Amen-em-het I in the prosopopeia which a scribe prepared for him about 1900 years before Christ.[14] The pharaoh gives the breath of life to his subjects;[15] he is the hero in battle who can, by his bravery, deliver himself and his army at critical moments, as did Ramses II in the battle of Kadesh at the beginning of the 13th century B.C., when his enemies, the Hittites, were closing in on him.

Nearer still to the Israelites, a Syrian-Semitic scribe (who spoke a language very close to Hebrew) copied a very important text about 1300 B.C. These are the reproaches that were addressed to a king who was no longer doing his duty:[16]

> Thou judgest not the cause of the widow,
> Nor adjudicat'st the case of the wretched;
> Driv'st not out them that prey on the poor;
> Feed'st not the fatherless before thee,
> The widow behind thy back.

This is a beautiful description of the salvific functions that were incumbent upon the king. One could find countless other examples of this kind in the pre-biblical ancient East, even if only by consulting the famous Code of Hammurabi (ca. 1750 B.C.) in which, from the very beginning (R. P. Scheil), relationships have been found with certain articles in the Torah of Moses.[17]

[14] This text can be found in Pritchard, *Ancient Near Eastern Texts related to the Old Testament* (Princeton, 1950), p. 418. Commentary in G. Posener, *Littérature et politique dans l'Egypte de la XIIème dynastie* (Paris, 1956), pp. 61ff.

[15] References in Erman-Grapow, *Wörterbuch der Aeg. Sprache* V, 352, n. 24.

[16] This text, found at Ugarit, Ras-Shamra by C. Schaeffer and translated for the first time by C. Virolleaud, is found in Pritchard, *op. cit.*, 149 (Ginsberg trans.)

[17] This text is found in Pritchard, *op. cit.*, 163–179 (Meek trans.)

The king has this salvific function because, like the son of David (2 Sam. 7, 4), he is the son of God, the heir of God and of the divine promises. As such he participates in God's power, although the nature of this sonship is not made fully clear. The scandal is that the beneficiaries of this salvific function can suffer illness and die: "How can one say that the son of El dies, the family of the beneficent and holy God?" [18] It is through his own descent that the king, the savior who must be saved, can finally fulfill his mission with regard to his people.

At the beginning of the second millennium, there was already among the Egyptians a great ceremony of succession which allowed the new pharaoh, identified with Horus, to avenge his dead father, a new Osiris destined for the kingdom of the dead. For our Syrian scribe it is the last child, the eighth daughter who cures her father. It is she who received the heritage of the firstborn in place of the firstborn son who called on his father to give up the throne because he was incapacitated. So it is that this royal ideology continues and nourishes itself in dynastic theology. To put it more succinctly: the people's hope of salvation rests on the succession of the king's son, object of the people's act of faith in his calling and selection. The faith and hope of Israel rested not so much on an aging David but on his descendants, finally on his descendant of the last days, the anointed king par excellence, the Messiah.

The Monarchy and Its Limitations in the Torah

The surrounding monarchical ideology underwent a profound change in Israel and in the Bible. Indeed the knowledge possessed by the people and scribes of the second millennium of this monarchical ideology offers, as it were, the thread of Ariadne which allows us to understand the theology assumed by the accounts of Genesis and of the Pentateuch, accounts so highly colored, so psychological, so concrete. Since the 19th century we have recognized among the texts of the Pentateuch, in which there are laws, names, genealogies and anecdotes, the

[18] Continuation of the text cited in footnote 16.

particular character of a series of texts that form, as it were, one continuous fabric. These have been grouped under the symbol J (Yahwist, from the German form "Jahvist")[19] because in these texts, without waiting for the revelation of the divine name at Horeb, the divinity was invoked under the name of Yahweh beginning with the son of Seth, who was substituted for the first-born Cain.

The remarkable author and religious genius who thus gathered together and grouped these traditions concerning the patriarchs and Moses did this dutiful and conscientious work not without thought of the salvation of a people who were living under a dynasty, certainly chosen by God, but in which dangerous foreign influences had become established, even under Solomon, the son of David, the founder of the temple. This son, not the first-born, the child of adultery, was legitimate as were the younger children Isaac, Jacob and Judah, Judah being the recipient of the prophecy of his father Jacob (Gen. 49).

Still, Solomon's reign could come to a bad end. The author warns the Israelites, tempted by foreign examples, that monarchy (even with a David as the head of the dynasty) is not in itself a pledge of salvation. If David had been chosen it was because he had respected the customs which went back to the first savior of the people, Moses. Moses had delivered the people from the evil hold of the Pharaohs, one of whose daughters Solomon had wed and whose ancient wisdom and "cunning" he admired (Gen. 3, 1).

Without having the title of king, Moses truly exercised the royal salvific function. For our author, who synthesized the old tribal traditions, Moses, the last of the patriarchs, foreshadows the true royal function in Israel. As in the case of the patriarchs and kings, the author is as concerned with Moses' mother as

---

[19] We should remember that besides this series, or *J* (Jahvist) stratum, biblical scholars distinguish an Elohist (*E*) stratum (of a prophetic spirit), the deuteronomic texts (*D*) and the priestly texts (*P*). For the present state of the criticism, cf. H. Cazelles, "Pentateuque," in *Suppl. Dict. Bibl.* VII, 736–858; *Introduction à la Bible,* ed. A. Robert and A. Feuillet (Paris/Tournai, 1959), I, 331–382; S. Mowinckel, *Erwägungen zur Pentateuch Quellenfrage* (Oslo, 1964).

with his father. He tells the story of the vicissitudes of his marriage in Midian, the religious influence of his wife (Ex. 4, 24f. on circumcision), the birth of his children. Moses was the object of a special vocation, like Tothmes IV at the feet of the Sphinx and many Assyrian kings. After negotiating for his people, he freed them and gave them a statute and ordinance (Ex. 15, 25), as did Hammurabi for the Babylonians. He fed his people in the desert as Amen-em-het I rightly did (cf. also Num. 11, 12). Like the Assyrian king he felt responsible for his people before the divinity. Philo of Alexandria was to attribute royal dignity to Moses.[20] While showing that Moses exercised this royal function, still this is not the title which he has in the Torah; the God of Abraham reserved for him mediation of a different order.

II

THE MEDIATION OF MOSES AS THE CONDITION
OF SALVATION IN THE TORAH

Through Worship

We can thus see emerging the originality of the biblical concept of salvation in Israel through the God of the Fathers. If the descendants of David enjoyed an eternal election (2 Sam. 7, 16), this dynasty did not owe its power to the superhuman value of David nor to a sort of natural kinship between the dynasty and the divinity, like pharaoh begotten by Amon on the walls of the temple at Luxor. David and his successors are the "anointed of Yahweh". The Torah of Moses connects the salvific function of royalty with a double dependence. The promise comes to the king only as the heir of the promises made to the patriarchs Abraham, Isaac and Jacob. Jacob, in Genesis 49, 10, secured the sceptre for a Jewish monarch although Judah comes only in the fourth place among the tribes. Furthermore, the orders which the king was to give in Israel are not orders which are sacred in themselves.

[20] *Vita Moses,* I, p. vii; II, p. 1.

Unlike Hammurabi who drew up a code, or some Egyptian pharaohs who issued decrees (like Horemheb and Senhi I in the time of Moses), law in Israel did not come from the king but from the Lord, through Moses. Such was the case in the law concerning the Passover (Ex. 12, 22) or the more general ritual law of Exodus (34, 17–26). If the dynasty of David is the depositary of eternal salvation for the faithful, it is because this dynasty is guaranteed by something which precedes and transcends it. Unlike Saul who disagreed with Samuel on questions of sacrifice and immolation, the son of David built a sanctuary where royal political skill would not prevail over the ancient divine prescriptions which were a part of the people's heritage from the desert, even in such a matter as the dietary taboo recalled by Genesis 2, 17. The ritual of feasts and sacred meals does not come from a royal order; it is offered as coming from the mediation of Moses before the conquest of Canaan by Israel.

The religious foundations of this Davidic monarchy, which in the end only one tribe recognized, go back to Moses who died on Mt. Nebo in Ruben before the conquest accomplished by his disciple Joshua.[21] It was he who established the foundations of the people's salvation and of his own life on the rules given him on the holy mountain in the name of the God of the nation. In the Yahwist accounts (J) the principal scene of Sinai is probably that of Exodus 24, 9–11: "Moses then went up with Aaron, Nadab, Abiu and seventy elders of Israel, and they beheld the God of Israel. Under his feet there appeared to be sapphire tilework, as clear as the sky itself. Yet he did not smite these chosen Israelites.[22] After gazing on God they could still eat and drink."

These chosen ones were able to eat the sacred banquet in the presence of God and even to see him without dying. So three times a year all the faithful had to go up to the national sanctuary to see the face of God, according to Exodus 34, 20. The

---

[21] Cf. Ex. 17, 9; 33, 1; Num. 11, 28; Josh. 1, 1. Elisha was at first the attendant of Elijah (1 Kgs. 19, 21; 2 Kgs. 3, 11).

[22] This rare and difficult term seems to signify something "set apart," a choice (Num. 11, 17). "To lay hands on" has a hostile and fear-inspiring connotation in Gen. 22, 12; 37, 22; 1 Sam. 24, 7.

faithful and the chosen do not see the divine essence through this act of worship, as proven by the metaphors used. The form of worship established in Jerusalem by David, and even more so by his son, is, rather, a memorial of the national deliverance in the month of Abib (Ex. 34, 18) and a pledge of divine salvific protection. Exodus 34, 23 comments: "Since I will drive out the nations before you to give you a large territory, there will be no one to covet your land when you go up three times a year to appear before the Lord, your God."

These liturgical traditions, pledge of life and protection for the people, have been collected by Sadoc and Abiathar to whom David, the Ephraimite from Bethlehem, entrusted the worship about the ark. Through Sadoc these traditions go back to Aaron, his ancestor who died on Mt. Hor near Cades (1 Chron. 6, 1–11). They go back also to Moses whose descendants through Gersam had charge of the sanctuary of Lais (Dan) (Judg. 18, 30). Unfortunately we have fewer witnesses in the Bible for the descendants of his second son, Eliezer (Ex. 18, 4), whose name is interpreted as a token of salvation ("God has brought me help"), and who very probably had charge of a sanctuary nearer Ephraim and Bethlehem-Ephrata.

Through the Decalogue

In the legacy of Moses there was more than this liturgy assembled in the capital by the dynasty of David and the priesthood of Jerusalem. The warriors of Ephraim who, under the leadership of Joshua, penetrated into the territory of the tribe (and even beyond) had brought with them traditions of a different order. With these warriors, some traditions and texts penetrated and were preserved in sanctuaries of the North, such as Transjordan. In these texts a different aspect of Moses' message shone forth— its moral aspect. To the degree that the corrupting influence of Phoenician and Canaanite worship showed itself more and more in Israel and its sanctuaries, the prophetic movement and the faithful Levites depended all the more on these texts. In effect, they showed, over against the pagan naturalism of the fertility gods, that Yahweh was not a Baal and that he was not unconditionally bound to the people of the twelve tribes. He had set down certain conditions in his covenant which the decalogue expressed and which Hosea, for one, recalled (Hos. 4, 1).

The prophetic movement no longer had to purify a monarchical ideology by bringing the monarchy in line with the promises given to the patriarchs and to the Mosaic (and Aaronic) cult. Rather, its duty now was to subordinate this same cult to the respect for one's neighbor and to the demands of a just God speaking to the conscience. They had been assured of the presence of a Baal by a statue of the god. Yahweh did not want a statue; he spoke to the conscience.

The ten commandments (Ex. 20, 2–17; Deut. 5, 6–22) are the expression on stone of the conditions of the alliance and of salvation.[23] If their existent redaction feels the effect of the prophetic influence, its fundamental elements (especially the short final phrases) correspond very well with what a scribe would have written who had been formed in the school of the political wise men in Egypt about 1300 B.C. He would have been a scribe, however, faithful to the God of his Fathers, who had directed their acts and their behavior.

We are at the crossroads of a human wisdom which has a highly advanced respect for the human person as one who is able to clearly envision such things in reading the writings of wisdom (which were well before Moses[24]), and the writings of a religion which is not the religion of an Osiris, a judge of the dead, or of a dynastic god such as Amon. The religion of the Fathers, of which Moses was the heir, is that of a personal God who supernaturally intervenes in the life of his faithful. Driven out of Egypt, the scribe Moses had recognized on Horeb the God of his Fathers who wanted to save his people at the very

---

[23] On the decalogue, cf. H. Haag, *Moral Theologie und Bible* (Paderborn, 1964), pp. 9–28; J. Gamberoni, *Bib. Zeitschr.* (1964) pp. 161–190; J. Stamm, *Der Dekalog im Lichte der neueren Forschung* (Bern, ²1962).
[24] Ptah-hotep, Merikare, Kheti. . . . Cf. Pritchard, *op. cit.*, pp. 412–440.

time when pharaoh needed labor to fortify the eastern part of the delta.[25]

What the decalogue demands is regard for one's neighbor, for his life and his goods, as well as fidelity to a God who is directly present: "You will have no other god before me." There are then to be none of those intermediary divinities between the faithful and the supreme divinity as so often represented in the glyptics of the time. The moral dimension of the decalogue bears a relation to the cultic. Not only is there question of idols and of the sabbath, but above all, according to the more important authors, it is probable that a similar text was read when the community assembled in worship and recalled the demands of the covenant.[26] Furthermore, it is quite probable that at the very source of this text Moses was inspired by an Egyptian custom in defining the conditions requisite for entry into the sanctuary and participation in worship. Those who had committed this or that act, transgression of a taboo, a rite, or a custom, were excluded. Egypt had a set list of conditions for entry for individual sanctuaries in local districts.[27] The decalogue broke with every sort of magic to concentrate its demands on the individual's relation with God and neighbor.

It was in this way that the faithful came to know the wishes of God. Not only did they know how to invoke God in their worship and hymns but they knew when they had sinned. No longer could the Jew say, as did the worshiper in Mesopotamia, that he did not know how he had offended his God, that he was ignorant of God's wishes, or that the divine plans are wrapped in enigma.

[25] It is also possible that Moses the scribe was aided by the intellectual and political effort which led to a short-lived monotheism of Amenophis IV. But the religion of Moses refers above all to the God of his Fathers, in the sense of very personal relations like those permitted in Babylonia at the beginning of the second millennium. Cf. *Suppl. Dict. Bibl.*, VII, 141ff.

[26] A similar reading of stipulations had been foreseen by the treaties and Deuteronomy 31.

[27] P. Montet, "Les fruits défendus et la confession des péchés," in *Les Sagesses du Proche-Orient ancien* (Strasbourg, 1962; Paris, 1963), p. 61.

The religion of Moses is a religion of the knowledge of God. To know God is to know that the Lord wishes to reunite his faithful ones into a people all living together and respecting one another, under the care of God who speaks to the heart of one's conscience. This God expressed his will and would judge in accord with the stipulations of a covenant. With the transgressions multiplied, the "people perish for want of knowledge" (Hos. 4, 6), but they can be pardoned by doing penance as at Horeb (Ex. 32, 35; 33, 6). The mistakes made in the desert are more cultic in nature than they are faults against the decalogue. Tradition, however, kept alive the memory of the Moses who was forced to flee to the desert for having avenged his oppressed brother (Ex. 2, 12ff.) before saving the daughters of Raguel.

We thus see how in the northern kingdom, which ignored the election of the dynasty of David, the prophetic movement had once again brought into prominence a fundamental aspect of Mosaism. The pre-exilic prophets are to recall with all their might the moral demands of the just God and to him will subordinate the propitiatory value of worship to such an extent that modern commentators have been led to believe that they were radically opposed to everything cultic. This position would make of the prophets men cut off from other biblical authors; and the intense cultic life that follows the return from exile would have been a cruel denial of their aspirations. In actual fact, they were quite aware that the religious festivals in which the people took delight and the sacrifices in which they placed their confidence were powerless to effect salvation if the substructure of the Torah of Moses were not respected. Its God could not have saved a people among whom the weak member was himself downtrodden. Not only the decalogue but the curses of Sichem (Deut. 27) against hidden faults and the code of the covenant (Ex. 20–23) express the concrete wishes of a God who knows his people.

Through Love

God's knowledge of his people issues in a love and societal life that is no longer one of simple justice. To live in Israel is to live a life of goodwill toward one's fellow man, a life of *hesed* (to use a Hebrew word which is difficult to translate). The members of this people are not simply juxtaposed but live a life intimately bound up one with another, entailing reciprocal obligations. Hosea speaks of this as does Exodus 34, 6. Now he is also the prophet most articulate about God's love for his people. The old terms of the alliance of the 2nd millennium already required a vassal to love his lord.[28] There can be some doubt about the depth of this love even when it is the expression of a just aspiration. We find an echo of this demand with a different resonance and a different depth when we read in one redaction of the decalogue of God "bestowing mercy down to the thousandth generation on the children of those who love me and keep my commandments" (Ex. 20, 6). But it is Deuteronomy in particular that will develop this love of God the savior. It asks the faithful one to open his heart if he desires to understand the will of God and to know him.

We do not have here the invention of the last book of the Torah. Already the ancient traditions recounted how Moses the shepherd had painfully collided with this stiff-necked people, himself the victim of a hardhearted pharaoh. Hosea, in chapter 11, describes the salvific ways of God from the time of the Israelites sojourn in Egypt to that of the monarchy as a mystery of the depths of divine love. "When Israel was a child I loved him, out of Egypt I called my son. . . . I drew them with human cords, with bands of love. . . . How could I give you up, O Ephraim, or deliver you up, O Israel? . . . My heart is overwhelmed, my pity is stirred. . . . For I am God and not man."

The complaints of Moses in the desert reflect the depths of a love that is revealed in the redemption of a sinful people. As early as the time of the negotiations with pharaoh (Ex. 5), we see Moses as the victim of recriminations because it is he who would have brought down upon the people the hatred of those

[28] Cf. W. Moran, "The Ancient Near Eastern Background of the Love of God in Deuteronomy", in *Cath. Bibl. Quart.* 25 (1963), pp. 80ff., esp. p. 85; should be read in conjunction with N. Lohfink, "Hate and Love in Osee IX:15," in *Cath. Bibl. Quart.*, 25 (1963), p. 417.

in authority. He turns to God. "Why did you send me on such a mission? Ever since I went to Pharaoh to speak in your name, he has maltreated this people of yours, and you have done nothing to rescue them" (Ex. 5, 22f.).

The people started grumbling again at Elim (15, 24), from Meribah to Cades (Ex. 17, 3ff.), to Horeb (Ex. 32, 11ff.). Moses intercedes, giving us a glimpse of the concern of a shepherd for his people. " 'Why do you treat your servant so badly?' Moses asked the Lord. 'Why are you so displeased with me that you burden me with all this people? Was it I who conceived all this people? Or was it I who gave them birth, that you tell me to carry them at my bosom, like a foster father carrying an infant, to the land you have promised under oath to their fathers? Where can I get meat to give to all this people? . . . I cannot carry all this people by myself, for they are too heavy for me. If this is the way you will deal with me, then please do me the favor of killing me at once, so that I need no longer face this distress' " (Num. 11, 11–15).

The lament of this shepherd reveals God's mandate. The people long to eat meat, long for the cucumbers they ate in Egypt; those responsible, sent to explore the country, discourage the people instead of lending them support. They enervate them by alarming them beyond measure, when more love and faith would have led to greater understanding of the ways of God. And so the author of Deuteronomy asks the Israelite to love "the Lord your God, with all your heart, and with all your soul, and with all your strength" (Deut. 6, 4). Thus would he insist on the circumcision of the heart which alone gives the strength of soul necessary to follow and keep the divine ordinances, to break through their stubbornness (Deut. 10, 16).

Most remarkable, and perhaps most disconcerting to our present-day mentality, is the fact that the same book which insists most on love between God and his people is the very one which develops at greatest length the divine institutions among this people. Revelation no longer bears only on the commandments or on the concrete laws which apply these commandments to the conditions of societal life in Israel. The faithful man lives in an organized community in which this life of love subsists due to the influence of these institutions. Furthermore all of these are subordinated to revelation: judge, king, priest and prophet.

The judge, with the scribe at his side but associated with the priest in the supreme tribunal (Deut. 17, 9) of the sanctuary, should hold office in each village. We can hear the words: "You shall not distort justice; you must be impartial. You shall not take a bribe; for a bribe blinds the eyes even of the wise and twists the words even of the just. Justice and justice alone shall be your aim. . . ." (Deut. 16, 19ff.)

The king is to be chosen by Yahweh among the Israelite "kinsmen". He will transcribe the Law which will be at his side all the days of his life. He must not act presumptuously or have many wives to lead his heart astray!

The Levitical priest shall have no heritage among his fellows, the Lord being his heritage and the offerings made to him. For he is chosen by God to minister to him and to pronounce blessings in his name. His dues from the sacrificial offerings are strictly defined (Deut. 18, 1–8).

Finally, the prophet is a new Moses (Deut. 18, 15–22), raised up by God to recall his revelation. He must confine himself strictly to what God commands or had commanded. According to the effect of his pronouncements, the faithful will judge if he has spoken presumptuously or overstepped his commission.

The development of these institutions in Deuteronomy is in direct line with a more ancient condition in which some more rudimentary divine institutions were meant to assure peace and brotherhood through the presence of the living Word of God. Nathan, Gad, or a tribeswoman had already reminded David the king that there are some things which are not done in Israel. (Cf. 2 Sam. 13, 12.) Through Nathan or Gad, the prophetic function was exercised alongside a guilty David at the same time as the priestly function watched over the Ark of the Covenant and the decalogue which was preserved in it (1 Kgs. 8, 9).

The texts which have a prophetic tone in the Pentateuch

recalled how the spirit of Moses had been communicated to the Elders (Num. 11, 25) and how this same Moses, on the advice of Jethro, had set up chiefs over groups of one thousand, one hundred, fifty, and twelve men to judge the less important cases. If, as is probable, Moses had edited the brief maxims of the decalogue regulating admission into the tent of worship, it is even more probable that at Cades or at Nebo he played a judiciary role vis-à-vis those who came to consult the divinity with a personal problem or to settle a dispute. It was customary in the temples of the East to consult the divinity this way and Isaiah reproached his contemporaries for running after necromancers instead of coming to the temple (Is. 8, 13.19f.). It is this ancient Mosaic institution that we see expanding and becoming diversified in Deuteronomy in order to establish the life of Israel (despite enemies within and without) in love and brotherhood.

III

SALVATION THROUGH HOLINESS IN THE TORAH

We are reminded of the impressive setting of the calling of the prophet Isaiah in the Temple (Is. 6). He perceives God's holiness proclaimed by the seraphs and this vision lets him see the radical uncleanness of the people of which he was a member. He is not competent to receive divine utterances until after the purification of his lips by a red-hot stone taken from the altar.[29] Because the people are unclean and God alone holy and transcendent, this people will be destroyed by the action of outside forces. But happily, by divine grace, there is in Israel a holy seed participating in the divine holiness over which the powers of destruction are powerless. Given the connection of this scene with the death of King Uzziah (and therefore with the accession of his successor), and given the insistence of the verses which

[29] The metal objects to be consecrated to God were to have been thus purified by fire (Num. 31, 22–23).

follow (Is. 7, 1–7) on the powerlessness of Damascus and
Ephraim to change the dynastic order willed by God, and finally
the affirmation of the hope of faith in the birth of Emmanuel
(Is. 7, 16f.) [the child upon whose shoulder will rest the government of the throne of David (Is. 9, 6)], the entire scene then
refers again to salvation through royal and dynastic election.
But it unfolds in the place chosen by Yahweh, the temple in
Jerusalem, the holy place par excellence, filled with the holiness
of the God enthroned there.

We know that in the second millennium before Christ, divinity is holy (or sacred) to the degree that it is awesome and
inhuman. Even Genesis takes care not to say of the God of the
patriarchs that he is holy because of its insistence on the close
bond between God and his faithful one. But, as soon as it touches
on deliverance from a pagan power, the Book of Exodus speaks
of holiness. At the very beginning, it mentions God's holiness
apropos of the holy place which is Horeb. The God of the
Fathers revealed to Moses both his name and his plan for salvation (Ex. 3, 5). Then, in the great canticle of Moses, after the
crossing of the Red Sea, the holiness of Yahweh is invoked.
"Who is like to you among the gods, O Lord? Who is like to
you, magnificent in holiness? O terrible in renown, worker of
wonders . . ." (Ex. 15, 11). Holiness signifies the transcendent
power of God who through Moses delivers his people.

In point of fact, the people have the greatest difficulty in feeling at ease with God's holiness and do not always have a clear
vision of its character. This holiness is very specially manifest
in his "sanctuary" and the Ark which it houses, an Ark dangerous to touch (1 Sam. 3–5). Nevertheless, God asks all the
Israelites to come to this sanctuary (Ex. 34, 23–26) and those
who do so are to "sanctify" themselves before appearing in the
presence of their God (Ex. 19, 10–11). It is not only a question
of washing one's clothes or of abstaining from sexual relations.
We have seen that the decalogue was probably referring in the
beginning to access to the sanctuary. The prophets insisted on
the moral demands of the Lord and showed clearly that the

holiness of God did not consist in any sort of ritual washing but in the perfect rectitude and perfect justice of this God, in his thought and in his actions. Isaiah, who recognized in God the "Holy One of Israel" (Is. 1, 4), asks not for sacrifices and holocausts as much as for the purification of "blood-stained hands." "Put away your misdeeds from before my eyes; cease doing evil, learn to do good; make justice your aim: redress the wronged, hear the orphan's plea, defend the widow. . . . But if you refuse and resist, the sword shall consume you" (Is. 1, 16–17.20).

Thus, to assure permanent protection and deliverance for his people, God, in the Torah of Moses, offers them a share in his own divine holiness. Then God will give his people a share in his own transcendence and in his immunity to the powers of evil. The Law relating to holiness, written down in Leviticus 17–26, is like a practical commentary on those principles which underlie the decalogue of Moses. Its rhythm is given by the refrain "Be holy, for I, the Lord, your God am holy" (Lev. 19, 2; 20, 26). Through the rites of expiation which are performed at the altar (Lev. 17, 11), lives can be saved and perfected, but only on condition of a real fidelity to the moral and ritual prescriptions of the God of Israel. Because the people have in the Torah the sanctifying presence of God, they must observe the proper traditional laws in the family order, the order of justice and of worship. Amid this vast codification of customs, which very often dates from the second millennium, is found the gem of the Gospel vaguely traced in Deuteronomy: "You shall love your neighbor as yourself" (Lev. 19, 18).

The election of this people is completed by a general alliance between God and humanity, with Noah the beneficiary (Gen. 9, 1–7), and especially by a more individual election, that of Aaron. The Aaronic priesthood has supplementary, more demanding regulations because it has charge of the purity and holiness of the people (Lev. 21). It is the central institution of this law that leads to holiness. "Honor him (the priest) as sacred who offers up the food of your God; treat him as sacred, because

I, the Lord, who have consecrated him, am sacred. . . . for with the anointing oil upon him, he is dedicated to his God, to me, the Lord" (Lev. 21, 8.12). It is the priest who in the name of his God receives the offering and the sacrifices. Chapter 26 is a résumé of all the blessings and punishments God will give his people depending on their fidelity to that holiness which they are offered while living among the secular powers of this world.

Conclusion

We have reached one of the highest peaks in the Torah, and Judaism has seized upon it and preserved its strength even after the destruction of the sanctuary and the rending of the veil in the temple. With the ruin of this temple and the downfall of its Aaronic priesthood, the Torah lives on only in the pharisaic and Christian interpretations. The faithful ones of the God of Abraham have no longer found the life-giving presence in a holy place, for it has been desecrated. They have ceased renewing their contact with the God of life through the liturgical cycle and its pilgrimages, through vows and spontaneous sacrifices. The people have no longer been made clean by the right of the scapegoat. The life-giving source, which used to spring from it (Ez. 47), has poured forth elsewhere.

Pharisaism has seen in the Torah a code of ethics and of Jewish civil rights and concerns. Let us not fail to appreciate its greatness and its worth: it has given to Judaism a lasting force throughout persecutions under the most diverse regimes, in the East as in the West. Every act is religious and meritorious for eternal life when it can be related one way or another to the demands of that Torah. Whether a person develops its casuistry, as was the tendency in one age, or whether he sees in it the eternal witness of the election of the children of Abraham, bearers of universal values for humanity, it is the text of the Torah which carries a permanent salvific value. It is this text which a person will venerate and which he will always consult to know the dealings of God with man.

For Christianity, the temple of stone has given way to the

temple of flesh, the physical and eucharistic Body of Christ (John 2, 21) just as Ezekiel declared that hearts of stone would become hearts of flesh under the action of the Spirit (Ez. 36, 26–27). The priesthood of Aaron has not disappeared with the downfall of the temple only to make room for the rabbinical teachers. It is assumed into a superior priesthood, that of Christ, priest according to the order of Melchizedek (Heb. 7). This Messiah Son of David assumes not only the priestly function of the Torah but the prophetic as well. Not only does he, like the prophet, have the "word" but he is the Word. Having entered by his blood, through the resurrection[30] into the heavenly sanctuary (Heb. 9), "therefore he is able at all times to save those who come to God through him, since he lives always to make intercession for them" (Heb. 7, 25).

In bestowing the Spirit, he diffuses through it living charity in our hearts. Thus, St. Paul is convinced that his teaching about faith does not destroy the Law but rather confirms it (Rom. 3, 31), because baptism makes us alive with the life of him who died and was raised from the dead (Rom. 6, 1–4). This is the "sprinkling with clean water" announced by Ezekiel (36, 25), which was to be followed by the gift of a new spirit, the transformation of heart and the practice of the Law. "I will give you a new heart and place a new spirit within you . . . and make you live by my statutes, careful to observe my decrees. . . . I will save you from all your impurities; I will order the grain to be abundant, and I will not send famine against you. . . . Thus the neighboring nations that remain shall know that I, the Lord, have rebuilt what was destroyed and replanted what was desolate" for "this desolate land has been made into a garden of Eden" (Ez. 36, 26–36). All the beauty of life sketched by the second chapter of the Torah is thus preserved.

---

[30] The "greater and more perfect" tent of worship of Hebrews 9, 11 is actually in all probability the risen Body of Christ. Cf. A. Vanhoye, in *Biblica* 46 (1965), pp. 1–28.

Johannes Willemse, O.P./*Nijmegen, Netherlands*

God's First and Last Word: Jesus (Mark 1, 1–13; John 1, 1–18)

One and the same event is seen and heard by various persons in different ways. Each person hears and sees in the context of his own peculiar background, against the horizon of his personal experiences and expectations and of his own appropriation of past and future as these are felt and lived by the community of which he is a member. As the Scholastics used to say: "Omne quod recipitur, recipitur secundum modum recipientis." The four Gospels offer a tragic example of this truth: not all of those who heard and saw Jesus heard and saw the very same thing. The high priests, scribes and pharisees saw and heard "Beelzebub, prince of devils". Those who saw did not see, but were blinded. Yet the eyes and ears of the blind and deaf were opened and publicans and sinners saw and heard the Son of God. The children of darkness who did not accept the light saw in Jesus the powers of darkness at work. The children of light beheld the Light of Jesus' glory, a glory as of the Only-begotten Son of the living God. They accepted him, they saw him as the Light of the world and heard him as the Word of Life.

Even among the faithful, however, the old adage holds: "Omne quod recipitur, recipitur secundum modum recipientis." The evangelists were men of the first century living in the eastern part of the Roman Empire. If they had had to write their Gospels

75

from their belief in the same Jesus but in the 20th century and in the northwestern part of Europe, they would have surely written otherwise; they would have seen and heard the same events differently than in fact they did see and hear. Actually, the four Gospels, although written during the same period and within the same world, differ even among themselves. And still, it is the identical Gospel which has found expression in often very dissimilar ways in these four accounts. It is, for example, the very same Jesus whom we first meet in the Gospel according to Mark in a passage on Jesus' baptism in the Jordan and whom we meet in the Gospel according to John in the Prologue. But what a difference! Upon closer examination, however, what is intended in these two introductions is seen to come down to precisely the same thing.

This unity within great, often very great, diversity—diversity in seeing and hearing, in thinking, in writing (literary genres), diversity also in the actual situation in which the writing took place (*Sitz im Leben*)—is found throughout the Sacred Scriptures. "From his fullness, we all have received", each in his own way, each also according to his art of representation. The Sacred Scriptures are the written report of many witnesses from many many periods: a report of what these countless witnesses received, each in his own way, in his own lifetime and situation, and within the framework of his own view of the world. It is a many-sided witness in which what has been received has been reworked, thought out, represented and worded from perspectives and within thought-forms that are often quite different.

Under the theme "the Word of God", this article is concerned with the Gospel, with Jesus. The wealth of data, interconnections and problems involved in this theme, however, forces us to limit our study to a first orientation. We shall try, on the one hand, to sketch the most important scriptural perspectives of this theme in their mutual relationships and, on the other hand, within these perspectives, to throw more light upon the above mentioned introductory passages of the Gospels according to Mark and John. In this way, one may come to see more clearly something of the substantial unity as well as of the rich diversity of detail, something of the unity in diversity as well as of the diversity in unity; there, also, where it is a question of the scriptural background of the language we use in speaking of the "Word of God" in connection with "Jesus of Nazareth, the son of Joseph" (John 1, 45).

God's Word: the Law and the Prophets

The New Testament was composed against the background of the Old Testament. The prominence accorded in the Old Testament to the speaking of God, to God's Word, corresponds to the importance of the prophetical influence upon the history and historical writings of the People of God. The decisive influence of the word of the prophets in Israel's history was undoubtedly just as decisive in Israel's vision of its God speaking to his people, in Israel's conception of God's Word.

In the history of Israel and in the life of the pious Israelite, other "speakers" besides the prophets played a role: the priests (and Levites) and the sages. Priest, sage and prophet spoke to Israel, each from his own world, each in his own way, each in the line of his special tradition. Despite mutual interaction, one finds clearly in the records of the Old Testament a striking difference in these modes of speaking. Typical of the sacerdotal-levitical tradition are the books of the Law, especially Leviticus; characteristic of the wisdom and prophetical traditions are, respectively, the "Wisdom literature" and the "Books of the Prophets". One has only to read first Leviticus 1, next Ecclesiastes 1 and, finally, Isaiah 1 or Jeremiah 1 to notice immediately the difference.

The distinction of priest, sage and prophet in their manner of speaking was also recognized in Israel itself, and is expressed in the following text: ". . . the law (instruction) shall not perish from the priest, nor counsel from the wise, nor *the word from the prophet* (Jer. 18, 18; Septuagint: *ouk apoleitai nomos apo hiereoos, kai boulè apo sunetou, kai logos apo prophètou*). Just as the law is characteristic of the priest and counsel of the sage, so is *the word* characteristic of the prophet. "The word" without equal is the word of the prophet. When we speak of "the Word of God", we find ourselves in a tradition dominated by the word of the prophets.

In the Old Testament, the word involves more than a mere expression of thought or will. Sustained by the breath, by the spirit of the speaker, the word is, as it were, invested with his might and power and goes into the world as a sort of independent and active reality.

The experience of the power and might of the word of the prophets plays probably a greater role in this conception than a primitive magic of the word (magic formula). The word by which the prophets spoke about events of their time was not so much a (passive) account of those events as an (active) judgment upon them, a judgment directed to the persons involved, touching the event itself and influencing it decisively. When the faithful People of God stood on the threshold of the New Testament, its history—both as (remembrance of its) past and as (expectation of its) future—was determined conclusively by the word of the prophets.

Faithful Israel recognized and acknowledged in the mighty and effective word of the prophets the Word of its God, the Word of God to his people, the Word of God as judgment (of the past) and as promise (for the future). To this recognition and acknowledgment corresponds the fact that the expressions "the Word", "the Words", "the Word of Yahweh" and "the Words of Yahweh" occur very often in the Old Testament and usually as signifying the Word coming from God to the prophets and announced by the prophets to Israel (in Samuel, 12 times; in Kings, 50 times; in Jeremiah, 52 times; in Ezekiel, 60 times[1]). This conception is shown also in the frequent use of the phrase: "And the Word of Yahweh came to . . ." (1 Kgs. 6, 11; 13, 20; Jer. 1, 4.11; 2, 1; 13, 8; 16, 1; 14, 4; 28, 12; 29, 30; Ez. 3, 16; 6, 1; 7, 1; 12, 1). So it is also that the prophetical books sometimes begin with the expression: "The words of

[1] *Bijbels Woordenboek* (Roermond, 1954–1957), col. 1867.

Amos" or "of Jeremiah" (Amos 1, 1; Jer. 1, 1; cf. Is. 1, 1; Nahum 1, 1), but preferably with "The Word of Yahweh which came to Hosea" or "to Micah", etc. (Hos. 1, 1; Mic. 1, 1; Zeph. 1, 1; cf. Mal. 1, 1). The introduction to Jeremiah in Hebrew is "The words of Jeremiah"; in the Greek of the Septuagint, "The Word of God that came to Jeremiah." A final correspondence is the fact that even in the New Testament the prophetical Word (or what is interpreted as being prophetical) is cited now as spoken by the prophet (*e.g.,* Acts 7, 48), then as spoken by God (*e.g.,* Heb. 8, 1–12), then again as the Word spoken by God through the prophets (*e.g.,* Matt. 1, 22; 2, 15).

Just as one recognizes a human master by the power of his word—"I say to one (of the soldiers under me), 'Go,' and he goes, and to another, 'Come,' and he comes, and to my slave, 'Do this,' and he does it" (Matt. 8, 9)—so Israel recognized and acknowledged in the might and power of the Word of the prophets the might and power of their Master, Yahweh, Israel's God. By his Word, sent to the prophets and announced by them, Yahweh the Lord God of Israel directed and controlled the history of his people. For the word of the prophets is not mere communication and/or announcement, not only preaching, but the actual accomplishment of what it conveys (*e.g.,* "Therefore I have hewn them by the prophets, I have slain them by the Words of my mouth"—Hos. 6, 5). The word of a real master *takes place.* This was the criterion for Israel's recognition and acknowledgment of the Word of its Master and God in the Word of the prophets: "So shall my Word be that goes forth from my mouth; it shall not return to me empty, but it shall accomplish that which I purpose, and prosper in the thing for which I sent it" (Is. 55, 11).

Faithful Israel, not least through the influence of the prophetical preaching, came to see and acknowledge Yahweh, Israel's God and the Lord of its history, not only as the unique and true God and the Lord of, and for, Israel, but as the unqualified unique and true God. Not only the history of Israel, but the whole universe from its creation to its final consummation was considered subject to the Lordship of God's Word. Everything that was, is, or will be is the work of God's Word. Through his Word God created the world: "By the Word of the Lord the heavens were made, and all their host by the breath of his mouth. For he spoke and it came to be; he commanded, and it stood forth" (Ps. 33, 6.9; cf. Gen. 1; Ps. 148, 5, etc.). Through his Word, Yahweh rules and governs the whole of nature: "He sends forth his command to the earth; his Word runs swiftly. He gives snow like wool; he scatters hoarfrost like ashes. He casts forth his ice like morsels; who can stand before his cold? He sends forth his Word, and melts them; he makes his wind blow, and the waters flow" (Ps. 147, 15–18; cf. Job 37, 5–13, etc.). Through his Word, Yahweh controls history: "The nations rage, the kingdoms totter; he utters his voice, the earth melts" (Ps. 46, 6); precisely through its mastery of nature, Yahweh's Word shapes the course of history: "At his command the waters (of the Red Sea and of the Jordan) stood as a wall" (Sir. 39, 17). Man is utterly dependent in every aspect of his life and every need of his existence upon the Word of Yahweh: "He sent forth his Word, and healed them, and delivered them from destruction" (Ps. 107, 20); "It is not the production of the crops that supports man, but your Word that preserves those who believe in you" (Wis. 16, 26). Creation and salvation history appear thus in a single perspective, the perspective of the word of the *Prophets*, of God's *Word*: the Word that simultaneously reveals and (re-)creates.

The (originally sacerdotal) tradition of the law also was deeply affected by the word of the prophets in the course of Israel's history and shows the influence of the prophetical tradition. The book of Deuteronomy is, as it were, a prophetical reinterpretation of the legal tradition. This is why the law appears in Deuteronomy as the *words* of Moses, the *prophet*: "These are *the words* that Moses spoke to all Israel" (Deut. 1, 1); "The Lord your God will raise up for you a *prophet like me* from among you, from your brethren . . ." (Deut. 18, 15ff.). Conforming to this, Psalm 119, for example, praises the law as "God's Word" (vv. 25, 49, 107) and the ten commandments are called the "ten words" (Ex. 34, 28; Deut. 4, 13; 10, 4): the "ten words" which form the constitution of Yahweh's covenant with his people and which rule the life of Israel and of every faithful Israelite as effectively as the prophets of Israel's history.

Leaving aside the historical evolution of Israel's conception of the Word of God, one may summarize this notion in the words of Bultmann: "In the Old Testament, God's Word is a mighty Word which acts as an event while and because it is spoken. God's Word is God's Act and he speaks in his action and, indeed, he speaks to man. His Word is a command binding nature and history insofar as it be grasped by man, insofar as it says something to man, that is, demands something of him, in the first instance, demands that man become conscious of his humanity in the face of God the creator, that he trust in the creator and praise him. God's Word in nature and history is not the epitome of a cosmic regularity—as the Stoic *logos*—which can be logically comprehended. God's Word is an imperative command, spoken by men (priests and prophets), that tells man what he ought to do. Here also God's Word is not the epitome of ethical norms which can be rationally explicated as a complex moral law from a single principle. In neither case is God's Word the epitome of a set of meanings or values beyond time, but an appeal that takes place, a happening in time and, as such, a revelation of God as creator and Lord." [2]

The Word of God, understood in this sense, was read by faithful Israel in the word of Moses and the prophets. In the light of such a reading of "the Law and the Prophets" or, more generally, of "The Scriptures", the authors of the New Testament understood and described the Christ-event.

The "Accomplishment" of God's Word

The Word of God, as law and as prophecy, demands fulfillment. The authors of the New Testament recognize and acknowledge in Jesus the "fulfillment" of the Word of God, of

[2] R. Bultmann, *Das Evangelium des Johannes* (Göttingen, 1941), pp. 6–7.

the word of Moses and the prophets, of the Scriptures. Dodd [3] has rightly identified as the substructure of the whole theology of the New Testament this recognition and acknowledgment as actually realized and developed by the early Christians in the phrases "according to the Scripture", "in order that the Scriptures might be fulfilled", etc. "This is what was spoken by the prophet . . ." (Acts 2, 16) begins the first systematic preaching by Peter on the feast of Pentecost, in which he continually refers to Old Testament passages. "But what God foretold by the mouth of all the prophets . . . he thus fulfilled" (Acts 3, 18) is also the principal theme of Peter's sermon before the Sanhedrin.

The same is true of the preaching of Paul: "And we bring you the good news that what God promised to the fathers, this he has fulfilled to us their children . . ." (Acts 13, 32), "saying nothing but what the prophets and Moses said would come to pass" (Acts 26, 22).

That which Philip announced to the Ethiopian is the fulfillment in Jesus of "the passage of the Scripture which he was reading" (Acts 8, 32).

Not only the preaching of the first disciples but even the first preaching of Jesus himself is described by Luke in the same terms: "(After his baptism in the Jordan and his temptation in the desert) Jesus returned in the power of the Spirit into Galilee . . . And he came to Nazareth, where he had been brought up; and he went to the synagogue, as his custom was on the sabbath day. And he stood up to read; and there was given to him the book of the prophet Isaiah. He opened the book and found the place where it was written, 'The Spirit of the Lord is upon me, because he has anointed me to preach good news to the poor. He has sent me to proclaim release to the captives and recovering of sight to the blind, to set at liberty those who are oppressed, to proclaim the acceptable year of the Lord'. And he closed the book and gave it back to the attendant, and sat down, and the eyes of all in the synagogue were fixed on him. And he began to

[3] C. Dodd, *According to the Scriptures. The sub-structure of New Testament theology* (London, 1952).

say to them, *'Today this Scripture has been fulfilled in your hearing'* " (Luke 4, 14–21).

The entire New Testament is one constant appeal—repeated in all sorts of ways—to join in Philip's avowal: "We have found him of whom Moses in the Law and also the prophets wrote, Jesus of Nazareth, the son of Joseph" (John 1, 45).

Jesus came to accomplish the law and the prophets. "Think not that I have come to abolish the law and the prophets; I have come not to abolish them but to fulfill them" (Matt. 5, 17).

The text just cited—the introduction to the Sermon on the Mount, the "Law" of the New Covenant—shows that the term "fulfill" means more than just "actualize". The relation between "the Law and the Prophets" appears to be more than simply the relation between "revelation-in-word" and "revelation-in-reality". For the "revelation-in-word" itself becomes fulfilled. Even the radical approach to the Law—to what "was said to the men of old"—in the words of Jesus "but I say to you . . ." appears in Matthew 5, 17–20 in the context of "fulfillment". Something similar occurs in the "reduction" of the Law by Jesus to the single command of love (Matt. 22, 36–40; John 15, 12), the "radicalizing" of the "ten words" to the "one word". "For he who loves his neighbor has fulfilled the law. The commandments, 'You shall not commit adultery, You shall not kill, You shall not steal, You shall not covet,' and any other commandments are summed up in this sentence, 'You shall love your neighbor as yourself.' Love does no wrong to a neighbor; therefore love is the fulfilling of the law" (Rom. 13, 8–10). "For the whole law is fulfilled in one word, 'You shall love your neighbor as yourself' " (Gal. 4, 14).

Jesus achieved this "fulfilled law" and in this sense also "fulfilled" it in loving his own "to the very end" (John 13, 1). For "greater love has no man than this, that a man lay down his life for his friends" (John 15, 13).

That in Jesus the "Law and the Prophets" are brought to an end and are accomplished, that the coming of Jesus meant the fulfillment of God's Word to his people is the background of the whole thought of the New Testament and is worked out in various ways in many passages. The remainder of this article offers an illustration of this from but two examples in the Gospels. The first is from the Gospel according to Mark, the Gospel closest to the source of the tradition from which derive all three synoptic Gospels. The second is from the Gospel according to John, the Gospel in which the theology of the Word reaches its summit. For comparison, we choose in both cases the passages in which the evangelists introduce Jesus to the reader. Keeping within the narrow limitations of the theme "God's Word", we shall try to show how Mark's treatment of Jesus' baptism in the Jordan portrays Jesus as *the* Prophet, as he who *speaks* (the fullness of) *God's Word,* and how John's Prologue presents Jesus as he who *is* (the fullness of) *God's Word.* At the same time, we shall try to show how both ways of presenting Jesus do justice to him as the "fulfillment" of God's Word, the Word that was with God in the beginning and that was spoken by God to his people in the law and the prophets.

Jesus, the Prophet

The passage in the Gospel according to Mark about Jesus' baptism in the Jordan (Mark 1, 9–11) is the central panel of the triptych which forms the prelude to the story of Jesus' public ministry (Mark 1, 14ff.) and of which the two side compartments are the accounts of the appearance of John the Baptist (Mark 1, 2–8) and of Jesus' temptation in the desert (Mark 1, 12–13). This triptych is even clearly recognizable in the Gospels according to Matthew and Luke as the original preface to the Gospel according to the synoptic tradition. The first half of the baptism account—the actual baptism of Jesus (Mark 1, 9)— forms a unit with the first panel of the triptych (*e.g.,* by reason of the appearance of John the Baptist common to both sections), whereas the second half (Mark 1, 10–11) is likewise related to the third panel (*e.g.,* by reason of the appearance of the Spirit common to both).

The reference to the ministry of John the Baptist in the first half of the preface corresponds, as we see from Acts 1, 21–22, to the original opening of the official testimony concerning the Christ-event: the substitute for Judas in the college of the twelve official witnesses must be "one of the men who have accompanied us during all the time that the Lord went in and out among us, *beginning from the baptism of John"*.

The Gospel according to Matthew reveals the significance of this concern with the ministry of John the Baptist as a direct reference to "the Law and the Prophets": "For all the prophets and the law prophesied until John" (Matt. 11, 13). John is "a prophet" (Matt. 11, 9) but in his function of preparing the way for Jesus he is "more than a prophet" (Matt. 11, 9). For he thus belongs in the fullness of time, the time of fulfillment: "This is he of whom it is written, 'Behold I send my messenger before thy face, who shall prepare thy way before thee' " (Matt. 11, 10).

The Gospel according to Mark begins with precisely this same reference to the fulfillment of the word of the prophet Malachi (3, 1), though the evangelist refers erroneously to the prophet Isaiah (Mark 1, 2). By allowing himself to be baptized, by subjecting himself to the prophetic ministry of John as Baptist, Jesus took upon himself in a tangible way (the fulfillment of) "the law and the prophets until John" in order to "fulfill all righteousness", as Matthew 3, 15 explains.

"And when he (Jesus) came up out of the water, immediately he saw the heavens opened . . ." (Mark 1, 10). When Jesus emerges from the water of the Jordan, the Gospel emerges from the literary genre in which the first half of the threefold preface had been immersed till then.

A first change in style is the method used to connect the fulfillment of "the Law and the Prophets" with "according to the Scriptures".

In the first half of the triptych (Mark 1, 2–9) the descriptive narration of the facts (vv. 4–9) is set apart from the commentary upon the meaning of the facts as fulfillment of the Scriptures (vv. 2–3), and the reference to the Scriptures is explicit. In the second half of the triptych (Mark 1, 10–13) the descriptive narration itself of the facts is composed of implicit references to (the fulfillment of) texts from the Old Testament. The passage is made up, as it were, of Old Testament allusions:

Mark 1, 10: the rending of the heavens—cf. Is. 63, 19; 64, 1; Ez. 1, 1.
　　　　　descent from the opened heavens—cf. Is. 64, 1.
　　　　　(descent of) Spirit upon Jesus—cf. Is. 11, 2; 42, 1; 44, 3; 61, 1.
　　　　　the Spirit as a dove—cf. (Ben Zoma[4] on) Gen. 1, 2.
　　　　　the dove above the water—cf. Gen. 8, 8–12.
Mark 1, 11: You are my Son—cf. Ps. 2, 7 (LXX).
　　　　　most beloved—cf. Gen. 22, 2; Is. 44, 2 (LXX).
　　　　　in you I am well pleased—cf. Is. 62, 4 (LXX).
Mark 1, 12: driven by the Spirit—cf. Ez. 3, 14; 11, 1.
Mark 1, 13: forty days in the desert—cf. Israel (Deut. 2, 7, etc.); Moses (Ex.
　　　　　34, 28); Elias (1 Kgs. 19, 8).
　　　　　forty (days) testing in the desert—cf. Israel (Ps. 95, 9–10;
　　　　　Heb. 3, 8–9).
　　　　　Satan and the wild animals—cf. Ps. 22, 12–22; Ez. 34, 5.8.29.
　　　　　(tame?) wild animals—cf. Is. 11, 6–9.
　　　　　wild animals and ministering angels—cf. Ps. 91, 11–13 (cited by
　　　　　Matthew and Luke).

That the transition from Mark 1, 2–9 to 1, 10–13 involves a change in literary style may be shown in still another way. When Jesus leaves the waters of the Jordan (Mark 1, 10), the text of the Gospel leaves the familiar geographical and historical region of John who baptizes and preaches in the desert and of the men of Judea—including Jesus, until he leaves the waters of the Jordan—and Jerusalem who flock to him. Then, from the rending of the heavens (Mark 1, 10) till the ministry of the angels (Mark 1, 13), we are in a strange and unknown world. That it is a world beyond reach of our (modern) scientific observation of nature and history is evident from what goes on there: the heavens are opened, the Spirit descends as a dove, voices come from the skies, the Spirit drives Jesus into the desert, Satan appears in person, angels are ministering. It is characteristic of

⁴ "A younger contemporary of the Apostles", cited in V. Taylor, *The Gospel according to St. Mark* (London, 1957), p. 161: "I was considering the space between the upper waters and the lower waters, and . . . as it is said, And the Spirit of God was brooding on the face of the waters like a dove which broods over her young but does not touch them."

this world that one can easily imagine there the mountain—
mentioned by Matthew and Luke—from which all the kingdoms of the world in their glory (Matt. 4, 8) can be seen in a
single instant (Luke 4, 5): a mountain which hardly belongs
in a modern atlas, or in a modern historical atlas, or even in
the "Atlas of the Bible".

Corresponding to the different worlds of the first and second
halves of Mark 1, 2–13 are two different confrontations. Mark
1, 2–9 describes the "historical" confrontation of John the Baptist and Jesus in the midst of the historical people of Jerusalem
and of the whole of Judea; Mark 1, 10–13 portrays the "trans-
historical" confrontation of Jesus as he stands wholly alone to
face God (vv. 10–11) and Satan (v. 13), the two extremes which
define the fulfillment of his mission as described in the Gospel
immediately following: the establishment of God's kingdom and
the victory over the kingdom of Satan.

We can better understand the way in which Mark 1, 10–11
is made up, as it were, of allusions to texts of the Old Testament
and, indeed, in the framework of a visionary world, if we study
the literary style of these verses more closely and, specifically,
compare them to other similar texts from the Old and New
Testaments. Then we shall be able to classify the literary style
of Mark 1, 10-11 as that of (a) a vision, as that of (b) a vision
of mission, as that of (c) a vision of a prophetic mission.

(a) "And when he (Jesus) came up out of the water, immediately *he saw* . . ." (Mark 1, 10). It is remarkable to find
the term "he saw . . ." (*eiden*) in a description of events, for
one cannot actually observe the observation of another. Yet this
peculiar way of describing events through the eyes of Jesus
occurs rather frequently in the Gospels: "He saw" (*eiden*, Mark
1, 16.19; 2, 14, etc.), "when he saw" (*idoon*, Mark 2, 5; 8, 33,
etc.). In these cases, however, the phrase "(when) he saw" is
always used *relatively, i.e.,* relative to Jesus' reaction to what is
seen—which reaction obviously presupposes that "he saw". This
use of "(when) he saw . . ." is thus, after all, a common way

of connecting up an event or situation with someone's action or speech. We all use this formula: "When he saw so and so, he said or did such and such."

But in Mark 1, 10 the word *"eiden"* is used *absolutely*. There is no mention of a reaction on the part of Jesus to what he saw! Yet we find this extraordinary application of the absolute *"eiden"*—often followed by *kai idou* (cf. Matt. 3, 16)—many times in the New and Old Testaments. The absolute "he saw . . ." is a standard formula for introducing visions and belongs to the literary characteristics by which one may recognize the literary style called "vision". This formula occurs frequently in the (apocalyptic) prophets of the Old Testament (especially Ezekiel) and in the (prophetical) Apocalypse of the New Testament.

In our case, the fact that "he saw" is a typical literary earmark of the vision-style, is confirmed by the presence of other characteristic features in each of the three elements "seen" by Jesus:

the heavens opened—cf. Rev. 19, 11; Acts 7, 56; 10, 11; John 1, 51.
the descent (from the heavens)—cf. Rev. 20, 1; Acts 10, 11; John 1, 51.
a voice (speaking) (from the heavens)—cf. Rev. 1, 10; Acts 10, 13; etc.

(b) The function of vision in connection with apocalyptic prophecies is the most striking of all because of its enigmatic quality. No less important and probably more ancient is its function in connection with the *mission entrusted to someone by God*. This use of vision is found in the Old Testament in regard to the missions to Israel of Elijah, Isaiah, Jeremiah and Ezekiel, and in the New Testament regarding the missions of Peter and Paul to the Gentiles.

Mark 1, 10–11 corresponds to the literary style of a mission-vision. It follows the structural scheme of this type of vision and immediately precedes Jesus' public appearance in the name of "him who sent me (Jesus)" (Mark 9, 36). To see the parallelism between Mark 1, 10–11 and, above all, the mission-vision of Ezekiel in the Old and that of Peter in the New Testament, compare the texts in the following scheme:

Ezekiel (1-2)	Jesus (Mark 1, 10-11)	Peter (Acts 10, 11-13)
1,1 kai egeneto . . . epi	kai egeneto . . . eis	kai theoorei
tou	ton	
potamou	Iordanèn	
kai ènoichthèsan hoi	kai . . . eiden	ton ouranon aneooig-
ouranoi	schizomenous tous	menon
kai eidon . . .	ouranous	kai katabainon
1,3 kai egeneto logos	kai to pneuma hoos	(skeuos ti)
Kuriou		hoos (othonèn . . .)
1,4 kai idon, kai idou	(peristeran) katabai-	kai egeneto phoonè . . .
pneuma	non eis auton	
2,1 kai èkousa phoonèn	kai phoonè egeneto	
huie anthropou	su ei ho huios mou	
2,2 kai èlthen ep'eme		
pneuma		

The significance of a mission-vision which precedes the story of one's ministry is clear: his action and speech are marked and authenticated as prophetical, as the words and deeds of a prophet sent by God to speak his Word in the power of his Spirit. He speaks in the power of his Spirit "because no prophecy ever came by the impulse of man, but men moved by the Holy Spirit spoke from God" (2 Pet. 1, 21; cf. already 2 Sam. 23, 2: "The Spirit of the Lord speaks by me, his Word is upon my tongue").

(c) "In many and various ways God spoke of old to our fathers by the prophets; but in these last days he has spoken to us by a Son" (Heb. 1, 1). These opening words of the Letter to the Hebrews agree with the presentation of Jesus in the Gospel according to Mark. In the mission-vision of Mark 1, 10-11, God finally sends after all the prophets his Son. ("Thou art my beloved Son" Mark 1, 11; cf. the parable in Luke in which after all the servants the "beloved son" is sent to the tenants.) The Son of God is sent to speak, after all the prophets, God's Word of the fullness of time, God's last Word, the fullness of God's Word: "And Jesus came into Galilee, preaching the Gospel of God, and saying, 'the time is fulfilled, and (now) the kingdom of God is (close) at hand" (Mark 1, 14-15).

The distinction between "the prophets" and "a Son" in Hebrews 1, 1 and between the mission (-visions) of the prophets in the Old Testament and that of the Son in Mark 1, 10–11 does not indicate that Jesus is no prophet. The contrary is true. Jesus calls himself a prophet (Mark 6, 4; Luke 13, 33); he is recognized and acknowledged by the people as well as by his disciples (Luke 24, 19) as "one of the prophets" (Mark 8, 28), as "a great prophet" (Luke 7, 16). Jesus prophesied "the end" just as the prophets did (Mark 13, 22–23), and the final event of his death and resurrection was recognized by his disciples as the fulfillment of "the Scripture and the Word which Jesus had spoken" (John 2, 22).

The distinction between "the prophets" and "the Son" is the same as that between "the prophesying of the prophets and the law until John" and their fulfillment in Jesus. As fulfillment of "the prophets and the law until John", Jesus is recognized and preached precisely as being *also* the *prophet* promised in Deut. 18, 5ff.: "Moses . . . said to the Israelites, 'God will raise up for you a prophet from your breathren as he raised me up' " (Acts 7, 37; 2, 22). Precisely as the fulfillment of "Moses and the prophets", Jesus is *also* invested with the fullness of the prophetical office, is also "more than a prophet" (Matt. 11, 9), is *"the* prophet who is to come into the world" (John 6, 14).

As "Son", Jesus is "more than a prophet", *i.e.*, more a prophet than "all the prophets until John". For "the Father loves the Son (cf. Mark 1, 11), and has given *all things* into his hands" (John 3, 35). "The prophets" are, in one sense, only part-prophets. When the Son speaks the Word of his Father, it is the fullness of his Word; it is God's last Word.

Finally, we note that the prophetical character of the mission-vision in Mark 1, 10–11 is indicated also in that the vision itself brings to mind that of the transfiguration (Mark 9, 2–8) in which Jesus appears "framed" by the prophets Moses and Elijah, as well as in the fact that the "forty days" immediately following the vision (Mark 1, 12–13) likewise remind us of Moses (Ex. 34, 28) and Elijah (1 Kgs. 19, 4–8—here also with the ministering angel!).

Jesus, the Word

"In the beginning was the Word, and the Word was with God . . . and the Word became flesh . . . Jesus Christ . . . the Only Son (of the Father, himself) God" (John 1, 1. 14. 17. 18).

The second half of the introductory chapter of the Gospel according to John (John 1, 19–51) covers practically the same ground and is thought out and written up for the most part in the very same categories of fulfillment of what "Moses in the law and also the prophets wrote" (John 1, 45) as in the triptych which introduced Mark's Gospel. But in the first half of John 1, the Prologue, these traditional categories have undergone, as it were, a radical re-formulation not to be found in the same extreme form in the rest of this Gospel. The Prologue is the furthest boundary, the horizon of the fourth Gospel, the testimony of the evangelist's belief concerning Jesus "to the very end" (cf. John 13, 1).

(a) The traditional presentation of Jesus as the Son of God (cf. Mark 1, 11) is expressed in its ultimate possibility in the Prologue: "The Only-begotten Son (of the Father, himself) God".

(b) The belief in Jesus as the fulfillment of "the Law and the Prophets" and as the accomplishment of the Word of God and, in this connection, the belief in Jesus as God's last Word and thus in Jesus as the one in whom God spoke to perfection receives its most radical formulation in the Prologue: in Jesus the Word has become flesh, in him God's Word is spoken and achieved definitively and exhaustively.

(c) The origin of the Christ-event, of Jesus' words and deeds, of Jesus' death and resurrection—as fulfillment of the Word of God—is brought back in the Prologue to its very first starting point: the Word that was in the beginning with God. Jesus is God's primeval Word. In the Word made flesh, God's original design for man is finally realized. Jesus is not only God's last Word but also God's first Word.

(d) The belief in Jesus as prophet, as he who speaks God's

Word, and in Jesus as *the* prophet, as he who speaks the fullness of God's Word, reaches in the Prologue its ultimate limit: Jesus not only *speaks* God's Word, he *is* the Word of God.

God's Word: the Gospel

The usual and predominant meaning in the Old Testament of the expressions "the Word" and "the Word of God" is the word of the prophets. In the New Testament, on the contrary, their normal and dominant meaning is the preaching of the Gospel (*e.g.,* 2 Tim. 2, 8–9), the word of those who "preach Christ" (*e.g.,* Phil. 1, 14–16).

Christian preaching, the announcing of the Gospel, appears to be the exact point where the two themes which command the Prologue of the fourth Gospel come together: "Jesus, the Word", and "Jesus, the Light".

In the Acts of the Apostles, preaching and the Gospel are often called simply "the Word" (*e.g.,* Acts 4, 4), "the Word of the Lord" (*e.g.,* Acts 8, 25), "the Word of God" (*e.g.,* Acts 4, 29. 31). Preaching is then "the ministry of the Word" (Acts 6, 4) and the faith corresponding to preaching is "the reception of the Word of God" (Acts 8, 14).

This word of preaching is a light that enlightens the faithful and shines in their hearts (2 Cor. 4, 6). Preachers are set up by God as "a light for the Gentiles" (Acts 13, 47) and are sent to the Gentiles to "open their eyes, that they may turn from darkness to light" (Acts 26, 18). Belief and disbelief are related as light and darkness (2 Cor. 6, 14; Eph. 5, 8; 1 Thess. 5, 4–5; 1 Pet. 2, 9). And the word of the prophets is there "as a lamp shining in a dark place, until the day dawns and the morning star (literally: the light-bearer) rises in your hearts" (2 Pet. 1, 19). The believers ought therefore to "shine as *lights* in the world, holding fast the *word* of life" (Phil. 2, 15–16). For "the grace which he gave us in Jesus Christ ages ago now (is) manifested through the appearing of our Savior Christ Jesus, who abolished death and brought *life* and immortality to *light* through the *Gospel* (= the word)" (2 Tim. 1, 9–10).

The Prologue adds to this manner of speaking the transition from the preaching to the one preached: Jesus himself is the Word, the Life and the Light. Such a transition is not difficult to make, for to preach "the Word" is to preach Jesus, and to believe in the Gospel is to believe in Jesus. The Word of the Gospel which is light and life for the believer is interchangeable with Jesus who died and rose again for us. As Barrett writes: "What John perceived with far greater clarity than any of his predecessors was that Jesus *is* the Gospel . . . That is, when the Gospel was offered to men it was Christ himself who was offered to them, and received by them." [5] In the preaching, the believers encountered Jesus as the Word of Life and Light.

"The Word of God and the Testimony of Jesus" [6]

A further examination of the theology of preaching found in the fourth Gospel also shows how characterizations of Jesus as Word and Light are bound up with this theology. Preaching is thought of in the Johannine writings as a *witnessing* and, indeed, of ear- and eye-witnesses: "That which we have heard, which we have seen with our eyes . . . concerning the Word of life — . . . and we saw it and testify to it . . . —that which we have seen and heard we proclaim also to you" (1 John 1, 1–3). The fourth Gospel offers itself precisely as a testimony (21, 24) of him who saw (19, 35; 20, 8) for those who did not see (20, 29) in order that they may (yet) believe (20, 29–30). This explains why, immediately after the *testimony* of John (1, 7–8. 15.19.32.34) concerning what he saw and heard (1, 32–34), the first disciples are called—to (come and) see (1, 39. 47.50.51)!—even before the beginning of Jesus' ministry (2, 1; cf. 2, 11). For they will be sent by Jesus later on to be *"witnesses,* because you have been with me from the beginning" (15, 27; cf. Acts 1, 21–22), to testify to what they heard and saw of Jesus and so to mediate between Jesus and ourselves who have not seen and heard him (20, 29–31).

[5] C. K. Barrett, *The Gospel according to St. John* (London, 1955), p. 58.
[6] Rev. 1, 2.9; 20, 4.

The fourth Gospel, however, is not concerned only with Jesus but with Jesus and *in Jesus with God*. There is a parallelism between the mediation of the disciples or the evangelist between ourselves as readers and Jesus on the one hand, and that of Jesus between the disciples and God on the other. Jesus says to the Father: "I have given them the words which you have given me" (17, 8), and "the glory which you have given me I have given to them" (17, 22), and "as you have sent me into the world, so I have sent them into the world" (17, 18). Jesus says to the disciples: "As the Father has sent me, even so I send you" (20, 21). Jesus says to us: "Truly, truly, I say to you, he who receives anyone whom I send receives me; and who receives me receives him who sent me" (13, 20).

This parallelism in mediatorship holds also for witnessing. The text just cited above goes on: "When Jesus had thus spoken, he . . . testified . . ." (13, 21). Just as it will be the mission of the disciples to give testimony (15, 27), so it is also the mission of Jesus to give testimony: "For this was I born, and for this I have come into the world, to bear witness . . ." (18, 37). The fourth Gospel makes frequent mention of the "testimony" of Jesus (3, 11.32.33; 5, 31; 8, 14; cf. Rev. 1, 2. 9; 12, 17; 19, 10; 20, 4); Jesus "testifies" (3, 11. 32; 4, 44; 5, 31; 7, 7; 8, 14. 18; 13, 21); Jesus is "the witness" (8, 18; cf. "the faithful witness" in Rev. 1, 5; 3, 14).

Just as it is true of us, for whom the fourth Gospel was written, that we have never seen or heard Jesus (20, 29–31), so also it is not only true of the "Jews" that "You have never heard the voice of God nor seen his form" (5, 37) but it is true of every man that "No one has ever seen God" (1, 18). Well then, just as the disciples bear witness to what they have seen and heard of Jesus whom we have never seen or heard, so also Jesus bears witness to what he has seen and heard of God whom no one has ever seen or heard: "No one has seen the Father except him who is from God; he has seen the Father" (6, 46); "He who comes from above . . . he who comes from heaven . . . bears witness to what he has seen and heard" (3, 31–32). The description in the fourth Gospel of the origin of Jesus as being "with God" seems thus to be in function of the unique role of Jesus as the witness of God; because he and only he was with God, he and only he has seen and heard God. Therefore he and he alone is able to bear witness to God.

But the Prologue goes still further. In the last analysis, faith in Jesus is not only belief in him who has seen and heard God, but ultimately belief in him who *is* what he saw: "the Light" (cf. 1 John 1, 5) and who *is* what he heard: "the Word". In the profession of faith of the Prologue, the unique quality of Jesus' witnessing to God transcends the category of testimony, just as the unique quality of his sonship of God transcends the category of sonship: Jesus *is* "the Word", he *is* "the Light", he *is* God.

In conclusion, an indication of the actual *Sitz im Leben* in which the Prologue came to be. Originally, the Prologue was very likely a hymn sung by the early Christians in praise of Jesus as the Word and the Light during the Church's celebration of Sunday. For, "the first day of the week" is not only the first day of creation—the day on which God *spoke*: "Let there be *light*" (cf. John 1, 1–5)—it is also the first day of the re-creation— the day of the Lord's resurrection—and, for this reason, the day on which the first Christians came together to break bread and listen to "the Word" (cf. Acts 20, 7–12), to the Word that "the true light is already shining" (1 John 2, 8), to the Word concerning Jesus who died *and is risen in glory*. The "day of the Lord" (Rev. 1, 10) is the day on which the first Christians assembled in faith to hear from the mouth of the preachers the Word concerning the risen Lord, who is "the first and the last" (Rev. 1, 17), who is the first and last Word of God, "the Alpha and the Omega" (Rev. 1, 18).

Franz Mussner/*Trier, W. Germany*

The People of God According to Eph. 1, 3–14

The Prologue to the Epistle to the Ephesians (1, 3–14)[1] has the character of a liturgical "eulogy", and in many respects reminds us of the second blessing-prayer called the "Great Love" which among the Jews preceded the morning-prayer.[2] In the Prologue the term "People of God" is not, to be sure, expressly employed, but the idea of a People of God is very clearly present in the background, as our exposition will show. This article aims, therefore, at clarifying this idea, biblical in origin, by an examination of Pauline theology and by exploring in depth the concept of the "People of God" which, through the efforts of the present Council, is being revitalized. For this purpose, as we will demonstrate, Ephesians 1, 3–14 is especially suited. In this section emerge ideas and images which are essentially part of the theological complex

[1] Cf. the recent lengthy analysis of J. Cambier, "La bénédiction d'Eph. 1, 3–14," in *Zeitschrift für die neutestamentische Wissenschaft und die Kunde der älteren Kirche* 54 (1963), pp. 58–104 (with extensive bibliography).
[2] Cf. S. Lyonnet, "La bénédiction d'Eph. 1, 3–14 et son arrière-plan judaïque," in *A la rencontre de Dieu. Memorial A. Gelin* (Le Puy, 1961), pp. 341–52; H. Strack and P. Billerbeck ed., *Kommentar zum Neuen Testament aus Talmud und Midrash* VI Vols. (Munich, 1928; reprint, 1956). Cf. IV, Vol. 1, *Exkurse zu einzelnen Stellen des N. T.,* p. 192.

known as the "People of God" [3] and which can serve to deepen Christian awareness.

I

THE CHURCH AS THE PEOPLE OF GOD OF THE "ENDZEIT" *

No nation falls out of the sky. It has a beginning, a history of growth. This holds good also for the People of God, with this distinction, that behind its origin there stands the sovereign and saving power of God. *God* it is who makes this nation into the People of God, and does so, first of all, by means of his own *choice.* God, in his own unfathomable freedom, has chosen the people of Israel to belong to him: this is one of the basic propositions of the Israelitic creed. The people of Israel were made aware of this divine choice by the Book of Deuteronomy.[4] We can consult Deuteronomy 7, 6ff.: "The Lord, your God has chosen you from all the nations on the face of the earth to be a people peculiarly his own. It was not because you are the largest of all nations that the Lord set his heart on you and *chose* you, for you are really the smallest of all nations. It was *because the Lord loved you* and because of his fidelity to the oath he had sworn to your fathers. . . . Understand then, that the Lord, your God, is God indeed, the faithful God who keeps

---

* The author uses the term *Endzeit* to express the finality of the revelation in Christ, as well as that era—necessarily in the future and the last age of the world—when the Kingdom of God will be fully realized because all men will be gathered into membership in Christ's Body. Because of the difficulty of conveying these ideas in a single English phrase, it is proposed to give the term *Endzeit* each time it occurs in the article.

[3] On the concept of the People of God in the New Testament, cf. the author's essay: " 'Volk Gottes' im Neuen Testament," in *Trierer Theologische Zeitschrift* 72 (1963), pp. 169–78 (with bibliography).

[4] Cf. T. Vriezen, *Theologie des Alten Testaments in Grundzügen* (Neukirchen, n.d.), pp. 46ff.; G. von Rad, *Theologie des Alten Testaments* I (Munich, 1957), pp. 228–30. English edition: *Theology of the Old Testament* (New York: Harper, 1962). The phrase *to choose* occurs in Deuteronomy alone 30 times, as indicated by L. Kohler, *Theologie des Alten Testaments* (Tubingen, ²1947), p. 65.

his merciful *covenant* down to the thousandth generation. . . ."

The choice of Israel by Yahweh makes of this nation his own peculiar possession. The unique motive for the election is Yahweh's love. In the Epistle to the Ephesians the same ideas occur again, but raised now to a new and surpassingly high level: God, "the Father of our Lord Jesus Christ . . . chose us in him (Christ) before the foundation of the world. . . . And in love[5] he predestined us to be adopted through Jesus Christ as his sons" (Eph. 1, 3–5). The chosen ones are his "possession" (1, 14) and are destined for the "inheritance" (1, 14). The Christian preeminence is shown in many ways: God is "the Father of our Lord Jesus Christ"; the choice was already made "before the foundation of the world"; the end is the "sonship" stemming from grace and the eschatalogical "inheritance". The inheritance promised to Israel in Deuteronomy consisted in the good things of this world: "He will love and bless and multiply you; he will bless the fruit of your womb and the produce of your soil, your grain and wine and oil, the issue of your herds and the young of your flocks, in the land which he swore to your fathers he would give you. You will be blessed among all peoples; no man or woman among you shall be childless nor shall your livestock be barren. The Lord will remove all sickness from you; he will not afflict you with any of the malignant diseases you know from Egypt . . ." (Deut. 7, 13–15); that is, Israel will be "in the whole of its real historical existence . . . established in salvation" (G. von Rad).[6] On the other hand, the Epistle to the Ephesians speaks of the "*spiritual* blessings" with which God has blessed us "on high in Christ" (Eph. 1, 3), that is, of the blessings experienced solely by the People of God in the New Testament, in the bestowal of spiritual and heavenly goods.

Mention is made of the redemption in Christ's blood (1, 7; cf. 1, 14); the forgiveness of sins (1, 7); the gift of the knowledge of the mystery of the divine will for the community of the

---

[5] With Cambier (and others), we join *en agápē* and *proopísas*.
[6] G. von Rad, *op. cit.*, p. 228.

faithful, namely, the eschatological *anakephalaiōsis* of the whole of creation "in Christo" (1, 9ff.); the signing with the Holy Spirit, the "seal" of the inheritance to come (1, 13ff.). Concerning the blessing of the People of God with the good things of this world there is not a word; the reference is wholly to salvation and to the manner of its coming. In this fact there is already a fundamental difference from the concept of the People of God in the Old Testament. Further distinctions will be made in later statements of the Epistle on the constitution of the People of God in the New Testament. For this new, eschatological People of God is now no longer limited to one particular earthly nation such as the Israel of the Old Covenant, but embraces all the peoples of the earth.

This is an immediate consequence, according to Ephesians 3, 3ff., of the "mystery of Christ" (3, 4) which "has been made known" to the Apostle in the form of a revelation. What in earlier times remained hidden from men is "now revealed to his holy apostles and prophets in the Spirit" (3, 5), and the terms of the revelation are: "The Gentiles (are) joint heirs, and fellow members of the same body, and joint partakers of the promise in Christ Jesus through the Gospel" (3, 6). The Gospel calls them into the community of the Body of Christ. The Apostle has already explained in detail (Eph. 2, 11–22) the mystery of salvation history which will be evident at the end of time (*Endzeit*). There it becomes plain whose "partners" the nations have become through the Gospel: their partners are the Judaeo-Christians, the representative "remnant" of the ancient People of God, who have become obedient hearers of the Gospel. From the "two" (2, 16.18) has been made the new, eschatological community of the Mystical "Body" of Christ (2, 16).[7]

This community has its origin not in the mere joining or add-

---

[7] Here the connection is clear in the Pauline writings between the idea of the People of God and the idea of the Church as *body*. See on this point the recent article by R. Schnackenburg and J. Dupont, "The Church as the People of God," in CONCILIUM I (Glen Rock, N.J.: Paulist Press, 1965), pp. 117–29.

ing of one party to another, but rather in an entirely new creation, because "of the two Christ (creates) in himself one new man" (2, 15).[8] The sacramental beginning of this new creation is baptism[9] (cf. also Gal. 3, 28 with regard to baptism: "For you are all one in Christ Jesus", and also Gal. 6, 15: "a new creation",[10] and 2 Cor. 5, 17: "If then any man is in Christ, he is a new creature"). Its ontological beginning, on the other hand, is Christ himself ("in him"!), by which is meant either his resurrected body as the origin of the new creature, or, what seems probable, Christ as the eschatological Adam (cf. 1 Cor. 15, 47; Rom. 5, 6), who becomes the progenitor of a new race of men, embracing his posterity within himself, and in this latter case the thought corresponds to the Semitic idea of the corporate personality.[11] Thus, the new creation coming out of Israel and out of the nations assembles in the community of the Church, the Body of Christ. In it there is no longer any "wall of partition", as the Law once stood between Israel and the nations, the visible and fear-inspiring expression of which was to be found in the stone walls which, in the Temple at Jerusalem, separated the court of the Gentiles from the court of the Israelites.[12]

[8] Cf. the details in my book: *Christus, das All und die Kirche* (Trier, 1955), pp. 85–100.

[9] Cf. also: N. Dahl, "Dopet i Efesierbrevet," in *Svensk Teologisk Kvartalskrift* 2 (1945), pp. 85–103; H. Sahlin, "Omskärelsen i Kristus: En interpretation av Ef. 2, 11–22," *ibid.* 4 (1947), pp. 11–24; R. Schnackenburg, "Er hat uns miterweckt: Zur Tauflehre des Epheser-briefes," in *Liturgisches Jahrbuch* 2 (1952), pp. 159–83.

[10] The expression comes from the language of the late Jewish period, and is particularly frequent in the theological writings of the proselytizers. Cf. details in H. Strack and P. Billerbeck, *op. cit.*, II. 421–3; III, p. 519; K. Rengstorf, *Theologisches Wörterbuch zum Neuen Testament* Vol. I, pp. 664–6; W. Phytian-Adams, "The Mystery of the New Creation," in *Church Quarterly Review* 142 (1946), pp. 61–77; E. Sjöberg, "Wieder-geburt und Neuschöpfung im palästinensischen Judentum," in *Stud. Theol.* 4 (1950), pp. 44–85; J. Jeremias, *Die Kindertaufe in den ersten drei Jahrhunderten* (Göttingen, 1958), pp. 39–43. English edition: *Infant Baptism in the First Four Centuries* (Philadelphia: The Westminster Press); G. Schneider, *Neuschöpfung oder Wiederkehr* (Düsseldorf, 1961), pp. 35–51.

[11] Cf. J. de Fraine, *Adam und seine Nachkommen* (Cologne, 1962).

[12] For details on this, cf. F. Mussner, *op. cit.*, pp. 81–4.

Hence, the eschatological People of God, created in Christ, transcends every national barrier raised by man throughout history, and makes of all men one community, bound together in one great brotherhood; the People of God makes of the nations the family of mankind: "There is neither Jew nor Greek; there is neither slave nor freeman; there is neither male nor female" (Gal. 3, 28; cf. 1 Cor. 12, 13). All are, rather, brothers of whom Christ, according to Romans 8, 29 (cf. Col. 1, 18), is the "firstborn".

And in our own time, we are given a great opportunity for a modern presentation of the concept "the People of God"—a concept which the Church has to bring up to date *as the sign of unity, of peace, of the great all-embracing brotherhood of the nations.* For Christ, "coming, announced the good tidings of peace to you who were afar off, and of peace to those who were near" (Eph. 2, 17). The People of God has a Gospel of peace to proclaim in the world!

II

THE PEOPLE OF GOD, THE WORD OF GOD, AND THE SPIRIT OF GOD

What constitutes, concretely, the eschatological People of God, according to the Prologue of the Epistle to the Ephesians? The answer is given in Ephesians 1, 13ff: "In him (Christ) you too, when you had heard the word of truth, the good news of your salvation, and believed in it, were sealed with the Holy Spirit of the promise, who is the pledge of our inheritance. . . ." It is, therefore, the acceptance of the Gospel in faith which makes a man (1) a member of God's people, together with (2) the signing with the Holy Spirit. Both aspects of the process were already in preparation in the Old Testament.

1. *Man: A Member of God's People*

"Israel's special relationship to God rests . . . from the beginning on the Word of God himself: the foundation of the

Sinaitic covenant, the decalogue, is called . . . 'the ten Words';[13] it was a mighty manifestation of God's will, by means of which the life of the nation was regulated and the groundwork of all future legislation laid. For in Deuteronomy the designation *dabarim* was affixed to all kinds of laws, so that 'the Word' gained a higher significance and became coextensive in meaning with 'the law of the nation', and in its turn gave the laws a share in the dignity of the revelation of the Law on Mount Sinai. So the whole way of life of God's people is governed by God's Word, in which is seen a clear and unequivocal expression of the sovereign's will" (W. Eichrodt).[14] Side by side with the legal "Word of God" stands the prophetic "Word of God" (*dabarim Jahwe*). The prophets become, "with the word entrusted to them, a power ready-to-hand, one which proves to be equal in force to any political or royal power" (*idem*).

In the view of history to be found in Deuteronomy, the Word of God becomes itself the guiding force in history.[15] "The Word is . . . the expression of the divine will to save; it is God's design for the world working itself out in history . . ." (*idem*). According to Deuteronomy 30, 19, God, with this Word, sets before Israel a choice: "life and death", a "blessing and a curse" (cf. also 32, 47); but the limitations of the Word of God seen as the present written *law* are also pointed out (cf. Deut. 4, 2; 30, 14; 32, 47).[16] The more man in exile saw himself constrained to place the reading from Sacred Scripture at the center of divine worship, the more obvious did it become that unchanging greatness was to be sought in the Word of the Bible" (*idem*).[17] Hence, there was the great danger in the later history of the Jews—and to this the Gospel bears witness—of falling into rigidity and formalism, and of presumption based on

---

[13] Ex. 20, 1; 34, 1. 27ff.; Deut. 4, 10. 13. 36; 5, 5. 19; 9, 10; 10, 2. 4.
[14] W. Eichrodt, *Theologie des Alten Testaments* II Vols. (Leipzig, 1935), II, p. 33. English edition, Vol. I.: *The Theology of the Old Testament* (Philadelphia: The Westminster Press, 1961).
[15] *Ibid.*, p. 34.
[16] Cf. also Num. 15, 31; 1 Chron. 15, 15; 2 Chron. 30, 12; 34, 21; 35, 6.
[17] W. Eichrodt, *op. cit.*, p. 36.

the exact observance of the letter of the law. The life-giving dynamism of the Word of God, its essential openness to a continuing and "surprising" use on God's part to bring salvation, was overlooked.

For when, in Christ Jesus, the Word of God became flesh in Israel, it came about that "his own" did not receive him. On the other hand, it is amazing how, in the mission of the early Church, the pagans received it with faith wherever the "Word of truth" was preached (cf., for example, Acts. 28, 28). And this is the case with the community being addressed in the Epistle to the Ephesians (Eph. 1, 13). So they have become the "joint heirs, and fellow members of the same body, and joint partakers of the promise in Christ Jesus through the Gospel" (Eph. 3, 6). By hearing alone (*akousantes*) of course, nothing is gained; faith must intervene (*pisteusantes*), so that the "sealing" with the sacred *Pneuma* may take place. Therefore, the Apostle points out the way in which, as a result of the concrete preaching-situation, the mission of the People of God comes into being: they have to hear, to believe, to be baptized—because the aorist (*esphragisthēte*) shows that the act of baptism is part of it.

Moreover, the Apostle is here moving entirely "in the terminology of the mission" (H. Schlier).[18] What is announced in the mission is "the Word of truth", "in which the truth itself becomes Word" (Schlier). Schlier quite rightly calls our attention to the fact that "the truth" must not be understood in the sense of "the true teaching" (as later on in the pastoral epistles). In an apposition, "the Word of truth" is here closely followed by and explained as "the Gospel of your deliverance (*tēs sōtērias hymōn*)." How this genitive is to be understood is made clear in Ephesians 2, 6–8: ". . . by grace you have been *saved* through faith"; and from the context it develops that a concrete redemption is meant: *a redemption, from the fate of death brought on by sin, into that inviolable realm of life of Christ the most high* (cf. 2, 1–7).

Here Paul, in the Epistle to the Ephesians—as in the Epistle

---

[18] H. Schlier, *Der Brief an die Epheser* (Düsseldorf, [3]1962), p. 69.

to the Romans—derives his theology from his concept of death.[19] The faithful acceptance of the Gospel means for the Apostle the faithful acceptance of the message that in Christ the predestined fate of death which weighed upon the whole world has been lifted, and the heavenly life of God has been won for the believer.

Therefore, "the Word of truth" is nothing else than "the Gospel of your salvation". What the Old Testament People of God sought (in vain) to attain by the way of the Law, namely, *life* (cf. Gal. 3, 12), has been won for the eschatological People of God by the acceptance in faith of the Gospel. The Gospel is for Paul first of all a power-of-life, which participates in the power of the firstborn from the dead, Jesus Christ. The Gospel is no mere message; it is in itself a life-giving power which presupposes that it will be accepted in faith (cf. Rom. 1, 16). Thus, it belongs according to its nature with the Spirit who is inseparable from it.

2. The Signing with the Holy Spirit

Now this "belonging-to" is also already foreshadowed in the Old Testament. Jewish thought was never able to effect any accurate delimitation of *the Word* from *the Spirit*.[20] Characteristic of this tendency is, perhaps, Isaiah 59, 21: "This is the *covenant* with them which I myself made, says the Lord: My *spirit* which is upon you, and my *words* that I have put into your mouth, shall never leave your mouth . . . from now on and forever, says the Lord." (Cf. also: 2 Sam. 23, 2; Zech. 4, 6; 7, 12; Prov. 1, 23.) "What the Spirit did in the issuing-forth of God's Word in the past, has also a normative meaning for the present, and he is at the same time the vital force of the community" (Eichrodt).[21] This corresponds to the nature of the Spirit, which, according to Genesis 1, 2, at the beginning of creation already hovered over the waters, in order to make of

[19] The author plans to publish an essay on this subject.
[20] Cf. W. Eichrodt, *op. cit.*, pp. 29ff.; 37ff.
[21] *Ibid.*, p. 29.

Chaos "the arena for the creation of life" (Eichrodt).[22] Man became a living being when God breathed into his nostrils the breath of life (Gen. 2, 7; 7, 22; Job 27, 3; 33, 4; Ps. 104, 30). When God summons back that breath of life, the act is equivalent to death for man (Job 17, 1; 34, 14ff; Ps. 104, 29; 143, 7; 146, 4).[23]

The Spirit is, according to the Old Testament view, simply the principle of "supernatural" life. This holds good, too, for the New Testament, especially for Pauline theology. Here the Spirit is the ontological foundation for the Christian life; cf. 1 Cor. 6, 11; 12, 13; 2 Cor. 1, 21–22 ("Now it is God who is warrant for us and for you in Christ, who has anointed us, who has also stamped us with his seal and has given us the Spirit as a pledge in our hearts."); Gal. 3, 2; Tit. 3, 5–6 (". . . he saved us through the bath of regeneration and renewal by the Holy Spirit; whom he has abundantly poured out upon us, through Jesus Christ our Savior").

As in 2 Corinthians 1, 21, so in Ephesians 1, 13 (cf. also 4, 30), the Apostle speaks of a "sealing" of the believer with the Holy Spirit. What is meant by this *sphragizein* here? Schlier[24] would prefer not to dismiss the conjecture "that the *sphragizesthai* . . . denotes the laying-on of hands" and with regard to "salvation through the act of taking-possession" it comes closest to "the process of eschatological preservation". According to E. Dinkler[25] it signifies the probability that the Apostle, with the ending *sphragizein* (2 Cor. 1, 22), "will have the expression mean both the act of juridical surrender to Christ and at the same time with it an eschatological 'signing' of the baptized person for the era of the coming of the kingdom (*Endzeit*)". Dinkler conjectures with regard to the phrase, "in spite of the fact

---

[22] *Ibid.*, p. 19.

[23] Cf. also P. van Imschoot, "L'Esprit de Jahvé, source de vie dans l'A.T.," in *Revue Biblique* 46 (1935), pp. 481–501.

[24] *Op. cit.*, concerning the place.

[25] "Die Taufterminologie in 2 Kor. 1, 21f.," in *Neotestamentica et Patristica, Freundsgabe für O. Cullmann* (Leiden, 1962), pp. 173–91, esp. 183–88.

that there is not sufficient evidence", to the existence of "a ritual of sealing or signing which is the fullness of the ceremony of baptism with water".

In the Epistle to the Ephesians, on the other hand, there is, according to Dinkler "the appearance, as it were, of a ready-made and accepted baptismal terminology, and by *sphragizein* the *whole* act of baptism and not just *a single element* of it is meant". This "sealing" in baptism takes place, according to the context, in Christ (*en hō*), that is, probably through the surrender to his "name", so that the baptized person becomes the property (*peripoiēsis*) of Christ and in baptism receives the Spirit as a "pledge" of the fullness of salvation (= "the inheritance") (perhaps indicated through the sacramental signing). "Thus, the gift of the Spirit terminates the act of sealing because the candidate for baptism, through the *karismata*, experiences his belonging to the Body of Christ, to the true Israel, even to the eschatological People of God, and he is inwardly made aware of the truth of the New Covenant *de iure et de facto*" (Dinkler).

In other words: the sealing with the Spirit at baptism makes of the baptized person a member of the eschatological People of God (cf. also 1 Cor. 12, 13; 2 Cor. 3, 3). In this baptism-in-the-Spirit, according to Ephesians 2, 18, "both", Jews as well as Gentiles, now have in the Church, in the living temple of God, in this era of the redemption, access to the Father. Thus the Word of God and the Spirit of God together constitute the eschatological People of God, for whom there is no longer any "wall of separation".

But what is the primary function of the eschatological People of God? According to the Prologue of the Epistle to the Ephesians, it is the praise of grace and of the glory of God (cf. 1, 6. 12. 14).

III

THE PEOPLE OF GOD, THE TEMPLE OF GOD, AND THE PRAISE OF GOD[26]

Ancient Israel, the People of God in the Old Testament, had their religious center in the Ark of the Covenant, or, after the days of Solomon, in the Temple at Jerusalem. Here dwelt the "majesty" of God; this was the single legitimate place for the offering of sacrifice in Israel; this was the focus of every feast and expiatory sacrifice-solemnity; this spot was the objective of votary and pilgrim; this was the spiritual center and the focus of the country's destiny; this was the origin, the symbol, the source of the divine nearness so rich in grace, the locus of prayer offered and prayer answered; in this place was centered the pride, the good fortune and the ardent desires of the devout as well as the object of their trust as believers.[27]

Now the People of God in the New Testament, since they are the true Israel of the *Endzeit,* will have a "temple" in which God is present, where individuals in the nation will have access to him, and where they will praise and bless the Lord. This "temple" can no longer be the Temple in Jerusalem which, moreover, long ago vanished from the face of the earth. We know, to be sure, that Jesus prophesied this fate for the Temple which played a certain role in his trial; he foretold the destruction of the Temple. In the controversy over the healing on the Sabbath (Matt. 12, 1–9) Jesus made a statement that is full of mystery: "But I tell you that one greater than the Temple is here" (12, 6) (*tou hierou meizon estin hōde*). Jesus is here speaking openly of himself "and of his own peculiar relationship to God and to the community. *Meizon* includes what the Temple is for the community, but it also goes beyond that to

---

[26] *Ibid.*

[27] This part of the article corresponds to my work in *Trierer Theologische Zeitschrift* 72 (1963), pp. 175–7. Cf. also F. Mussner, *op. cit.,* pp. 76–118 (with more extensive bibliography).

what Jesus gives to the community" (A. Schlatter).[28] And Jesus explains to the Samaritan woman, according to John 4, 21: ". . . the hour is coming when neither on this mountain (*i.e.,* on Garizim), nor in Jerusalem will you worship the Father."

With these words, certainly, the Old Testament Jewish teaching on the unique place appointed for divine worship is removed. For present purposes, even more valuable is the statement: "Where two or three are gathered together for my sake, there am I in the midst of them" (Matt. 18, 20). In John's Gospel Christ explains his resurrected body as the new temple of the era of redemption (cf. John 2, 19–23). The old Temple in Jerusalem signified the presence of God; so now Jesus himself means God's presence (cf. especially John 10, 30. 38; 14, 11; 17, 21–23); according to Colossians 2, 9, "all the fullness of the Godhead dwells in Christ *bodily*". The faithful make up his "body" and by abiding in Christ receive a share in the divine fullness (Col. 2, 10; Eph. 1, 23). Consequently, Christians who abide in the Spirit are themselves "the Temple (the House) of God" (2 Cor. 3. 9. 16. 17; also cf. 1 Cor. 3, 9; 2 Cor. 6, 16; 1 Tim. 3, 15; Heb. 3, 6; 1 Peter 2, 5: *oikos pneumatikos*).

Before all else, there is still *one* text to cite in which this matter has been given detailed expression and in which the whole of the Christological redeeming-action is to be found: Ephesians 2, 11–22. Here the Church is seen as the fruit of the tree of Christ's cross, a Church which embraces the whole of a new mankind in place of the old folk-community of Israel, in which every wall of separation has been brought low, and all men—whether formerly Jews or Gentiles—have access to the Father in one Spirit through Christ, since this same new union of peoples in Christ represents the spiritual temple of the era of redemption, "in him you too are being built together into a dwelling place for God in the Spirit" (Eph. 2, 22). Whence follows undoubtedly also the experience in worship of the new People of God who are the Christian community: in their service of God, especially in the sacrifice of the eucharist, they already have experience in a very

[28] Cf. F. Nötscher, "Tempel," in *Echter-Bibel.*

direct manner in the community-as-mission of the fact that all there, whether Jew or Gentile, Greek or barbarian, freeman or slave, man or woman, have the selfsame access to the common Father of all, and indeed directly, without barriers of separation and intimidating protocol. The veil is rent asunder, the All-Holy is accessible, God is present in his People as never before. Ephesians 2, 11–22 exhibits in a straightforward manner the high point and the classical summation of the New Testament theology of the People of God.

In this spiritual "temple" the Church assembles the eschatological People of God, made up of Jews and Gentiles, and *summons them to praise the common Father*. The existence of Israel had as its final end a cultic purpose.[29] "Unceasingly has Israel sung God's praise" (G. von Rad).[30] Therefore, God has chosen for himself a nation out of all peoples (cf. also Eph. 1, 5ff., 11ff., 14). Now, in the "temple" of the Church, is fulfilled, according to Romans 15, 6–11, the word that all men, Jews and Gentiles, "one in spirit, and with *one* mouth . . . may glorify the God and Father of our Lord Jesus Christ . . . Christ Jesus has been a minister of the circumcision in order to show God's fidelity in confirming the promises made to our fathers, but that the Gentiles glorify God because of his mercy, as it is written, 'Therefore will I praise thee among the Gentiles, and will sing to thy name' (2 Sam. 22, 50; Ps. 18, 50). And again he says, 'Rejoice you Gentiles, with his people' (Deut. 32, 43). And again, 'Praise the Lord, all you Gentiles; and sing his praises all you peoples' " (Ps. 117, 1). The concrete beginning of this praise of God is *the Church* in which the New Testament People of God are assembled and have access to the Father.

The Constitution on the Sacred Liturgy of Vatican Council II helps to make it clear that the People of God should enter more fully into a living praise of God as expressed in the Prologue to the Epistle to the Ephesians.

[29] A. Schlatter, Der Evangelist Matthäus (Stuttgart, ²1948), concerning the place.
[30] Cf. also G. von Rad, *op. cit.*, pp. 353–67; A. Deissler, "Das lobpreisende Gottesvolk in den Psalmen," in *Sentire Ekklesiam* (Freiburg, 1961), pp. 17–49.

PART II

BIBLIOGRAPHICAL
SURVEY

Bruce Vawter, C.M./*St. Louis, Mo.*

Recent Literature on
the Prophets

The Old Testament prophets and the institution of prophecy continue to engage scholarly attention to a degree that is probably proportionately greater than that devoted to any other aspect of Sacred Scripture. To deal adequately and exhaustively with this contemporary study within the compass of the present article is an evident impossibility. Merely to list the titles of books and articles that would fit within any reasonable definition of what is "recent" would more than fill the pages that we have at our disposal.[1] The writer makes no apologies, therefore, for having sharply limited his subject to some of the more significant literature that has become known to him and has most attracted his interest. He has done so in the hope and with a good measure of confidence that his choices will also respond to what are among the primary concerns of the readers of this publication.

---

[1] The best sources for *mise en scène* regarding prophetic as well as other biblical literature remain the annual *Elenchus Bibliographicus* of *Biblica* (books, articles, reviews, generally without comment) and the periodical *Internationale Zeitschriftenschau für Bibelwissenschaft und Grenzgebiete* (articles, books by exception; often with a considerable time-lag but with abstracts).

112

I

THE PROPHETS AND ISRAEL'S WORSHIP

In his survey of "The Prophetic Literature" contributed to a collection of essays published by the British Society for Old Testament Study in 1951,[2] Otto Eissfeldt noted as a welcome trend in modern scholarship the recognition that the prophetism of the Old Testament—including the "classical" prophetism of "literary" prophecy—had a definite relation to the cult of Israel.[3] It was welcome, he said, because it appeared to mark the beginning of a better understanding of various prophetic traits which had hitherto been enigmatic. In the second section of this article especially we may be able to see the extent to which this hope has been realized.

Certainly there has never been any doubt about the close relation between the cult and postexilic prophecy.[4] The deep involvement of a Haggai, a proto-Zechariah,[5] and a Malachi with

[2] *The Old Testament and Modern Study* (Oxford: Clarendon Press), pp. 115–61 (reprinted as an Oxford Paperback in 1961). A thorough survey of literature on prophecy and the prophets up to 1950 was that of Georg Fohrer, "Neuere Literatur zur alttestamentlichen Prophetie," in *Theologische Rundschau* 19 (1951), pp. 277–346; 20 (1952), pp. 193–271; 295–361.

[3] Some of the more important works that have contributed to this scholarly development are Sigmund Mowinckel's *Psalmenstudien III: Die Kultprophetie und prophetische Psalmen* (Oslo: Dybwad, 1923), many of whose conclusions are summarized in his *The Psalms in Israel's Worship* (Oxford: Blackwell, 1962), a translation and complete revision of his *Offersang og Sangoffer* of 1951; Alfred Haldar, *Associations of Cult Prophets Among the Ancient Semites* (Uppsala: Almquist & Wicksells, 1945); A. R. Johnson, "The Prophet in Israelite Worship," in *Expository Times* 47 (1935/36), pp. 312–19, and *The Cultic Prophet in Ancient Israel* (Cardiff: University of Wales, [2]1962).

[4] Cf. T. Chary, *Les prophètes et le culte à partir de l'exil* (Tournai: Desclée, 1955).

[5] Zech. 9–11, Zech. 12–14, and Mal. 1–3 are commonly considered to have been originally three anonymous prophetic collections (each beginning with the same catch-phrase), of which the last is easily the oldest. Paul Lamarche, S.J., *Zacharie IX–XIV* (Paris: Gabalda, 1961), has attempted to defend the unity of authorship of Zech. 9–14 and an earlier dating; the chapters are, in any case, dependent on Zech. 1–8 and the Second Isaiah.

the cult is altogether apparent: not only do they reflect cultic themes and language, they also presuppose the transition from a regal to a sacerdotal concept of soteriology that characterizes the postexilic Judaism,[6] as well as the beginnings of the liturgical "realized eschatology" that achieves varying expressions in the Chronicler and Ben Sira.[7] In the eyes of many authors, passages like Isaiah 24–27 (the "apocalypse of Isaiah") and the book of Joel make their best sense when they are conceived in a cultic setting. The book of Ezekiel, too, after a short generation of critical near-anarchy, is once again recognized as substantially the work of a prophet who was intensely involved with the Zadokite priesthood and its Law of Holiness and who could not conceive of an Israel in which the cult did not have a central place.[8]

It was the pre-exilic prophets who raised a serious question with regard to the role of the cult in the continuity of Israelite tradition. Passages like Isaiah 1, 10–17; Hosea 6, 6; Amos 5, 21–27, etc., are quite obviously not calculated to certify the prophets as in the forefront of the Israelite liturgical movement of the 8th century B.C. It could be, and was, pointed out, of course, that in their existential situation the sacrifices and ritual condemned by the prophets were the meaningless formalities of men who possessed no genuine knowledge or love of the moral God of Israel, that in other situations the prophets need have

[6] The translation of *The Prophetic Books* by the Catholic Biblical Association of America (1961) explicitly recognizes the transition by restoring the name of Zerubbabel to the text of Zech. 6, 9–15.

[7] It is impossible to agree with Martin Rehm, "Das Opfer der Völker nach Mal. 1, 11," in *Festschrift Junker* (Trier: Paulinus-Verlag, 1961), pp. 193–208, that Mal. contemplated a cessation of the Jerusalem priesthood. Cf. the author's "Levitical Messianism and the New Testament," in *The Bible in Current Catholic Thought* (New York: Herder and Herder, 1962), pp. 83–99.

[8] For example, see the commentary of Georg Fohrer (Handb. z. A.T. 13, Tübingen: Mohr, 1955). Cf. also H. H. Rowley, "The Book of Ezekiel in Modern Study," in *Bulletin of the John Rylands Library* 36 (1953/54), pp. 146–90; Walther Zimmerli, "Der Eigenart der prophetischen Rede des Ezechiel," in *Zeitschrift für die alttestamentliche Wissenschaft* 66 (1954), pp. 1–26.

found nothing more reprehensible in the same rites than Isaiah would have found in the prayer that he condemns in 1, 15.[9] It could also be maintained that such prophetic condemnations fit into the pattern of "dialectical negation" not otherwise uncommon in biblical language,[10] that is, one that means "not so much this as that". All this is very true, and for some while now it has been fairly generally agreed in biblical circles that the differences between priestly and prophetical religion had been greatly exaggerated through a misguided scholarly "Protestantization" of prophetism in the 19th century,[11] though we still do find authors maintaining that the opposition of the pre-exilic prophets to cult was an opposition in principle, to a ritualistic system that had no roots in the authentic Yahwistic tradition.[12]

The direction of the presumption has now shifted, as historical and form critical studies have pointed to the need for synthesis after a generation of atomization. The antiquity of the cult, of the law, of the covenant concept, and the like, make it far more likely that the prophets should have had at least a normal Israelite's share in cultic concerns than that they should have stood in opposition to it.[13] The recognition of the links between the

[9] Cf. H. H. Rowley, "The Meaning of Sacrifice in the Old Testament," in *Bulletin of the John Rylands Library* 33 (1950), pp. 89–93, and *The Unity of the Bible* (New York: Meridian Books, 1957 [1953]), pp. 38–62.

[10] Cf. Roland de Vaux, O.P., *Les Institutions de l'Ancien Testament II* (Paris: Cerf, 1960), pp. 308f., 344–47 (Eng. Tr.: *Ancient Israel, Its Life and Institutions* [New York: McGraw-Hill, 1961], pp. 428f., 454–56).

[11] See G. Henton Davies, "The Yahwistic Tradition in the Eighth-Century Prophets," in *Studies in Old Testament Prophecy* (Edinburgh: Clark, 1950), pp. 37–51, and Norman W. Porteous, "The Basis of the Ethical Teaching of the Prophets," *ibid.*, pp. 143–56.

[12] Some of the writings of Norman H. Snaith and J. Philip Hyatt come immediately to mind. In the second edition of *Die zwölf kleinen Propheten Handb. z. A.T.* 14, Tübingen: Mohr, 1954), Theodore H. Robinson professed that he had found little in the past seventeen years of study (other than philological studies) to cause him to change his opinion in commenting on Hosea through Micah. His co-author Friedrich Horst, however, had given considerate attention to more recent form critical studies, even if to reject them. This volume has now appeared (1964) in a "third," essentially unrevised edition.

[13] Cf. G. E. Wright, "Cult and History," in *Interpretation* 16 (1962),

older *nabiism* and "classical" prophecy and of the degree to which the latter, despite its undeniable uniqueness in the history of religion, does in some part conform to a Near Eastern pattern, has contributed to the same end, as has the stress on the connections of prophetism with a basically common religious tradition.[14] It is true, Isaiah's presence in the Jerusalem temple at the time of his inaugural vision (Is. 6) may have been as an ordinary Israelite spectator and not as a member of the cult personnel, but there is no reason whatever to question that it was as one who was deeply involved in the liturgy of Israel.[15] Furthermore, when we take into consideration his association with Urijah the chief priest and the qualification of his wife as a *n^ebî'â* (Is. 8, 2f.), his dependence on the sacral and regal traditions of Jerusalem in preference to those of the Mosaic age, his capacity for "nationalistic" prophecy, and the like, it does not seem at all improbable that in descending upon Isaiah the spirit of Yahweh may have chosen a professional *nābî'*/as it had done so often in the past.

Acknowledgment that there could be cultic influence on classical prophetism is a commonsense conclusion that results in more sensible interpretation. The oracle of the eschatological Jerusalem verbally identical in Isaiah 2, 2–4 and Micah 4, 1–3 is best explained neither as the borrowing of one prophet from the other (leaving the commentators to argue the priority) nor as an interpolation into both texts, but as the common use of a

---

pp. 3–20. See also Sigmund Mowinckel, *Religion und Kultus* (Göttingen: Vandenhoeck & Ruprecht, 1953); Helmer Ringgren, *Israelitische Religion* (Stuttgart: Kohlhammer, 1963).

[14] Cf. Walther Eichrodt, *Theologie des Alten Testaments* 1 (Stuttgart: Ehrenfried Klotz, 5.1957), pp. 225–63 (Eng. Tr.: *Theology of the Old Testament* [Philadelphia: Westminster, 1961], pp. 339–91); Johannes Pedersen, "The Role Played by Inspired Persons Among the Israelites and the Arabs," in *Studies in OT Prophecy*, pp. 127–42; Jean Steinmann, *Le prophétisme biblique des origines à Osée* (Paris: Cerf, 1959), pp. 241–48; Bruce Vawter, C.M., *The Conscience of Israel* (New York: Sheed & Ward, 1961), pp. 13–43 (Ger. Tr.: *Mahner und Künder* [Salzburg: Otto Müller, 1963], pp. 21–53).

[15] Cf. P. Béguerie, "La vocation d'Isaïe," in *Etudes sur les prophètes d'Israël* (Paris: Cerf, 1954), pp. 11–51.

cultic chant, to which the psalms afford numerous parallels. Even the line which now serves as the exordium to the prophecy of the dour Amos (Am. 1, 2), far from being the addition of a later editor, can be seen as the normal conviction of a man of Judah whose cultic convictions would be implemented a century and a quarter after in the Deuteronomic reform under King Josiah.[16] Ezekiel and the postexilic prophets fall more readily into place in the continuing tradition of Israelitic prophetism. The ritual character of parts of Habakkuk, Nahum, Zephaniah no longer seems anomalous. And just as the later classical prophets could concern themselves with cultic matters, the attribution to earlier cult and court prophets like Samuel, Nathan, and Elijah of the moralizing kind of prophecy habitually associated with Amos and his successors certainly needs be no anachronism, whatever earlier commentators may have thought.

In a word, we are encouraged to understand better the implications of a prophetic succession to which an Amos acknowledged himself to belong even while dissociating himself from it. Salvation oracles, for which the cult had a special predilection, can no longer be denied to the preexilic prophets on principle; the judgment must be made in each case respecting the individual prophetic genius and not peremptorily. Perhaps one of the more important considerations in this connection will be the reexamination that is yet awaited of the entire question of prophetical messianism.[17] The psalms presuppose on numerous occasions the presence of prophets (Pss. 20, 7; 60, 8–10; 95, 7b–11, etc.); it was prophets who authored most of the messianic "royal" psalms (Pss. 2; 20; 21; 45; 72; 89; 101; 110) which are rooted in the pre-exilic cult of the Jerusalem temple.[18]

[16] Robinson himself is of this opinion in his commentary.
[17] The literature on messianic prophecy is immense. Two collections of articles that should by no means be overlooked are those of Vol. 19 (1957) of the *Catholic Biblical Quarterly* and *L'attente du Messie* (Tournai: Desclée de Brouwer, 1954). In 1956 an English translation and revision of Mowinckel's classic *Han Som Kommer* (1951) was published: *He That Cometh* (New York: Abingdon).
[18] Cf. Hans-Joachim Kraus, *Psalmen* (Neukirchen: Buchhandlung des Erziehungsvereins, 1960) 1, lixf. and *passim*. See also Joseph Coppens,

Between the royal messianism of the psalms and that of the classical prophets, even a prophet as attached to the Jerusalem tradition as Isaiah, there is an obvious difference, but there is also a connection. There have been many studies of specific prophetic texts, some of which have reached apparently definitive conclusions;[19] other passages remain as controverted as ever.[20] It may be hoped that the way is open for studies that will attack the problem afresh on more general premises.

The newer perspective in which prophetism is being viewed is, in part, a reaction to the evolutionism and arbitrary historicism that have become associated, rightly or wrongly, with the name of Julius Wellhausen. As is true in most reactions, there have occurred undoubted excesses and exaggerations.[21] The classical prophets were not cult prophets; their religion did differ from the priestly *torah;* they did utter new words that altered the tradition. All this must be gladly admitted. At the same time, however, it can undoubtedly be better understood the more it is now related to the other Israel that was itself, in its own way, also prophetic.

II

THE PROPHETS AND THE COVENANT

One of the most interesting and important developments in form critical study of the Old Testament has been the determination of the antiquity of the covenant concept and theology as rooted in historical fact. This, too, has been in reaction to the older critical theory as finally synthesized by Wellhausen: the covenant was an idea that developed late in Israelite history to

---

"Études récentes sur le psautier," in *Le Psautier* (Louvain: Publications Universitaires, 1962), pp. 1–71.

[19] For example, W. L. Moran, S.J., "Gen. 49, 10 and Its Use in Ez. 21, 32," in *Biblica* 39 (1958), pp. 405–25.

[20] See the bibliography amassed by Joseph Coppens, "L'interprétation d'Is., VII, 14, à la lumière des études les plus récentes," in *Festschrift Junker*, pp. 31–45.

[21] Cf. Georg Fohrer, "Remarks on Modern Interpretation of the Prophets," in *Journal of Biblical Literature* 80 (1961), pp. 309–19.

afford a theological explanation to account for the disasters that
had overtaken Israel the nation. According to this same theory,
the law, as the consequence of covenant, was wholly the product of Israel's history and played no constitutive part in its
origins. Israel and its religion were explained in terms of the
evolution of the religious process in an ethnic group like that
of the Badawin and the Wahabi, whose ways could still be
studied in Arabic society.

The rejection of this reconstruction has followed on a history
of research that need only be briefly summarized here. Form
critical studies into Israel's origins have shown that Causse's
formulation which served as the title of a book in 1937, *Du
groupe ethnique à la communauté religieuse,* was almost precisely the opposite of the historical truth: Israel was first a religion, then a people, whose origins are to be more profitably
examined in the context of the ancient amphictyonic principle
than in that of nomadic institutions.[22] Israel's law, too, must be
set in principle at its very origins, intimately connected with its
cult.[23] Finally, form critical analysis of the covenant structure
itself by George Mendenhall and others has led convincingly to
a *Sitz im Leben* of the Mosaic age.[24] One or another aspect of
this development has come under challenge, sometimes serious

[22] Two of the fundamental studies were Martin Noth's *Das System der
zwölf Stämme Israels* (Stuttgart: Kohlhammer, 1930) and Gerhard von
Rad, *Das formgeschichtliche Problem des Hexateuch* (Stuttgart: Kohlhammer, 1938) (=*Gesammelte Studien zum Alten Testament* [Munich:
Kaiser Verlag, 1958], pp. 9–86). Lineally descended from these, but
building on additional epigraphical and archaeological data is the recent
important work of George E. Mendenhall, "The Hebrew Conquest of
Palestine," in *Biblical Archaeologist* 25 (1962), pp. 66–87.

[23] Fundamental studies were those of Anton Jirku, *Das weltliche Recht
im Alten Testament* (Gütersloh: Bertelsmann, 1927); Albrecht Alt, *Die
Ursprünge des israelitischen Rechts* (Leipzig: Hirzel, 1934) (=*Kleine
Schriften zur Geschichte des Volkes Israel* [Munich: Beck, 1959], pp.
278–332); Martin Noth, *Die Gesetze im Pentateuch* (Halle: Schriften
der Königsberger Gelehrten Gesellschaft, 1940).

[24] George E. Mendenhall, "Ancient Oriental and Biblical Law," in
Biblical Archaeologist 17 (1954), pp. 26–46; "Covenant Forms in Israelite Tradition," *ibid.,* pp. 50–76; K. Baltzer, *Das Bundesformular* (Neukirchen: Buchhandlung des Erziehungsvereins, 1960); W. Beyerlin, *Her-
kunft und Geschichte der ältesten Sinaitraditionen* (Tübingen: Mohr,
1961); Jean L'Hour, "L'alliance de Sichem," in *Revue biblique* 69
(1962), pp. 5–36; 350–68.

challenge;[25] however, there seems to be no doubt that its basic structure will prevail.

The prophets are obviously much involved in this development. The prophetic doctrine of the covenant, of love as its motive and motif, of moral religion as covenant obligation and response, we must recognize, is not the invention of the prophets but rather their development of an historical revelation bound up with Israel's origins. That their development was decisive no one, of course, will deny. It was their theology, their superior insights, and their continued mediation of the Word of God, which made possible the resultant Deuteronomic formulations, which without the prophets would have been inconceivable. Nevertheless, it was upon *tradita* that the prophets built, and it is in this light that their preaching and teaching must be evaluated. Eschatology, too, which is so intimately associated with covenant religion, must be recognized as original to the Israelite revelation.[26] The prophets moralized, or further moralized, an eschatology which inhered in Israel's faith; they did not discover it. In this regard the relation between prophetic and apocalyptic eschatology can be seen anew.[27]

Because the covenant was enacted, perpetuated and renewed in the cult, it is evident that the consideration of the previous section of this paper is quite relevant here in respect to prophetic

[25] Cf. Dennis J. McCarthy, S.J., *Treaty and Covenant* (Rome: Pontifical Biblical Institute, 1963); C. F. Whitley, "Covenant and Commandment in Israel," in *Journal of Near Eastern Studies* 22 (1963), pp. 37–48; Erhard Gerstenberger, "Covenant and Commandment," in *Journal of Biblical Literature* 84 (1965), pp. 38–51.

[26] See Ladislav Černý, *The Day of Yahweh and Some Relevant Problems* (Prague: Charles University, 1948), and recently, H. P. Müller, "Zur Frage nach dem Ursprung der biblischen Eschatologie," in *Vetus Testamentum* 14 (1964), pp. 276–93. Cf. Gerhard von Rad, "Die Stadt auf dem Berge," in *Evangelische Theologie* 8 (1948/49), pp. 439–47 (=*Gesammelte Studien*, pp. 214–24): Wir sehen die Propheten vielmehr als Träger und Verkündiger von eschatologischen Vorstellungen, die in der Volksüberlieferung schon in allem Wesentlichen durchaus fertig ausgestaltet vorlagen" (439/214).

[27] Cf. George Eldon Ladd, "Why not Prophetic-Apocalyptic?" in *Journal of Biblical Literature* 76 (1957), pp. 192–200; Bruce Vawter, C.M., "Apocalyptic: Its Relation to Prophecy," in *Catholic Biblical Quarterly* 22 (1960), pp. 33–46; H. H. Rowley, *The Relevance of Apocalyptic* (London: Lutterworth, ²1963).

interpretation. That the prophets condemned Israel in the name of covenant violation is, perhaps, a commonplace of prophetic exegesis. That this is true also of Amos, who did not employ the word "covenant" to designate Israel's relation to Yahweh, would also doubtless be acknowledged by all today. That these condemnations were also phrased in the cultic language of the covenant is, however, a new discovery of form criticism that affects the precise understanding of many prophetic words.

We may consider, for example, the "prophetic lawsuit," which in Isaiah 1, 2f., Jeremiah 2, 4–13, and especially Micah 6, 1–8,[28] achieves a special and significant form. The juridical indictment is, of course, a common prophetic literary form, which appears in numerous guises. In these instances, among others, it appears precisely as a denunciation of covenant violation, seemingly closely related to the covenant treaty form which has been discerned by Mendenhall and others.[29] Here Yahweh appears not as judge but as plaintiff: the appeal is lodged before the mountains, the hills, the heavens, the elements which were the witnessing deities to the Hittite suzerainty treaties of the Mosaic age. The cultic overtones are most apparent in the Mican passage; it could well have served as a covenant ritual even as it has been so naturally adapted to the Christian ritual of Good Friday. The themes of these passages are not isolated, but occur throughout the Old Testament. It is, of course, by no means necessary to imagine that in their denunciations the prophets were functioning as cult officials. They did couch their message in language and concepts that were originally cultic, however.

The same kind of background has been invoked to explain the

---

[28] It is not necessary here to argue the "authenticity" of Mi. 6, 1–8. However, it may be observed that the more the conventional style of such oracles is recognized, the less cogent are the arguments from the standpoint of Micah's usual style, actual or presumed.

[29] Cf. E. Würthwein, "Der Ursprung der prophetischen Gerischtsrede," Zeitschrift für Theologie und Kirche 49 (1952), pp. 1–16; F. Hesse, "Wurzelt die prophetische Gerichtsrede im israelitischen Kultus?" in Zeitschrift für die alttestamentliche Wissenschaft 65 (1953), pp. 45–53; R. Press, "Die Gerichtspredigt der vorexilischen Propheten und der Versuch einer Steigerung der kultischen Leistung," ibid., 70 (1958), pp. 181–87; Herbert B. Huffmon, "The Covenant Lawsuit in the Prophets," in Journal of Biblical Literature 78 (1959), pp. 285–95.

prophetic "oracles against the nations" which begin with Amos.[30] Part of the treaty provisions was the community of friends and enemies. In prophetic teaching, this was never un-critically assumed; but on the other hand, prophetic insistence that Yahweh's protection was conditioned on obedience takes on new meaning in the light of the treaty formulations. The pro-phetic sermons closely parallel various of the *torah* rituals of the psalms. Even more basically, the very character of the prophet as herald of the covenant King (cf. Is. 6, 8–10), as "watchman" (Jer. 4, 5–12, etc.), mediator and intercessor be-tween God and people, can be most convincingly related to the rites and ritual language of the covenant.[31]

Still in this line of thinking, a recent study of Walter Brueggemann offers suggestions that could lead to a reinterpretation of such an apparently uncompromising "prophet of doom" as Amos.[32] If his analysis is correct, Amos' prophecy is less the inexorable death warrant of Israel than it is a summons to covenant renewal couched in the ancient cultic language of covenant and holy war.[33] Within this pattern the famous doxologies (Am. 4, 13; 5, 8f.; 9, 5f.), long recognized as cultic in origin but variously explained as interpolations or adaptations,[34] now find a logical place. It is easy to see that form critical study of this kind can have far-reaching implications for the interpreta-tion of prophecy.

[30] Cf. F. C. Fensham, "Clauses of Protection in Hittite Vassal-Treaties," in *Vetus Testamentum* 13 (1963), pp. 133–43.

[31] Here we may refer to the works of H. Graf Reventlow, especially *Das Amt des Propheten bei Amos* (Göttingen: Vandenhoeck & Ruprecht, 1962); *Wächter über Israel: Ezechiel und seine Tradition* (Berlin: Töpel-mann, 1962); *Liturgie und prophetisches Ich bei Jeremia* (Gütersloh: Gerd Mohn, 1963). See also James Muilenburg, "The Form and Struc-ture of the Covenantal Formulations," in *Vetus Testamentum* 9 (1959), pp. 347–65.

[32] "Amos IV 4–13 and Israel's Covenant Worship," in *Vetus Testa-mentum* 15 (1965), pp. 1–15.

[33] In this regard, see also H. P. Müller, "Die kultische Darstellung der Theophanie," in *Vetus Testamentum* 14 (1964), pp. 183–91.

[34] F. A. Vaccari, S.J., "Hymnus propheticus in Deum Creatorem," in *Verbum Domini* 9 (1929), pp. 184–88; J. D. W. Watts, "An Old Hymn Preserved in the Book of Amos," in *Journal of Near Eastern Studies* 15 (1956), pp. 33–9.

III

PROPHETIC INSPIRATION

We may conclude this brief survey with an even briefer consideration of what is doubtless one of the most fundamental of all questions concerning prophecy, the nature of prophecy itself or of prophetic inspiration. How did prophecy come to man, what were its effects on him, and what precisely do we understand by "the prophetic word"? These are but a few of the many ramifications of this problem.

It is unfortunate that in the theology usual in Catholic circles the treatment of this vital topic has been largely approached from sources other than the biblical data, despite the fact that it was biblical prophecy, after all, with which this theology has been exclusively concerned. Even St. Thomas' tractate *de prophetia,* while qualified by his usual balance and good sense, is seen more and more nowadays to be inadequate to the demands of critical biblical study. Beginning with Augustine, the Scholastic tradition relied far too heavily on aprioristic theories of prophecy derived from pagan, rabbinical and Muslim concepts, and far too little on what the Bible actually had to say about it or demonstrate about it.[35] The earlier Protestant biblical criticism, however, scarcely offered anything better, as the preceding pages may have suggested. If for no other reason, it was inhibited by its philosophical inadequacies from elaborating its ideas systematically and relating them realistically to the historical situation it studied so assiduously.

What prophecy was, or is, we can learn only from the prophets, especially from prophets like Isaiah and Jeremiah, who have explicitly or implicitly told us the most about the prophetic process.[36] To these might be added Ezekiel, who was also forced to

[35] Cf. Oswald Loretz, *Die Wahrheit der Bibel* (Freiburg: Herder, 1964), pp. 12–14.

[36] An older work that has been of much help to the author in this respect is that of Ivar Seierstad, *Die Offenbarungserlebnisse der Propheten Amos, Jesaja und Jeremia* (Oslo: Dybwad, 1946). An even older classic

be extremely conscious of his own prophetic character.[37] From these and other isolated prophetic references we know that the prophetic consciousness consisted in a strong moral relationship to God, a transforming experience by which a "call" was known. It was a constitutive experience: the prophet was quite as much a prophet in what he did and in what he was as in what he said, just as the biblical "Word" of God is more often what God has done than what he has said.[38] The prophet, said Jeremiah (23, 18.22), stands in the *sōd* of Yahweh, that is in his intimate friendship and council.[39]

What was the nature of this experience? Older prophets, even "false" prophets, doubtless appealed to the visible presence of an ecstatic "spirit" (cf. 1 Kgs. 22, 24). This never seems to have occurred to the classical prophets (cf. Jer. 28, 5–9). Even when, as in the case of Ezekiel, we have good reason to suspect that ecstacy played a part in prophetic vision, it is fairly evident that the prophetic oracles as such were never formulated as the utterances of an ecstatic.

In recent times, many have suggested the mystical experiences of some of the saints as a means of understanding prophetic inspiration. In his monumental work on prophecy, Johannes Lindblom examines and qualifies this solution.[40] Relying in part on Scandinavian parallels to biblical prophecy, but mainly confining himself to the biblical evidence, Lindblom accurately distinguishes prophetic inspiration from mysticism—a God who is known rather than ineffable, of extramanence rather than immanence, of history rather than of individual experience. Lind-

---

in this field is John Skinner's *Prophecy and Religion: Studies in the Life of Jeremiah* (Cambridge University Press, 1922), recently reissued in paperback form.

[37] Cf. Walther Zimmerli, "Das Wort des göttlichen Selbsterweises (Erweiswort), eine prophetische Gattung," in *Mélanges Robert* (Paris: Bloud & Gay, 1957), pp. 154–64.

[38] Cf. Gerhard von Rad, *Theologie des Alten Testaments II: Die Theologie der Prophetischen Überlieferungen Israels* (Munich: Kaiser-Verlag, 1960), pp. 62–72.

[39] The parallel passage in Am. 3, 7 is probably dependent on Jeremiah.

[40] *Prophecy in Ancient Israel* (Oxford: Blackwell, 1962). This is not a revision but a complete reworking of his earlier (1934) *Profetismen i Israel.*

blom's lengthy discussion is of considerable value in this as in many other areas of prophetic study, even though it leads to few positive formulations.

Another approach is that made by Abraham Heschel in his *The Prophets*.[41] Heschel's explanation of prophetic inspiration is the prophet's being caught up in, and made participant of, the divine "pathos" and concern for the creature man and his history. He, too, distinguishes prophetic inspiration from mysticism and ecstaticism, though his own treatment often approximates the mystical and is unrelentingly biblical in its anthropomorphisms ("The grandeur of God implies the capacity to experience emotion"). It is this "emotion" of God into which the prophet enters in a personal relationship.

These studies emphasize the unique character of biblical prophetism. They also stress the all-important truth, which must always be taken in balance with what was discussed in the first sections of this article, that however dependent the prophet was on Israelite tradition and however he may have stood in the mainstream of its religion, he was always first and foremost a charismatic character and his word was always "new". It should be evident how vital this consideration is, not simply as an isolated *theologoumenon,* but also for its practical consequences on all of biblical interpretation and understanding. On it depends in large measure the progress of the well-known discussion on the "senses" of Scripture, the distinction of prophetic from other biblical inspiration, the determination of what is meant, in all its nuances and in the final analysis, by "the Word of God".

[41] New York: Harper & Row, 1962. This, too, is the redoing of an earlier work of 1936, *Die Prophetie*.

Roland E. Murphy, O.Carm./*Washington, D.C.*

The Wisdom Literature of the Old Testament

In view of the avowedly pastoral intent of CONCILIUM it might appear that the sapiential books of the Old Testament (Proverbs, Job, Ecclesiastes, Sirach [Ecclesiasticus] and Wisdom) have less to offer than other parts of the Bible. Fortunately, this is not so because the direction of the wisdom literature is comparable to that of Schema 13 of Vatican Council II. It presents Israel facing the world, involved in the world, judging the values in the wisdom tradition of its neighbors, looking to the concrete reality of conduct and success in worldly affairs, and to the meaning of this success. While the Law and the Prophets have received the lion's share of attention, the wisdom literature has been the subject of an ever-increasing number of studies.[1] Although Sirach and Wisdom do not belong to the Jewish or Protestant Canon, they are necessary for a proper evaluation of the wisdom movement in Israel. Moreover, the discovery of the Dead Sea Scrolls has underscored the importance of this "intertestamental" literature. Fragments of

[1] In a general survey published in 1951 [*The Old Testament and Modern Study*, ed. H. Rowley (Oxford), pp. 210–37], W. Baumgartner allotted a modest treatment to wisdom literature, but he noted an upsurge of interest at that time. Our report will emphasize the developments since 1951.

Sirach have been found in the Qumran caves, and the Qumran literature has several contacts with the Book of Wisdom.[2]

I

WISDOM: INTERNATIONAL AND ISRAELITE

Progress in Old Testament studies has been due primarily to the archeological explosion which enabled scholars to hear the Word of God more literally and historically in its own milieu. Thus, G. Mendenhall and K. Baltzer have greatly clarified the Israelite notion of covenant, thanks to the discoveries of the ancient Hittite treaties. Likewise, the affinities of Israel's wisdom literature with that of Egypt and Mesopotamia have become ever more clear. Since the publication of the Wisdom of Amen-em-ope in 1923 the Egyptian literature has provided the favorite comparisons with Israelite wisdom, especially with the Book of Proverbs.[3] From the third millennium B.C., down into the Hellenistic period there are extant about a dozen examples of Egyptian *Sebayit,* or teachings, which purport to be instructions which X makes for his son (or student) Y. They have a very practical purpose: to instruct a young man how to cope with the practical problems of life, especially life at court. He is expected to be diligent, honest, capable of exercising self-control, etc.

In Mesopotamia the wisdom writings cover a broader area.[4]

[2] On Sirach see A. di Lella, "Qumran and the Geniza Fragments of Sirach," in *Cath. Bibl. Quart.* 24 (1962), pp. 245–67; for the Book of Wisdom see A.-M. Dubarle, "Une source du livre de la Sagesse?" in *Revue de sciences philosophiques et théologiques* 37 (1953), pp. 425–43.

[3] The most striking example is the dependence of Proverbs 22, 17–24, 22 upon the Wisdom of Amen-em-ope; this opinion is admitted by most scholars despite the recent objections of E. Drioton. Accurate translations of the more famous Egyptian works are available in J. Pritchard, *Ancient Near Eastern Texts* (Princeton, [2]1955). Informative essays on Egyptian wisdom literature and its contacts with Israel are contained in *Les sagesses du proche-orient ancient* (Paris, 1963), especially those of J. Leclant and S. Morenz, pp. 5–26; 63–71. See also E. Würthwein, *Die Weisheit Aegyptens und das Alte Testament* (Marburg, 1960).

[4] The Assyro-Babylonian works are translated in W. Lambert, *Babylonian Wisdom Literature* (Oxford, 1960). J. Nougayrol gives a survey in

Besides court etiquette there is an emphasis on popular sayings, fables, etc. And there are several literary works that are in the same spirit of Job and Ecclesiastes, such as the "Dialogue about Human Misery", the "Dialogue of Pessimism", etc. Hence, perhaps the most striking feature of the wisdom literature of the ancient Near East is its international character. This was not an area where the most distinctive beliefs of a people came to expression. It is not surprising that in 1 Kings 4, 29–34, Solomon's wisdom was reputed to be greater than that of the Egyptians and the "sons of the East". The comparison itself shows that Israel was aware of the rich wisdom heritage of her neighbors. While Israel's debt to her neighbors is to be acknowledged, we shall see that there is a special stamp to the sapiential writings preserved in the Old Testament.

II

THE WISDOM MOVEMENT IN ISRAEL

The orientation of Israel toward Egypt is an important key to the life-setting and the beginnings of the biblical wisdom literature. The life-setting was the Jerusalem court, always influenced by Egyptian methods, where the young men were trained for their responsibilities in political life. In Proverbs 10–22 and 25–29 we find the same kind of advice that was featured in the Egyptian *Sebayit:* self-control, correct attitudes, etc. The popular wisdom which derived from the rugged Jewish peasant (*e.g.,* Proverbs 10, 5; Tobit 4, 1ff.), also found its way into these collections. Recently J.-P. Audet has pointed out that one cannot exclude the home as a life-setting of wisdom and teaching in ancient Israel.[5]

Les sagesses . . . (cf. footnote 3), pp. 40–51; cf. also G. Castellino, *Sapienza Babilonese* (Turin, 1962). For the sapiential literature of ancient Sumer see J. van Dijk, *La sagesse suméro-accadienne* (Leiden, 1953); E. Gordon, *Sumerian Proverbs* (Philadelphia, 1959); S. Kramer, *History Begins at Sumer* (New York, 1959).

[5] Audet's view is described by G. Couturier, "Sagesse Babylonienne et Sagesse Israélite," in *Sciences ecclésiastiques* 14 (1962), pp. 293–309.

But it remains true that it was in the court that the sayings of the sages were cultivated and given adequate literary expression before being collected (*e.g.*, by "the men of Hezekiah"—Prov. 25, 1). In the atmosphere of the court in Jerusalem wisdom seems to have been but one of the preoccupations of the scribe and counsellor.[6] Their life was also taken up with the manifold duties engendered by bureaucracy and officialdom. The prophets seem to have taken a dim view of the sages (Is. 29, 15; 30, 1; Ezek. 7, 26; 11, 2), as though their advice ran counter to the prophetic viewpoint. They formed a class clearly distinct from priest or prophet (Jer. 18, 18), and the collections of sayings in the later chapters of Proverbs are to be attributed to them.

The paradox of Israel's wisdom literature is that most of it was actually composed during the postexilic period, when there was no longer any court. This important fact helps to explain the peculiar stamp assumed by Old Testament works. Despite the royal and courtly origins of the movement, the literature assumed a definitely religious orientation. One can see this most clearly in the introduction which was composed (chapters 1–9) for the collections in Proverbs. The author of this introduction found a value in the older collections, and he sought to preserve and also to develop them for the guidance of the community. The saying: "The fear of the Lord is the beginning of wisdom" (Prov. 1, 7; 9, 10; cf. Job 28, 28; Ps. 110/111, 10; Sir. 1, 16) is an indication of this point of view. The old sayings are brought under the authority of the ethical demands of Yahweh.[7]

Now the hortatory tone of the Deuteronomic preaching is echoed in the appeal of the wisdom teacher to his student. Not only were the traditional sayings judged to be in harmony with the Law, they promoted a maturity demanded by the ethical

[6] Cf. H. Duesberg, *Les scribes inspirés* (Bruges, 1938–39); A.-M. Dubarle, *Les sages d'Israel* (Lectio Divina I) (Paris, 1946); P. de Boer, "The Counsellor," in *Wisdom in Israel and in the Ancient Near East,* ed. M. Noth and D. Thomas (*Suppl. Vet. Test.* III, Leiden, 1955).

[7] Cf. S. Plath, "Furcht Gottes," *Arb. zu Theol.* II, 2 (Stuttgart, 1963), pp. 58–76; R. E. Murphy, "The Concept of Wisdom Literature," in *The Bible in Current Catholic Thought,* ed. J. McKenzie (New York, 1962), pp. 46–54.

training of youth. The good life held out by the earlier sages was seen to be identical with the rewards promised by the Deuteronomic preachers (Deut. 5, 33; 30, 15-20). The postexilic sages formed disciples who perpetuated their religious teaching, as one may judge from the epilogue to Ecclesiastes (Eccles. 12, 9–14) and from the prologue to Sirach (cf. also Sir. 51, 23-30). In this postexilic development the literature becomes more universal, less concerned with any single class, such as courtier. It is oriented toward *all* Israel, and the religious thrust continues until Sirach is able to identify wisdom with the Law (Sir. 24, 23). As we shall see, even the "problem" of the righteous sufferer, the mystery of divine retribution, eventually receives a distinctively Yahwist treatment and solution.

III
THE WISDOM WRITINGS

Proverbs

In the last few years several commentaries on Proverbs have appeared.[8] While there is a reasonable difference of opinion reflected in the translation and understanding of some individual passages, one should note a general agreement on the meaning of the various collections that make up this book. A. Barucq and B. Gemser have paid due attention to the character of chapters 1–9, and both take into account the definitive study of the late A. Robert which established the anthological composition present in this introduction.[9] This method of composition means the re-use of earlier biblical phraseology in expressing one's message. Robert pointed out the dependence of these chap-

[8] R. Scott, *Proverbs. Anchor Bible* 18 (New York, 1965); A. Barucq, *Le Livre des Proverbes* (Paris, 1964); B. Gemser, "Sprüche Salomos," in *Handb. z. A.T.* 16 (Tübingen, ²1963); H. Ringgren, "Sprüche," in *A. T. Deutsch*, 16/1 (Göttingen, 1962); J. v.d. Ploeg, "Spreuken," *Boeken O.T.*, VIII, 1 (Roermond, 1952).

[9] Robert's studies appeared in a series of articles in the *Revue Biblique* in 1934–35. The analysis of the literary structure of these chapters has been done by P. Skehan, *Cath. Bibl. Quart.* 9 (1947), pp. 190–8.

ters upon Deuteronomy, Jeremiah and Isaiah. This method was a characteristic device of the later sages and was exploited in Sirach and in the Book of Wisdom. It helps to explain the religious orientation discussed above.

Exegetes have moved away from the recognition of any real hypostasis in Proverbs 8 (cf. Sir. 24; Wis. 7).[10] A.-M. Dubarle has described the function of personified wisdom better than anyone else: "If this transcendent figure prepares in some manner for the Christian dogma of the Trinity, it is not by insinuating a plurality of persons in God, but rather by showing how infinitely close God is to his work, and how he desires to communicate himself in some way. . . . Divine perfection does not mean solitude, but on the contrary, communication of self. One can easily understand how such an idea leads to a doctrine which will place in God himself a giving, a flowering of himself, which constitutes a new divine person." [11]

The sayings in the older collections (Chapters 10ff.) have been somewhat harshly judged as eudaimonism, a pragmatism that inculcates merely what is profitable, what contributes to a successful life. But comparison with Egyptian literature indicates that utilitarianism does not properly describe the viewpoint of the sages. Rather, like their Egyptian counterparts, they attempted to find the divine order (Egyptian *ma'at*) established in the world. This order must be recognized; man must integrate himself into the divinely established harmony.[12] As G. von Rad has put it, the wisdom movement is an attempt to master reality, to perceive the (divine) laws operating in nature and human society and man himself.

[10] On this topic see H. Ringgren, *Word and Wisdom* (Lund, 1947); R. Marcus, "On Biblical Hypostases of Wisdom," in *Hebr. Un. Coll. Ann.* 23 (1950/51), pp. 157–71; R. Stecher, "Die persönliche Weisheit in den Proverbien," in *Zeitschr. für katholische Theologie* 75 (1953), pp. 565–80.

[11] *Les sagesses* . . . , *op. cit.*, p. 204.

[12] Cf. H. Gese, *Leben und Wirklichkeit in der alten Weisheit* (Tübingen, 1958); G. von Rad, *Theologie des Alten Testaments* I (Munich, 1957), pp. 415ff. (English tr.: *Old Testament Theology* [New York, 1962], pp. 418ff.)

132   ROLAND E. MURPHY, O. CARM.

Job

It is somewhat discouraging to admit that the text of Job is perhaps the most poorly preserved in the Old Testament, and that scholars are still far from agreement in determining the original reading.[13] There is almost no one today who would translate the highly difficult text of 19, 25ff., as Jerome did in the Vulgate, which carries a clear statement of the resurrection of the body. But even with this difficulty several good commentaries have added to our understanding of the book.[14] Exegetes are fairly unanimous in questioning the pertinence of the Elihu speeches (chapters 32–37) and the poem on wisdom (chapter 28), which seem to be later insertions in the work. The Lord's reply to Job in chapters 38–41 has also been questioned, because these chapters do not really "answer" Job's complaint. But R. MacKenzie has argued that the chapters are designed to express "what the presence of God is like".[15] The integrity of Job's life is no longer an issue, as it was in the dialogue with the Three Friends, and hence it is ignored in the reply of the Lord, on whom Job has no claim.

The precise message of the book is not easily formulated.[16] Several viewpoints concerning suffering can be detected in the work: it is a test (chapters 1–2), a medicinal corrective for man (Elihu in 33, 19–22). Chapter 28 seems to imply that suffering is an enigma insoluble for man who has no access to wisdom (except by fear of the Lord, 28, 28). The total thrust of the book is to refute the conventional idea of divine retribution as it was cultivated among the sages (e.g., Ps. 36/37). The rigid

[13] This is readily apparent in the most recent translation, M. Pope, *Job*. *Anchor Bible* 15 (New York, 1965).

[14] The best commentary is G. Fohrer, "Das Buch Hiob," in *Kommentar z. A.T.*, XVI (Gütersloh, 1963). See also S. Terrien, "Job," in *Comm. de l'A.T.*, 13 (Neuchâtel, 1963); F. Horst, "Hiob," in *Bibl. Komm.*, XVI (Neukirchen, 1960); F. Stier, *Das Buch Iyyob* (Munich, 1954).

[15] "The Purpose of the Yahweh Speeches in Job," in *Biblica* 40 (1959), pp. 301–11. The authenticity of these speeches has been strengthened by the literary analysis of P. Skehan, *Biblica* 45 (1964), pp. 51–62.

[16] An excellent summary of a vast literature is given by H. Rowley, "The Book of Job and Its Meaning," in *Bulletin of the John Rylands Library* 41 (1958), pp. 167–207.

optimism of the sages (virtue brings prosperity as a reward from God) is shattered. At the same time there is no real attempt to discourse on the "problem" of the righteous sufferer. The tendency of modern exegetes is to recognize that the treatment is existential—how is one to live with suffering. This answer is reflected in the changed attitude of Job in chapter 42, where his vision of God, or encounter with him, is singled out as the reason why he can cling to him in faith.

Comparisons with the Sumerian and Babylonian counterparts of Job contribute little to our understanding of the book. It is clear that a literary tradition concerning the righteous sufferer existed before the Hebrew work, but there is no indication of literary dependence. The evidence of the Bible itself (the bracketing of Job as a just man with Noah and "Danel" in Ezekiel 14) had already suggested that the framework of the Job story (chapters 1–2 and 42) reached back into folklore, and was taken over by the author with little change. His genius and originality lay in his conception of the relationship between man and God, which is expressed in the superb poetry of the debate with the Three Friends and the encounter with Yahweh.

Ecclesiastes

Although Ecclesiastes has often been made out to be a hedonist, pessimist, and/or skeptic, recent commentaries are returning to a more sober and exact judgment.[17] The realization has grown that his disturbing questions proceed from faith, and receive their poignancy from his orthodoxy. It is true that in the tradition of the wisdom writers he does not argue his point by referring to explicit items of Yahwist faith, such as the salvation

[17] O. Loretz, *Qohelet und der alte Orient* (Freiburg im Br., 1964); H. Hertzberg, "Der Prediger," in *Kommentar z. A.T.* XVII, 4 (Gütersloh, 1963); W. Zimmerli, *"Das Buch des Predigers Salomo,"* in *A. T. Deutsch* 16/1 (Göttingen, 1962); R. Scott, *Ecclesiastes. Anchor Bible* 18 (New York, 1965); R. Gordis, *Koheleth, the Man and His World* (New York, 1955); J.v.d. Ploeg, "Prediker," in *Boeken O.T.* VIII, 2 (Roermond, 1953). *L'Ecclésiaste* by E. Podechard (Paris, 1912) still remains valuable, despite the questionable supposition that additions were made to the book by a sage and a pious glossator for the sake of ensuring orthodoxy.

history experienced by Israel, or the Law. This stance is typical
of a sage, and it is changed only by Ben Sira (Sir. 44–50; cf.
also Wis. 11–19). But Qoheleth, as the author calls himself,
remains a Jew, even while his attitude challenges the accepted
values of his day: wisdom, riches, divine government and retribution.

Because his work is to be dated in the fourth or the third
century, many authors succumbed to the temptation to explain
Qoheleth by means of Hellenism. A very thorough study of
O. Loretz has disposed of the alleged Greek influence.[18] Loretz
argues also against Egyptian influence and instead presents a
convincing case for that of Mesopotamia; that is, Qoheleth had
his roots in the Semitic thought world that dominated the ancient
Fertile Crescent. Loretz points specifically to the problem of
God's justice, which forms the theme of the Mesopotamian
works: "I will praise the lord (Marduk) of wisdom", the "Babylonian Theodicy", and appears also in the Gilgamesh epic. There
are also several themes in common: the symbol of wind/breath
for something that is transient, the preoccupation with the name
or memory of a person as it lives on after his death, and finally
the striking similarity between the advice of Siduri to Gilgamesh
(tablet 10, col. 3) and the advice that Ecclesiastes constantly
reiterates (9, 7–9; cf. 2, 24f.; 5, 17–19; 11, 7–10).

This influence does not mean, however, that Ecclesiastes was
any the less a faithful Yahwist. It is unsafe to conclude otherwise
from his consistent use of Elohim (the generic name for deity)
instead of Yahweh. This preference would seem to be dictated
by the position he adopts: to solve human problems in the light
of human wisdom. His questionings mesh with a commonplace
of the wisdom literature, viz., the inaccessibility of wisdom,
which is with God (Eccles. 7, 23–24; 8, 16–17; cf. Job 28).

The other staple of the sages—fear of the Lord—is represented in his work (3, 14; 7, 18), but he is also cognizant of the
fact that fear of the Lord does not explain the ways of Providence (8, 12–14).

[18] Op. cit., 45ff.

More concretely, he recognized the truth of the *Deus absconditus,* the Hidden God (Is. 54, 15; cf. Eccles. 3, 11. 18; 7, 23–25). In his comment on Eccles. 3, 14, W. Zimmerli has well characterized the sage's understanding of the fear of God: "Not to walk in paths of light which secure for those who walk therein the harvest of life's fruits and honor. Fear of God here means walking under a heaven that is mysteriously closed, walking without the assurance that lightning might suddenly shoot out and strike you as you go—at every step relying upon the free gift of God, but with every step also summoned to suffer the riddle and oppression that God can inflict."

Sirach

There is a dearth of full-length commentaries on Sirach,[19] and few critical translations, based on both the Hebrew and Greek evidence, have been made.[20] The difficulty lies in the imperfection of the ancient translations, while the Hebrew text —known to the Western world only since the discovery by S. Schechter in 1896—is about two-thirds complete and is itself poorly preserved.

Ben Sira, or Sirach, is far from being an uninteresting person, even though he wrote as if the rebellious voices of Job and Ecclesiastes had never existed. He has revealed something of his personality in his work, both his optimism and his conservatism. As his grandson relates in the prologue to the Greek translation, Sirach was steeped in the traditions of his people, which he handed down in the style of a wisdom teacher. He lived in the ominous period just before the Maccabean revolt and doubtless he intended his teaching to be a bulwark against the incipient Hellenism. He succeeded in incorporating the wisdom heritage into characteristically Jewish belief: wisdom is clearly and ex-

[19] The most recent is M. Segal, *Sēper ben Sîrā' haš-šālēm* (Jerusalem, ²1958). See also V. Hamp, "Sirach," in *Echterbibel* (Würzburg, 1951); C. Spicq, "L'Ecclésiastique, in *La Sainte Bible* VI (Paris, 1946). The older commentaries by R. Smend (1906) and N. Peters (1913) are still invaluable.

[20] The situation is well described by L. Hartman, "Sirach in Hebrew and Greek," in *Cath. Bibl. Quart.* 23 (1961), pp. 443–51.

plicitly identified with the Mosaic Law (24, 23; 39, 1, etc.).
Wisdom did not lose its mystery: "There is but one, wise and
truly awe-inspiring, seated upon his throne: It is the Lord; he
created her . . ." (1, 8–9). However, "fear of the Lord is the
beginning of wisdom" (1, 14; cf. 15, 1), and "perfect wisdom
is the fulfillment of the Law" (19, 17). This legalism of Sirach
has occasioned some criticism, but Otto Kaiser has given a sym-
pathetic interpretation of Sirach's synthesis.[21] The devotion to
the Law, so characteristic of postexilic Judaism, necessarily colored Sirach's approach to wisdom. At the same time, very many
of his admonitions derive from the experiential wisdom of old.
Why? Because he joined legal observance with the sage's ideal
of discipline (musar); the man who obeys the law is the dis-
ciplined man, the wise man.

Exegetes have been unanimous in pointing out Sirach's significant departure from the style of previous sages. He devoted
several chapters (44–50) to the "praise of the Fathers", i.e.,
salvation history in terms of personalities, the heroes of Israel's
past.[22] This approach to Israel's history has parallels within the
Bible (the "historical" Psalms, 77/78, 104/105, 105/106; Wis.
10; 1 Mc. 2, 49–61; Heb. 11), not to mention the genre of
De Viris Illustribus which was to reach such a vogue. Sirach's
purpose was doubtless to concretize the instructions imparted in
his book, to present models of Israelite wisdom.

Wisdom

The Book of Wisdom, like Sirach, has not received many
commentaries since the excellent one by J. Fichtner in 1938.[23]

---

[21] "Die Begründung der Sittlichkeit im Buche Jesus Sirach," in *Zeitschr.
für Theologie und Kirche* 55 (1958), pp. 51–63. E. Bauckmann, "Die
Proverbien und die Sprüche des Jesus Sirach," in *Zeitschr. für die alttes-
tamentische Wissenschaft* 72 (1960), pp. 33–63, thinks that Sirach "sac-
rificed" the Law to Wisdom. Rather, Sirach supplied additional motives
from the area of the wisdom literature for keeping the Law.

[22] Cf. T. Maertens, *L'Eloge des pères* (Bruges, 1956); R. Siebeneck,
"May Their Bones Return to Life!—Sirach's Praise of the Fathers," in
Cath. Bibl. Quart. 21 (1959), pp. 411–28.

[23] "Weisheit Salomos," *Handb. z. A.T.* 5 (Tübingen, 1938). Since then
one can point to J. Reider, *The Book of Wisdom* (New York, 1957);
A. Drubbel, "Wijsheid," in *Boeken O.T.* VIII, 4 (Roermond, 1957);

But it has prompted many studies centering on its theology, its teaching of immortality, and the "historical" development in chapters 11–19. By and large, the tendency of these studies has been to recognize the authentic Jewish viewpoint that is expressed by a Greek-speaking (Alexandrian?) Jew of the first century, B.C. There is clear evidence that he was influenced by Greek thought (*e.g.*, 7, 7–20; 8, 7, etc.), and authors never fail to mention this fact. But it should also be admitted that his work remains intensely Jewish. This Hebraic aspect is justly assessed in the dissertation of G. Ziener,[24] and it is confirmed by other studies. An example can be found in the doctrine of immortality clearly affirmed by the author (Wis. 1, 13–16; 2, 21–3, 3; 5, 15–16). It is often assumed that this is due to Greek influence. One would not wish to deny the catalytic action of Greek philosophy and its ideas about the natural immortality of the soul. But the fact is that the author does not conclude to immortality from the nature of the soul. He seems to share the Greek understanding of the soul in 8, 18–20 and 9, 15, but there is no trace of this in his teaching concerning immortality. Rather, this is expressed in typically Jewish fashion without speculation upon the nature of man: immortality is attached to justice (Wis. 1, 14; cf. 15, 3), and it consists in being associated with the members of the heavenly court, the "sons of God" (5, 5), who experience his grace and mercy (4, 15).[25]

As in Sirach, a distinctive treatment of salvation history appears in Wisdom 11–19,[26] where the exodus stories are re-told.

J. Fischer, "Das Buch der Weisheit," in *Echterbibel* (Wurzburg, 1950).

[24] "Die theologische Begriffsprache im Buche der Weisheit," in *Bonn. Bibl. Beitr.* 11 (Bonn, 1956).

[25] For this point of view see P. Skehan, *Cath. Bibl. Quart.* 21 (1960), pp. 525–27; P. Grelot, "A la rencontre de Dieu," in *Mémorial A. Gelin* (Lyons, 1961), p. 176. P. Beauchamps has recently argued from Wisdom 19, 6–21 that the body is involved in the reward and salvation envisioned by the author: "Le salut corporel des justes . . . ," in *Biblica* 45 (1964), pp. 491–526.

[26] In contrast to earlier opinions, most scholars today are willing to recognize one author for the whole work. But the structure itself has been subject to more analysis; cf. P. Skehan, "The Text and Structure of the Book of Wisdom," in *Traditio* 3 (1945), pp. 1–5; A. Wright, "The Structure of Wisdom 11–19," in *Cath. Bibl. Quart.* 27 (1964), pp. 28–34.

There is a growing consensus among scholars that these chapters present a good example of Old Testament midrash (G. Camps, R. Siebeneck, A. Wright, etc.), *i.e.,* that they are an explanation of the Scriptures, designed to make them intelligible and relevant to a later generation. The marvels of the exodus are described with many interpretative embellishments (*e.g.,* the plagues in chapters 16–18), and the whole material is handled in such a way as to show how the Lord "magnified and glorified" his people (19, 22).

IV

WISDOM AND THEOLOGY

The doctrine of personal immortality affords perhaps the most interesting example of development of doctrine, or of progressive revelation, within the Old Testament. And it lies largely within the ambit of the wisdom literature. The early works are clearly unaware of any true life after death; one "lives on", but this is the bleak, dreary existence of the shades in Sheol, which Ecclesiastes described as without work, reason, knowledge and wisdom (9, 10; cf. also Job 10, 21–22; 14, 7–12; 17, 13–16), and which several psalms portray as without contact with God (Pss. 6, 6; 29/30, 10; 87/88, 11–13).

It is precisely the awful fact of death, which men share with animals, that constantly entered into Ecclesiastes' discussions (Eccles. 2, 15–17; 3, 19–22; 9, 4–6). The early sages (and even Sirach! cf. Sir. 41, 1ff.) accommodated themselves to the ineluctable fact of death. They laid great stress on the blessings imparted by God to the wise man in *this* life. We must not misunderstand this emphasis on earthly rewards; these temporal blessings were "sacraments", signs of divine favor. The equation set up by the sages was this: wisdom (justice) = life. But their unbounded optimism (cf. Prov. 3, 1–10; 10, 30; Ps. 36/37, etc.) was shattered by the experience of Ecclesiastes and by the author of Job. They brought the traditional view to an impasse that was eventually resolved in the period of the martyrs (the Maccabean revolt) when the doctrine of the resurrection of the just was affirmed (Dan. 12, 2). A similar solution was reached, as we have seen, by the author of the Book of Wisdom. It is a long road from the early sages to the author of Wisdom, but the steps along the road are logical. The equation, wisdom = life, is proved inadequate (Job, Ecclesiastes), but it reappears with a deeper meaning in "justice is immortal" [Wis. 1, 15; justice (Wisdom) = life (immortal)].

The study of Old Testament theology justly stresses what is distinctive of Israelite belief, such as the covenant, salvation history, the prophetical teachings, etc. This emphasis has been so thoroughgoing that the role of the wisdom literature within biblical theology has been questioned by G. E. Wright.[27] A very successful answer has been given by W. Zimmerli.[28] Zimmerli admits that wisdom lies outside salvation history (which should not be understood as *exhausting* Old Testament theology). It lies within the perspective of creation as it is developed in Genesis 1–2. Here man is blessed and empowered to "name" the animals; man is to rule creation, and the function of wisdom is to enable him to exercise this rule. Wisdom attempts to master reality, the secrets of man, his conduct, and his relationship to the world. Should wisdom overstep its bounds, should it attempt to control God and his way of governing the world, then the corrective is supplied by works such as Job and Ecclesiastes, who are the "watchmen" of the divine independence. From this point of view the pertinence of wisdom literature to biblical theology is eminently justified; wisdom theology is "creation theology".

But we are far from being able to anwer many of the questions that enter into a theology of wisdom. We are still ignorant of the circumstances surrounding the personification of Wisdom as a woman (Prov. 8, etc.).[29] The very antinomies of Wisdom—ac-

[27] "God Who Acts," *St. Bibl. Theol.* 8 (Chicago, 1952), pp. 102–5.
[28] See his essay in *Les sagesses* . . . (cf. footnote 3), pp. 121–37. (English Tr.: "The Place and Limit of the Wisdom in the Framework of the Old Testament Theology," in *Scottish Journal of Theology* 17 [1964], pp. 146–58). See also G. von Rad, *op. cit.*, I, pp. 448–51 (English Tr.: *Old Testament Theology* [New York, 1962], pp. 446–53).
[29] W. Albright has suggested Canaanite origins for Proverbs 8; see *Wisdom in Israel* . . . (cf. footnote 6), pp. 1–15.

cessible (Prov. 1–9; Wis. 6, 9–21, etc.) and inaccessible (Job 28; Bar. 3, 23–26; Eccles. 7, 23–25)—are puzzling. They seem to represent different approaches of sages of varying epochs. M. Noth has pointed out that the attribution of wisdom to the Lord is found only in later strata (postexilic) of the Bible.[30] This suggests that wisdom may have had some unhappy associations in its early existence in Israel. Perhaps it was identified too exclusively with the human level in that its international origins were remembered. Perhaps there were some Canaanite memories associated with wisdom in such a way that prohibited its early attribution to the Lord. This is the kind of historical question that can only be answered by historical evidence that is not yet available.

The wisdom literature of the Old Testament is in a sense timeless; unlike most of the other books it is not easily tied to concrete historical circumstances, and the Persian period (ca. 539–333) of Israelite history is a relatively unknown era.[31] We are only beginning to assess the relationship between the sages and the priests and prophets in Israel, and to determine the mutual influence between the sapiential books and the rest of the Old Testament.[32] But if the present renewed interest is sustained, we may look forward to answering these and more questions which this intriguing section of the Old Testament raises.

[30] *Ibid.*, pp. 225–37.

[31] The Dead Sea scrolls have contributed greatly to our knowledge of the intertestamental period. But it is surely ironic that the wisdom literature, which we have always had, has not been adequately exploited to illumine this period.

[32] Wisdom and the prophetical writings are examined by J. Lindblom in *Wisdom in Israel . . .* (cf. footnote 6), pp. 192–204; on the Psalms and wisdom, cf. S. Mowinckel, *ibid.*, pp. 205–24, and R. Murphy, *Suppl. Vet. Test.* IX (1962), pp. 156–67; L. Alonso-Schökel has described the relationship of Genesis 2–3 to the wisdom literature in "Motivos sapienciales y de alianza en Gen. 2–3," in *Biblica* 43 (1962), pp. 295–316.

The survey articles on Wisdom in *Die Religion in Geschichte und Gegenwort* (H. Gese) and in Kittel's *Theologisches Wörterbuch zum Neuen Testament* (G. Fohrer) are to be recommended. The best general introduction to the wisdom literature remains those by H. Duesberg and A.-M. Dubarle (cf. footnote 6).

PART III

DO-C DOCUMENTATION

CONCILIUM

DIRECTOR: Leo Alting von Geusau
Groningen, Netherlands

ASS'T DIRECTOR: M.-J. Le Guillou, O.P.
Boulogne-sur-Seine, France

Gustavo Pérez Ramírez/*Bogotá, Colombia*

Family Planning and Latin-American Problems: Perspectives in 1965

ADDRESS DELIVERED AT THE FIRST PAN-AMERICAN CONFERENCE ON POPULATION, CALI (COLOMBIA), AUGUST, 1965

Introduction[1]

Not since the Reformation has there been such an upheaval in the Catholic Church as we are now witnessing, nor such a time of change as rapid and unexpected as it is welcome. This upheaval is a gigantic effort at revival and "aggiornamento" that the Church of Christ has undertaken, a process of truly deep renewal and revision in the knowledge that the truth will make us free. Concepts such as natural law, authority, religious liberty, the Church in the modern world, the hierarchy, the laity, missionary activity, the ideal of service, have all been scrutinized. The irrational, stereotyped modes of thought produced over the centuries on the basis of these concepts have been examined in the light of modern scientific disciplines, theological as well as biological and physical. The whole message of salvation, which must inform a changing world with a changing scale of values, is being reinterpreted in terms of modern needs. Family planning

[1] In view of the complexity of this subject, some clarification is necessary at the outset. This article has a sociological approach. It is an analysis of a series of facts which must be taken into account in any objective assessment of the demographic problems of Latin America. It also refers to the present doctrinal position of the Catholic Church and the efforts at exegetical and theological interpretation currently being devoted to the subject, in accordance with the spirit of the Council. So it does not claim to make judgments which are reserved to the competence of the magisterium of the Church, particularly in view of the Papal Commission studying the subject in its scientific and other aspects.

142

is one of the subjects under review. This review has brought hope to nations whose development is continuously retarded and frustrated by the "population explosion", and to individuals who face the task of integrating the teaching of Christ with present-day realities.

The advances made in the natural sciences and the achievement of more hygienic living conditions have reduced the mortality rate, prolonged the expectation of life and consequently increased the sum total of the population to a point where it is obvious that it cannot go on expanding indefinitely. Fortunately, man is endowed with reason, and bound to obey its dictates. His scientific inquiries have led to advances in the fields of social anthropology, physiology, biochemistry, social psychology, sociology and other disciplines. He has thus come to know himself better and to penetrate further into the secrets of the natural law. For its part, theology, faced with these facts and scientific discoveries, has been clarifying its postulates and ethical norms, following a homogeneous line of development interrupted at times, it would appear, by historical circumstances.

I propose to deal briefly with the situation in Latin America with regard to family planning and the use of contraceptives, and then with the Council debates and the attempts made by the Church, as an organized institution, to combine the demands of day-to-day existence with the general lines of doctrine appropriate to its mission.

I

ASPECTS OF THE LATIN-AMERICAN SITUATION WITH REGARD
TO FAMILY PLANNING

The sociologist's task is to consider social facts established by observation, to distinguish and relate them to particular cultures and to analyze systems of values and modes of behavior. So a dual approach to the Latin-American situation is required: structural, on the one hand, and ethico-cultural on the other.

Structural Conditionings

The birth of a child in a pre-technical, traditional society had, by reason of the very structure of the society, social implications very different from those of today. The family was the basic unit of production and performed a multiplicity of functions. Grandparents and relatives lived together, thereby simplifying the tasks of education and household chores. The high rate of mortality, particularly infant mortality, required a higher birth rate simply for the sake of survival of the race. In these circumstances a far higher birthrate per family was required for the survival of a certain number of children, for many did not survive; in the present day, practically speaking, every birth means a child who will survive to adulthood. The demands of education are greater, too, in a modern society, to say nothing of the difficulties of finding work, housing, etc.

In terms of world population and the community of nations, the problem is no smaller. The task of adequate distribution of limited natural resources will become increasingly harder as the present excess of fertility throughout the world grows to such an extent (already on the horizon) that the only rational alternative to reducing the population by war or wholesale slaughter would appear to be the limitation of the birthrate, always supposing that this is done by means acceptable to the ethical dictates of human nature and of religious values.

It is worth noting here that Malthus came forward with his theories in the full tide of the Industrial Revolution, when scientific discoveries were multiplying and the process of urbanization was beginning, factors which helped to bring into being the consciousness of population as a problem. Latin America, however, remained apart from these developments because Spain for a long time stayed on the fringes of the Industrial Revolution. Furthermore, till but a few decades ago, Latin-American society was traditional in structure, agrarian and lacking in realization of the problems caused by the rapid expansion of the population. Now, the obsolescence of the agrarian structure of society is realized, but the task of facing the population problem is being put off. The problem will, however, inexorably demand attention even in societies enjoying the most equitable distribution of resources and wealth.

The Structural Frame of Reference

The first point to be emphasized under this heading is that the cultural background of Latin America is, as we have seen, non-Malthusian. There are certain cultural factors which affect the demographic problem and are not sufficiently allowed for in population studies, such as, for example, the fatalistic attitude toward death.

The Latin concept of death embraces high rates of mortality, in general, and of infant mortality in particular, as something fated, irremediable and *inevitable*. The cult of the dead and the pomp of funerals in Latin America are not inspired only by motives of prestige or religiosity. They reveal the importance accorded to death, and the acceptance of its inevitability, of the precariousness of life and of the supremacy of natural forces as something imposed by fate. Remember that the concept of reason ordering nature springs from the philosophies of Kant and Hegel, equally absent from the cultural substrata of Latin America.

The Cultural Ethos and Catholic Morality

To the foregoing must be added other cultural features in the ethical field, peculiar to the Latin-American system of values, whose influence has not been considered in terms of the population problem. For example, *Machismo,* the cult of aggressive maleness, showing itself in pride in the number of children procreated and freedom of sexual conduct, on one side, with the idealization and false mystification of womanhood, mingled with Moorish elements such as the stigma of sterility, on the other. These two elements produce a traditional, double sexual standard: permissiveness for men and restriction for women. A gnostic-manichaean dualism adds a de-humanizing note to this framework, reducing human sexuality to something almost morally despicable, practically on a level with animal sexuality, a simple matter of reproduction.

These are just the salient features of the ethical cultural framework, not to be taken in a determinist sense, within which Catholics must approach the problem of conjugal morality. The ethical background shows a *simpliste* traditional ethos, inherited from Western Christendom, alien to the advances of science and unchanged, due to the defensive attitude of the Church, since the Reformation. Attention was paid only to the unchanging natural laws of recurrence and regularity, and nature was given a sacred, untouchable character.

The elaboration of doctrine was pursued with great zeal till the 13th century. The 14th, 15th and 16th centuries saw the heyday of the *"Summae* for the use of Confessors" designed as simple guides to the confessional. The juridical element predominated in them, without any deeper attempt to relate moral actions to the whole of Christian teaching. This line of "practical-practice" led to the crisis of the 17th and 18th centuries. The very approach of the casuists, concerned with finding the minimum requirements for valid confession, led many to laxity. Their excesses provoked a rigorism, culminating in Jansenism, which has done much harm in Latin America as well as in other parts of Christendom, down to our own days. Its errors persist, despite the preaching of St. Alphonsus, the Thomist revival and the contemporary movement of a morality of response and engagement.[2]

It is only within the framework of the recent doctrinal and moral renewal that the serious problems of sexual morality are being studied again in the light of scientific advances.

So, some years ago, faced with the discoveries of Ogino and Knaus, the Church accepted the "rhythm method". The introduction of this innovation was by no means smooth: in one

[2] Cf. Bernard Häring, *The Law of Christ* 2 Vols. (Westminster, Md.: The Newman Press), vol. 1, pp. 35–53; J. Ferin and L. Janssens, "Morale conjugale et Progestogenes," in *Ephemerides theologicae Lovanienses* 22 (1963), pp. 787–826.

American country, all reference to the Ogino-Knaus method was removed from the early editions of *Casti Connubii;* this did not prevent the method from spreading rapidly.

Linked with this process of evolution, we cannot ignore a divorce between Religion and Science, Church and World, on the level of practical conduct, a divorce between a physical-naturalistic ethic and one with a broader scientific base, which would enable moral decisions to be taken from a broader base and facilitate the ordering of life in obedience to the call of Christ. In the field of practical decisions there is widespread deviation from the traditional norms still in force governing the sexual act and its ends. Confessors will bear witness to the constant drama of uneasy, anguished, traumatized and rebellious consciences which this entails. The phenomenon has, however, still not been studied sufficiently within a sociological framework, nor has its extent been measured.[3]

For a sociological study of the etiology of contra-normative attitudes, their motives and their relationship with actual behavior must be known. I feel that the theory devised by Professor Kingsley Davis on the sociology of deviation or anomie is the correct focus from which to study this problem as a sociological feature of Catholicism in Latin America. He starts from the fundamental premise that conscious motives or desires can either conform or not conform to actual behavior. Then, both desires and behavior can either conform to or deviate from the norm. He draws up a double-entry table cross-referencing these possibilities, to show the interrelations between conformity and deviation on the one hand, and motives and behavior on the other.[4]

Briefly, the motivation of behavior can be said either to conform with, or to deviate from, the norm governing that behavior,

[3] *Limited surveys have in fact been made in several countries, usually betraying the opinions of those responsible for the survey and of a sufficiently amateur nature to justify, at least in part, the suppression of their findings.* (Trans.)

[4] J. Blake and K. Davis, "Norms, Values and Sanctions," in *Handbook of Modern Sociology*, ed. R. Faris (Chicago, 1964), pp. 468ff.

Motivation or desires	Behavior Conformity	Violation
Conformity	(1) + +	(2) + −
Violation	(3) − +	(4) − −

and this double motivation can lead either to conformity with, or deviation from, the motivation itself.

In position (1) are those who conform: those whose conduct is in accord with their desire to act in conformity with the norm. They are the Catholics who reject the use of contraceptives, desire to do so, and act in conformity with the present rules of the Church. Their number may well be less than is supposed, as various investigations in hand are beginning to show. We shall give an example of this later.

In position (4) are the rebels or innovators, whose behavior goes against the norms, by their deliberate choice. Many have left the Church for various reasons, but statistics show that many, while violating the norms by their use of contraceptives, do not for this reason abandon their faith or religious practices, even including the reception of communion. This group of innovators does not wait for the religious authorities to adopt their position, believing their conduct justifiable. As Professor Davis remarks: "Reflection on history leaves the impression that the reproductive folkways and mores of the common man have varied more in relation to the conditions of his life than with reference to religious or philosophical doctrine. Although contraception has become a Western folkway, no major religion advocated its use *prior* to its popular adoption." [5]

Positions (2) and (3) demonstrate complications in that

[5] Kingsley Davis, "Values, Population, and the Supernatural," in *Studies in Population,* ed. George Mair (Princeton University Press, 1949), p. 137.

motivation and conduct are at variance. Position (2) shows that, as one would expect, conduct deviating from the norm is not necessarily the fruit of will not to conform. A husband and wife, deeply Christian, sincerely wishing to follow the rules of the Church with regard to the use of contraceptives, can have the best of intentions but in practice violate the ecclesiastical laws, and not necessarily only through "human weakness". Causes of deviant conduct other than deviant motivation, where, in fact, the motivation is toward conformity, must be sought. For example, lack of a deep fellowship in the Church and of a feeling of belonging to the Church can help to make her teaching still more difficult to observe. The norms of the primary group, in fact, exert a stronger pressure and tend to prevail when in conflict with those of other less intimate groups.

Finally, position (3) indicates that contra-normative motivation or desires are not always translated into contra-normative behavior. This is the case with innumerable Catholics who manage to act in accordance with the present teaching of the Church, even while they feel the need to integrate the demands of modern life, of urbanization, of adequate education for their children, of the economic needs of the nation, with a morality of living in Christ, in the hope of eternal supernatural life and spiritual peace, as members of a religion of salvation.

All this poses questions, such as: How can conformist motivation be prevented from producing non-conformist conduct? There are certainly factors in existence which tend to inhibit contra-normative conduct, and not only deep acceptance of the rules, fear of punishment, or social control. But the problem is more complex than it might appear. The solution will not be found without a calm dialogue, facing the discoveries of science honestly, with a total fidelity to truth, and an inter-disciplinary revision of the norms and the suppositions on which they are based.

An intensive and persuasive process of interiorizing the norms can only be justified in an integrated, cohesive and stable society.

Repression, intransigence and refusal to discuss, as means of guaranteeing conformity to the norm, lead, as Professor Davis rightly remarks, to social collapse, not social change.

The study carried out by CELADE (the Latin-American Demographic Center of Santiago, Chile) in seven large cities in Latin America, throws some light on the contra-normative phenomenon as lived by Latin-American Christians in the use of contraceptives.[6] The study was carried out simultaneously in Bogotá (Colombia), Buenos Aires (Argentina), Caracas (Venezuela), Mexico City (Mexico), Panama City (Panama), Rio de Janeiro (Brazil) and San José (Costa Rica). At the time of writing, the results have not yet been fully tabulated. Only partial data are available, such as the following tables showing, for these Latin-American cities, the proportion of married women using contraceptives in relation to the frequency with which they attend religious functions of the Church.

TABLE 1.   Use of contraceptives by married women in relation to the frequency of their attendance at Church

Frequency of Church attendance	Percentage of women using contraceptives		
	Panama	Rio de Janeiro	San José
Once a week or more	59.3	57.9	65.2
Once a month or more	64.4	47.1	54.2
Sometimes in a year	—	51.1	53.2
Once in a year	58.2	59.7	62.4
Once in years	—	64.0	78.0
Never	50.0	58.0	71.9

Granted their validity, these figures show clearly enough how far married women who call themselves Catholics are deviating

[6] Cf. León Tabah, "Plan de recherches de sept enquêtes comparatives sur la fécondité en Amérique Latine," in Population 1 (1964), pp. 95–126. This article explains the methodology employed and the hypothesis of the study.

from the known laws of the Catholic Church. What is statistically most significant is that most of those who go to church *use* contraceptives.

Unfortunately, not having had access to the original figures, I cannot analyze these facts any further to establish interrelation with new categories and compare these figures with other important findings that emerge from the survey. The phenomenon of conduct deviating from the norm is, however, confirmed and strengthened even more in the following table:

TABLE 2.   Use of contraceptives by married Catholic women (legal marriage or by consent) in relation to the frequency of their reception of Communion.

Frequency of reception of Communion	Percentage of women using contraceptives		
	Caracas	*Bogotá*	*Mexico*
Once a month or more	56.7	39.9	34.8
Less than once a month	64.2	37.7	34.8
Never	54.8	49.7	39.5

Source: Miró-Rath, *Preliminary findings of comparative fertility surveys in three Latin-American Countries, Annex, table 14.*

Again, we lack sufficient data to qualify these figures enough before coming to conclusions. It would, for example, be necessary to establish a separate category of women living in marriages of consent, who might well be in the category of those who never receive communion. We should also point out that frequent communion is not always a good criterion by which to measure religious faith, without taking into account the possible degree of influence of the Jansenist heresy, which keeps some otherwise strictly practising Catholics away from reception of the sacrament, believing themselves unworthy to receive God frequently.

II

THE POSITION OF THE CHURCH

The traditional doctrine governing conjugal morality teaches that the sexual act is legitimate only within marriage and when nothing is done to interfere artificially with its natural fecundity. This means that artificial contraception—not periodic abstinence—is immoral, and not only simply immoral: Pope Pius XI in his encyclical *Casti Connubii* condemned contraception as "intrinsically and gravely immoral." [7]

Some theologians, including several Jesuits,[8] hold that this famous paragraph from the encyclical has an infallible "ex cathedra" status. They advance the natural law principle according to which the procreative end inherent in the marriage act must always be respected, as the basis for the condemnation of contraception.[9] The situation is further complicated by the declaration of Pius XII, that the condemnation of contraception is "as valid today as it was yesterday and will be tomorrow and forever".

The problem could not be a more burning one. But it is under study and its solution rests with the magisterium of the Church. The study starts from the assumption, which can be supported with arguments, that the declarations of previous popes are not infallible. One proof of this would seem to be the very declaration of His Holiness Paul VI, in his statement on birth control in June 1964. While stating that the norms laid down by Pius XII in this respect remain valid, he gave to understand that they are not unchangeable, since he added, "consequently, these

[7] Encyclical: *Casti Connubii*, in *Acta Apostolicae Sedis* 22 (1930).
[8] Capello, Vermeersch, Creusen, Zalba, Cartechini, etc.
[9] Cf. J. Ford and G. Kelly, "Will the Church's Teaching on Birth Control Change?" in *The Catholic World* 198 (November, 1963), pp. 87–93. The article begins with the following statement which sums it up: "In the Catholic Church the condemnation of contraception is unquestionably irrevocable."

norms should be considered valid *at least until we feel obliged in conscience to change them.*" [10]

These words would seem to clear the air to a considerable extent, particularly if they are considered within the context of the announcement made by His Holiness in the same statement: "The question is being submitted to a study as wide and deep as possible, as serious and honest as a matter of such importance requires." And His Holiness announced that he hoped soon to present the conclusions of this study, in which many eminent experts were collaborating, "in the form that can be considered most appropriate to this matter and to the ends that must be achieved." Furthermore, in his allocution to the members of the Commission on March 27, 1965, His Holiness exhorted them in the following terms: "We ask you insistently not to lose sight of the urgency of a situation which requires most clear indications from the Church and her supreme authority. We cannot allow the consciences of the faithful to remain exposed to the uncertainty which today, too often, prevents married life from unfolding according to the divine plan. Furthermore, apart from such urgent problems for married couples, there are also certain economic and social problems which the Church cannot ignore." [11]

The following statement by Fr. Häring, one of the most distinguished of contemporary moral theologians, should also be taken into account: "In the field of morals, moreover, many problems are posed altogether differently with the passage of time. Sometimes a long struggle is needed to work out all the necessary distinctions in sufficient clarity." [12] As an example he advances the Church's prohibition of interest on loans. The Council of Vienne (1311–2) "threatened theologians who might dare to justify loans against interest with chains and imprisonment. At the end of a long process of development, we have

[10] See *L'Osservatore Romano,* June 24, 1964.
[11] See *L'Osservatore Romano,* March 27, 1965.
[12] Bernard Häring, "Responsible Parenthood," in *Commonweal* 80 (June 5, 1964), p. 327. A special issue on responsible parenthood.

Pius XI's encyclical *Quadragesimo Anno,* which, in the modern economic structure, unequivocally concedes to capital the right to a reasonable rate of interest." [13] As Fr. Häring comments: "Something similar has happened in the case of conjugal morality." Let us hope that the process will be much shorter in this case and will have been concluded in the Fourth Session of the Second Vatican Council, now that philosophical and theological reflections, as well as scientific discoveries, have served to show the question in a clearer light. There is a heartfelt clamor from all Christendom for the "very clear guidance from the Church" which His Holiness Paul VI has spoken of.

The encyclical *Casti Connubii,* published 35 years ago, "at that time constituted a milestone on the road to a more positive spirituality of marriage, but the formulations concerning abuses on marriage were framed with a backward glance at an era which had not yet come to a close, not in anticipation of what was to become an increasingly general attitude and social structure." [14]

I propose here, then, to limit myself to an overall view of the principal lines of thought which are still the subject of debate. Vatican Council II had originally included the debate on this matter in Schema 13, dealing with the relationship between the Church and the Modern World, thereby setting a problem which directly affects the community of nations within its fundamental framework, the dialogue with the world.[15]

Last year, the problem of population and the use of contraceptives was debated, shortly before the end of the third session. Although it was the shortest debate, the points made with such vigor provide rays of light to illuminate the work of investigators. The words of Cardinals Suenens of Belgium, Léger of Canada, Alfrink of Holland and Patriarch Maximos of Antioch will be

---

[13] *Ibid.*

[14] *Ibid.*

[15] Schema XIII, Chap. 4, §21, "On the dignity of marriage and the family." *This subject was in fact not debated in this context, as the author of the article hoped it would be, for it was considered that the Pope had reserved to himself the right to pronounce on this matter by the establishment of his special Commission.* (Trans.)

well known.[16] "May this Council," pleaded Cardinal Léger by way of conclusion, "without fear and without reticence, clearly proclaim the two ends of marriage (human conjugal love and procreation) as equally good and holy. Once this has been established, moralists, doctors, psychologists and other experts will be much better able to determine in particular cases the duties both of fecundity and of love."

Patriarch Maximos referred to the faithful who "find themselves driven to live in breach of the law of the Church, far from the sacraments, in constant anguish, for want of being able to find the viable solution between two contradictory imperatives: conscience and normal conjugal life." He also pointed out the other aspect of the problem, that of population as a social question, the fact that "the demographic pressure in certain countries, especially in large agglomerations, is in the present circumstances in opposition to any raising of the standard of life and condemns hundreds of millions of human beings to a misery that is unworthy and without hope."

On the basis, then, of what was said in the Council debates, and of the writings of outstanding theologians and scientists who have declared themselves in favor of "responsible parenthood", we can summarize the arguments as follows:

1. *Revision of the Natural Law Concept*

The basis of the problem and of its practical solutions will be found in whatever view of the natural law is taken.

"Any formulation of the natural law is the fruit of reflection on man's rights and duties in his human situation; it is difficult to conceive of the natural law in any way other than as orientated towards the fulfilment of human nature in its totality, and inspired by respect for the human person and human life. Man's intervention in nature can raise delicate problems, but he has a norm for their solution in the overall good of the individual and

[16] Reprinted in F. Drinkwater, *Birth Control and Natural Law* (London: Burns & Oates, 1965), Appendix I.

mankind. It is not a question of denying the absolute sovereignty of God, but of recognizing man's part in the creative process for which God has endowed him with intelligence and will." [17]

Those who think thus consider that there can be no conflict between a natural law based on respect for human values and a control of human fecundity orientated toward man's total well-being. It should be pointed out that "nature" has a double meaning, and confusion between the two meanings may be the root of the difficulties. In the first place it means the intrinsic principle of operation, or essence; it also means the principle established by what happens in the majority of cases (*ut in pluribus*). So, in the case of a sterile woman, the sexual act takes place *ut in pluribus* without the fact of her not conceiving altering the specific nature of the act.

Applying this distinction to the natural law, it is clear that those "primary" principles that belong to humanity cannot change without changing man in his essence. The "secondary" principles of natural law refer to the most rational manner in which to carry out the inclinations of human nature, and these can be subject to variation and change, insofar as they are natural only in the sense of applying in the majority of cases —*ut in pluribus*.

2. Developments in Anthropological, Sociological and Psychological Ideas

New anthropological ideas also offer valid grounds for accepting a "responsible parenthood". Man is viewed as an indivisible whole, made up of body and soul, against the dualist conception of man which seeks to minimize the body. So human sexuality differs from animal sexuality, in that human conjugal love, which embraces both body and soul, is a true end of marriage. Love is not merely to be placed at the service of fecundity, but must

---

[17] "Address to Vatican Council II on the Subject of the Problems of the Family," sent to the Holy Father and the Bishops of the Catholic Church by an international group of lay Catholics, October, 1964. Reprinted in Drinkwater, *op. cit.*, Appendix II.

be considered a true end of marriage, "as something which is good in itself and which has needs and laws of its own".[18]

Human sexuality cannot be seen exclusively in terms of procreation. The sexual relationship between husband and wife embraces their whole human personality, and so is an essential element in the achievement of unity between them. Many Catholic scientists believe that advances in psychological knowledge and the growing emphasis on the importance of personal human relationships have also promoted new awareness of the positive contribution made by affective and physical elements to the development of unity in marriage—a relationship in which the spouses are not merely procreators, but persons who love one another for their own sakes.

From the sociological point of view, the process of social change operative in society has had a profound influence not only on systems of values and behavior, but on the very relationship between human beings, on their roles in society and on the basic institutions of society. The process of forming and dispersing a family, for instance, has altered substantially, as was pointed out at the beginning of this article.

The "dialogue with the world" postulated by Schema 13 opens the way for sociological analysis to help toward finding solutions. As His Holiness Paul VI stated when defining the aims of the Council: "The Church must understand herself, renew herself . . . and establish a dialogue with the modern world. These ends cannot be achieved without sociological analysis and without defining the sociological conditions."

3. New Findings in the Fields of Physiology and Bio-Chemistry

"Another dimension of the problem has been opened up by advances in our understanding of physiology which have greatly clarified the meaning of sexuality. In the first place, there is the knowledge of the continuous and exuberant character of spermatogenesis. . . . In the second place, the occurrence of the condition of fertility in woman is now known to be discon-

[18] Cardinal Léger, in Drinkwater, p. 71.

tinuous and strictly limited in time. Furthermore, woman's sexual behavior, unlike that of the lower mammals, is not absolutely controlled by periodic hormone secretions." [19] It is thus clear that even on the physiological level the sexual act is not necessarily linked to procreation, and so fertility cannot be the direct end or meaning of each individual act. The obligation of fecundity cannot be seen to rest with the physiological attributes of each act, but with the totality of acts and circumstances, as much psychological as physiological, that make up the whole of married life. Given that the definition of the ends of marriage includes the upbringing of children, this natural order by which the parent-child relationship springs not from one isolated act but from the relationship of a whole married life between husband and wife, appears extremely logical. Cardinal Léger expressed this in his Council speech: "It would be good if the duty toward fecundity should be attached less to each act than to the state of marriage itself."

New possibilities of finding a solution to the problem are also presented by the progestogene and steroid drugs discovered a little over a generation ago but still being experimented with and evaluated. The present investigations are concerned basically with revising the action mechanism of the steroid deviates, whose fertility-inhibiting action has been considered equivalent to that of the natural progestogenes. Leaving the exact mechanism of the steroids aside, since it is not immediately relevant, and because it is still today a subject of debate and study, I would like merely to point out that, whatever the exact process is, it is not a sterilization. The use of anovulatory pills would seem not to be bad in itself, therefore, and could be justified by the end for which they were employed.

Another point worth noting is that "the closer look at life which modern biology provides indicates that a biological action is ordinarily multifunctional, and that the inhibition of a function which is not needed is the typical means of achieving the

[19] "Address to Vatican Council II," in Drinkwater, p. 88.

integrated control required by living things."[20] The sexual act appears to be clearly a multifunctional one, an action which satisfies various physiological demands besides that of procreation, and which also performs a psychological function. Hence, from a biological point of view, contraception cannot be called contrary to nature, because it is natural for biological systems to inhibit one phase of a multifunctional activity when its effects are not required. This is clear from the fact that in pregnancy, and also to a certain extent during lactation, there is hormone activity to prevent the formation of new ova and so the start of another pregnancy.

All these new viewpoints and discoveries make for greater clarity in the attitudes taken by Catholic theology. For example, theologians now agree to the use of progestogenes for therapeutic purposes, and some would accept their use as simple contraceptives, basing their arguments on the fact that birth regulation is a moral good in itself.[21]

4. Advances in the Exegetical and Theological Understanding of Marriage

The interventions of the Council fathers in favor of a revision of the Church's present position vis-à-vis the problem of birth regulation were based ultimately on a new, deeper, understanding of the relevant biblical texts. It has been suggested that the Church's present pro-birth attitude has been encouraged by the fact that the Fathers used to quote the "increase and multiply" of Genesis (Gen. 1.28; 9.1) as an affirmation of the essential goodness of procreation, against the gnostic heretics who condemned procreation as being, as it were, an imprisonment of the spirit in evil matter. Professor Janssens, of the Theological Faculty of the University of Louvain, has shown how St. Augustine's false interpretation of the doctrine of marriage contained

---

[20] J. Pleasants, "The Lessons of Biology," in *Contraception and Holiness* (London: Collins, 1965), p. 82.
[21] W. van der Marck, O.P., quoted by L. Dupré in *Commonweal* 80 (June 5, 1964), p. 340.

in Genesis and the Epistles of St. Paul has been the root of a matrimonial ethic imbued with neo-Platonism and agnosticism of a Manichaean type.[22] We have in fact become more used to the version of Genesis on the origin of marriage which insists on its procreative character, with the "increase and multiply", and we tend to forget chapter 2 of Genesis, probably more ancient, which describes the marital union in psychological terms: "so a man shall leave his father and mother and cleave to his wife, and they shall be two in one flesh" (Gen. 2, 20–24).

St. Paul, for his part, in the Epistle to the Ephesians gives conjugal love the highest religious sense that any human relationship can possess, quoting chapter 2 of Genesis, which clearly speaks of conjugal love: "Husbands, love your wives, as Christ loved the Church and gave himself up for her" (Eph. 5, 25–33). Conjugal love is evidently spiritual in character but is distinguished from every other love by the sexual attraction between persons of different sex. So Professor Janssens, clarifying the specific character of married love, insists that *eros* must be included in the *agape* of love between husband and wife.

While for St. Paul husband and wife have full rights over each other's bodies, St. Augustine appears to restrict this right to the exclusive end of procreation alone. The interpretation usually given to his words is that he considered all sexual pleasure and desire intrinsically wrong, and that the sexual act could be made good only by the end of procreation and the intention of preserving marital fidelity. It was not for several centuries that it came to be admitted that there could be sexual relations without sin even though they contained neither the desire nor the need for procreation. Until then sexual relations between husband and wife once the wife had conceived were forbidden, as the finality of the act was then held to have been fulfilled.[23]

In the present critical situation, the Church in Council has sought the truth with a sincere intention of serving, and of find-

---

[22] J. Ferin and L. Janssens, *art. cit.*
[23] John Noonan, *Contraception. Its Treatment by the Catholic Theologians and Canonists* (Harvard University Press, 1965).

ing its bearings in the Gospels, to be able to tackle any class of conflict: war, violence, structural reform, the population explosion, etc.

Within such a context of social change such as that of Latin America, the social patterns and relationships belonging to the recurring fulfillment of everyday obligations must be combined with those belonging to the general lines of orientation which guide the Church as an organized institution. This will enable the Church to mobilize its leaders and members in a way that will make them more effective in the performance of their functions, which are tied in so many ways to the solution of the Latin-American crisis.

This is a dynamic, many-sided task, embracing frameworks of reference and practical decisions. Its action must bear on:

(a) *The cultural framework of reference,* through a confrontation between values accepted in the traditional framework and the new scientific discoveries outlined above. This implies a solution of resistances and conflicts arising between the traditional and the new. Part of the process of rationalization must be the adoption of frameworks of interpretation which will be open enough to leave room for the assimilation of new values, flexible in the use of means, dynamic in the ordering of their objectives and conscientious in regard to decisions taken, bearing in mind the variety of situations to which they will apply.

There are incongruities of every type to be resolved, but particularly in the field of cultural patterns and values. The doctrine of marriage expressed in current rituals, manuals and books of spirituality, for example, must be brought up to date.

(b) *The process of "socialization",* since values and patterns are accepted without reflection, without the necessary degree of interiorization or "cathesis" of values discussed by Parsons (which does not mean that norms and values should be given a determining character above social phenomena). This process of socialization must begin with the family. Neurotic families will not solve the crisis of this continent. Educational institutions can

162   GUSTAVO PÉREZ RAMÍREZ

also play their part by teaching the positive value of sex and
creating a sense of altruism and responsibility. Preaching, too, is
important. Unfortunately it is all too often imbued with an exaggerated "pro-birth" mentality or with gnostic-manichaean dualism. Equally important is the socialization of leaders of opinion
and of religious leaders in general in relating family planning to
sociological perspectives and the advances of science. The task
also implies a need for the revision of the system of social control, away from a Codex system of rewards and punishments.

(c) *Adaptation of the aims and the daily pastoral administration of family life:* I refer to the needs of Christians who come
to the confessional faced with the necessity, referred to in the
Address to the Second Vatican Council already quoted, "of
achieving a mutual interpretation of the realities of today's world
and the teaching of Christ". "The human significance of these
problems," the signatories to this document, many of them scientists, continue, "can hardly be over-emphasised. In the first place,
it is well known that millions of well-intentioned Christian
couples find great difficulty, within the framework of the existing
directives, in reconciling the different ends of marriage: procreation and education of children, and mutual love. Their difficulty is leading, in countless cases, to conflict, to warping of
conscience, to lapsing from the Church and to loss of harmony
between the partners."

We share these anxieties, and also the hopes of all those in
the Third World who desire to see the problem of social and
cultural incoherencies resolved by the working out of more consistent responses.

PART IV

CHRONICLE OF THE
LIVING CHURCH

In Collaboration with
Katholiek Archief
Amersfoort, Netherlands

Aggiornamento in the Mission Field

Some five hundred participants, comprising missionaries, future missionaries, theologians and missiologists, met at Louvain (August 23–27) for the thirty-fifth Missiology Week. They came from 26 different countries, representing 74 groups of religious, male and female, to study the missionary situation in 28 mission countries spread over the five continents.

The theme was both topical and complex. Its object, "New Thinking about the Missions", aimed at preparing the ground for the *aggiornamento* in practice and at a reexamination of the basic principles. The subject was divided into several stages of which the first was the *scriptural foundation of the mission*.

Canon Giblet, Professor at the University of Louvain, commented on the actuality of the mission in the Scriptures and explained the missionary mandate at the time of Christ and at the beginning of the Church. He stated that it was more a matter of "living the missionary spirit" rather than studying it methodically, although there were plenty of very striking attitudes and directives.

Going on from this point, Fr. Yves Congar showed that the mission flowed from the love of the Blessed Trinity and dealt with the "missions" of the Son, the Spirit, the Church and the

165

missionaries. He defined the mission as the Church's inner move-ment toward expansion, a movement destined to continue toward a *Parousia* which has already begun. The mission, therefore, belongs to the nature of the Church until the end of time.

But does this really imply that we should go to such lengths as we are now doing? *Is it not possible to be saved outside the visible Church?* Are there no hidden Christians (*i.e.,* pagans, faithful to the light God has given them)? Fr. Masson recog-nized this, but maintained that it was not merely a question of saving man by a process which led to minimal and exceptional results. According to God's infinitely generous plan, the way of mankind's normal and full salvation passes through the visible Church. To glorify God in his plan we must do our best to offer it to all.

Canon Thils, another Professor of Louvain, added that there is no need to deny that God actually works in the consciences of men who live in a non-Christian religious environment. *The non-Christian religions* have the value of an historical and concrete religious environment for those who live in it; they are saved in these religions. Theology is still trying to discover exactly what the role may be of these religions in the plan of God's salvation; but they contain unquestionably purifying and edifying values. This task also expects the contribution of the Church and de-mands her presence.

Fr. Le Guillou then reminded the audience of the scandal caused in mission countries by the divisions prevalent among Christians themselves. He showed how both theology and reli-gious practice combined in stressing *the urgency of the ecumeni-cal movement,* both for and in the mission field, and he illus-trated this by concrete examples.

Fr. Mueller, S.V.D., Study Secretary of his Congregation, gave a fine analysis of *missionary spirituality* on the basis of three scriptural texts: "Go and make disciples"; "the Father works (with you) up to the present" and "you are established as a sign".

These first six, very compact papers outlined an image of the mission, corresponding to the tendencies of that "dynamic Church" which lies at the heart of Vatican Council II.

But the essential problem of method also needed clarification. It was first dealt with scripturally by Fr. de la Potterie, of the Biblical Institute of Rome, who showed that there was a close connection between *the profession of faith and the reception of baptism* in the synoptics and in St. Paul. This connection must find expression as far as possible in concrete missionary activity in all ages, but particularly our own. Grace is normally "sacramentalized". This idea was taken up and developed by Fr. Dejaifve, of the Jesuit Faculty of Louvain, who showed that the Church, to be established in the mission field, is simultaneously and indivisibly the *People of God in the spiritual sense and a structured and visible congregation,* with its teaching, its sacraments and its hierarchy. For this he made abundant and felicitous use of the Constitution on the Church.

This, then, is *the Church,* in its essential features, as she must present herself to the world. But what is *this world,* what does it think of us and who wants to go and meet it?

Albert Dondeyne gave a clear analysis of the *major, constant factors of this world, which are important for the mission.* From the religious point of view, the modern world finds it more difficult to believe in God than the civilizations of the past; we are, therefore, confronted with the mounting popularity of an atheistic humanism. On the other hand, there is an impressive renewal taking place within the Church; it is no longer a renewal of purely outward appearances but of the faith itself; we are rediscovering Christianity as the salvific action of God in Jesus Christ, projected in the Church and in each individual Christian, for the salvation of the whole world. In connection with this renewal the speaker asked us to beware of hasty research and vague solutions, too quickly popularized.

In the field of the "profane" (the secular), Dondeyne pointed to the unification of the world through the disappearance of distance, the fact that the masses living in underdeveloped countries are more aware of the unfair differences that exist between one nation and another, and the awakening, almost everywhere, of a sense of responsibility that extends to the whole world and emphasizes interdependence. He insists on the *encounter of the various cultures,* a phenomenon which the Church should take even more seriously than the others. In view of the complexity of these dominant factors of modern society, the speaker stressed the urgency of the need to give missionaries a formation that would include anthropology, linguistic studies and the science of religions, all at university level. But do we have the necessary institutions for this?

The world is one, but there are, nevertheless, various civilizations. Each of these civilizations presents its own image to the mission and sees and judges the mission in the light of this image. The general diagnosis must, therefore, be adjusted to the various situations. This was done for India by Fr. Parel, for Japan by the Anglican Canon Hammer and for Islam by Fr. de Prémare. Whatever the local differences, some attitudes seem to be present everywhere: Christianity is often suspected of *"playing the Western game"* and it also appears to these people as both *strange and foreign.* As much and as soon as possible the mission must be fully integrated into the life of the various civilizations, share their fate and adopt their culture in order to enliven it. The ghetto mentality must disappear; there must be Christians who take a generous share in responsibility for their people. The papers mentioned worked out the details for the application of these general principles to each case.

A last group of papers studied the *aggiornamento* of those who work in the mission field, whether lay (Fr. Frisque), religious (female: Sr. St. Paul) or priests of the various missionary congregations. This last paper by Fr. Volker, Superior General of the White Fathers, recommended the continuation of strictly missionary Institutes but demanded a vigorous overhauling in order to meet the new situations of belief and non-belief in an underdeveloped society that has become independent and aware of its own character

The Secretary, Fr. Masson, underlined some of the more important ideas brought out by this conference, by way of provisional conclusions. The mission, being an essential and, therefore, enduring activity of the Church, will never disappear, but it needs revision on the following lines: there must be a better balance of the spiritual and visible aspects of the Church in presenting her to non-Christians; there must be more respect for the pre-evangelical values put by God in the heart of the various peoples and their religions; there must be an atmosphere of grown-up freedom, both in the evangelization and the person evangelized; there is an urgent need of a better formation of missionaries at university level insofar as ethnology, linguistic studies and cultural studies are concerned. Without the fortuitous support coming from the West, the mission can henceforth rely only on one's own total gift of oneself to the other and on the goodwill of the other. And so we find again the missionary function in its original purity: "I have only wanted to know Christ among you."

Cardinal Suenens visited on his own initiative and spoke to the participants. He emphasized that, in spite of all the difficulties and in agreement with the demands imposed by a better understood respect for the non-Christian, the function of the missionary which is to evangelize and to establish the Church, must continue at all costs. Referring to some theories that would reduce the mission to a silent, living witness, he called upon the members of the audience to "exorcize this dumb demon" and to proclaim the Good News indefatigably throughout the world.

BIOGRAPHICAL NOTES

PIERRE MAURICE BENOIT, O.P.: Born August 3, 1906, in Nancy, France, he became a Dominican and was ordained in 1930. He pursued his studies at the Saulchoir in Belgium and at the Ecole Biblique in Jerusalem, obtaining degrees in theology and Sacred Scripture. He has been Professor of New Testament studies at the Ecole Biblique since 1934, and in 1965 became its Director. As a peritus at Vatican Council II, he was a Consultor on the Preparatory Commission on the Oriental Churches. His numerous books and articles are widely known and greatly respected.

ROLAND E. MURPHY, O. CARM.: Born July 19, 1917, in Chicago, Illinois, he entered the Carmelites and was ordained in 1942. After studying at The Catholic University of America and at The Pontifical Biblical Institute in Rome, he received his doctorate in theology and degrees in Semitic Studies and in Sacred Scripture. He is Professor of Old Testament at The Catholic University of America, and in 1964 was Visiting Professor at the Pittsburgh Theological Seminary (Presbyterian). The Editor-in-chief of the *Catholic Biblical Quarterly*, he has written *The Dead Sea Scrolls and the Bible* (Newman, 1956), and *Seven Books of Wisdom* (Bruce, 1960).

BASTIAAN VAN IERSEL, S.M.M.: Born September 27, 1924, in Herlen, Netherlands, he joined the Montfort Fathers and was ordained in 1950. After studies at the University of Louvain and the University of Nijmegen, he received his doctorate in theology in 1961. He holds a high academic post at the University of Nijmegen, and is Editor of the journal *La Terre sainte*. He has contributed to many scholarly journals, including *Novum Testamentum* and *Vox Theologica*.

HEINRICH KAHLEFELD: Born January 6, 1903, in Boppard, Germany, he was ordained for the Diocese of Meissen in 1926. He made his philosophical and theological studies at Cologne and at Innsbruck, and after further study at Tübingen and Leipzig, he became Professor of New Testament Kerygmatics at the German Catechetical Institute in Munich. He is the author of essays and monographs on the theology of worship and on biblico-theological studies.

HENRI CAZELLES, S.S.: Born June 8, 1912, in Paris, he entered the Sulpicians and was ordained in 1940. After studying at the Institut Catholique, at the Ecole Biblique and at the Sorbonne, he received degrees in political science, law, and a doctorate in theology. He was Professor at the Major Seminary of St. Sulpice d'Issy from 1942 to 1954, and at present is Professor of Old Testament Studies at the Institut Catholique. He has written and edited books on Old Testament studies, and contributes to such journals as *Catholic Biblical Quarterly, Revue Biblique, Biblica,* and others.

JOHANNES WILLEMSE, O.P.: Born March 16, 1931, in Schiedam in the Netherlands, he joined the Dominicans and was ordained in 1957. He has studied at the University of Nijmegen and at the Ecole Biblique in Jerusalem, receiving his doctorate in theology in 1965 after completing a study of the structure of the Gospel of St. John. He is Professor of Theology at the Dominican Seminary in the Netherlands, and a contributor to *Tijdschrift voor theologie* and *New Testament Studies.*

FRANZ MUSSNER: Born at Edlham in Upper Bavaria on January 31, 1916, he was ordained for the diocese of Passau in 1945. He attended the University of Munich and The Biblical Institute in Rome, receiving his doctorate in theology in 1952 and the licentiate in biblical studies in 1952. He was Professor of New Testament Theology in the Graduate School of Theology at Trèves from 1953-1965. The most recent of his many published works are commentaries on the Epistle of James and on the Epistle to the Colossians: *Der Jakobusbrief. Kommentar* (Freiburg, 1964) and *Der Kolosserbrief. Ein geistlicher Kommentar* (Leipzig-Düsseldorf, 1965).

BRUCE VAWTER, C.M.: Born August 11, 1921, in Fort Worth, Texas, he joined the Vincentians and was ordained in 1947. After studying at the Angelicum in Rome and the Pontifical Biblical Institute, also in Rome, he received the licentiate in Sacred Scripture in 1951 and the doctorate in Sacred Scripture in 1958. He has been Professor of Sacred Scripture at the Major Seminary in Denver, Colorado, and Visiting Professor at The Catholic University of America and at De Paul University in Chicago. His books are: *A Path through Genesis, The Bible in the Church,* and *The Conscience of Israel,* and he is a frequent contributor to *The Catholic Biblical Quarterly* and other scholarly journals dealing with Scripture studies.

GUSTAVO PÉREZ RAMÍREZ: Born October 31, 1928, he was ordained for the diocese of Bogotá in 1952. After studies at the Gregorian University in Rome and the University of Louvain, he received his doctorate in political and social sciences in 1958. He is the President of the Asociación Colombiana de Sociologia, a member of the American Sociological Association, and Director of the Centro de Investigaciones Sociales in Bogotá. He contributes to the journal *Social Compass,* and has written extensively on ecclesial, sociological and demographic problems in Latin America.

Subject Index to CONCILIUM (Volumes 1-10)

FIGURES IN BOLD FACE INDICATE VOLUME NUMBER, WITH PAGE REFERENCES IN LIGHT FACE.

Aaron, priesthood of, **(1)** 55–56

Abhishiktesvarananda, Swami, teachings of, **(9)** 148

Abinnaean Archives in Egypt, non-magisterial documents on military service, **(7)** 115

Abortion in India, **(3)** 61

Abrecht, Paul, on the changing Churches, **(3)** 103

Absolute, Japanese thirst for the, **(9)** 106–107

Absolution, for dying non-Catholics, **(4)** 38; power of, **(2)** 30

Acacius, schism of, **(8)** 71

Acculteration, historical phenomenon of, **(1)** 172

Actio liturgica of the priest, **(1)** 58

Action, Aristotelian concentration on, **(9)** 22–23; Catholic, in France, **(9)** 128, 130; of God, immanentization of, **(9)** 32

Acts of the Apostles, a *derived* witness, **(4)** 49

Adam, representative function of, **(1)** 73

Adelphotês, term in the early Church, **(1)** 48

Administration, as a charisma of the Holy Spirit, **(4)** 51

Administrator, diocesan, dismissal and resignation of, **(8)** 43; diocesan, procedure for the election of, **(8)** 41–42

Adoption, divine sonship by, **(6)** 21

Adorno, T. W., on ideology, **(6)** 122–123; on the sociological theory of knowledge, **(6)** 114

Advaita, Hindu notion of, **(3)** 169; **(9)** 147

Adventists, **(6)** 158

Afanassieff, N., on *communicatio in sacris,* **(8)** 148; on concelebration,

(2) 143n.; on eucharistic ecclesiology, **(4)** 131f.

Africa, bibliography on pastoral sociology in, **(3)** 141; catechesis in, **(4)** 199–207; cultural evolution in, **(1)** 105; cultural studies of, **(1)** 175; heresies as impediments to the evangelization of, **(4)** 6; militant expansion of Islam in, **(4)** 15; tension in communities of, **(1)** 174

Agapê, meaning of, **(1)** 59, 100; Western Christian precept of, **(9)** 89–90

Agapitus, Pope, letter to Patriarch Peter of Jerusalem, **(8)** 73

Aggiornamento, in India, **(3)** 72; in seminary training, **(2)** 188

Agni, Hindu notion of, **(9)** 144–145

Agnosticism, **(1)** 112

Agricultural schools, in India, **(3)** 65, 71

Ain-Traz, synod of, **(8)** 61

Ajanta Caves, **(9)** 148

Alanus, on juridical and teaching authority in the Church, **(7)** 10

Alba-Julia, synods of, **(8)** 60

Alberigo, Giuseppe, **(7)** 177; on episcopal power in Tridentine debates, **(7)** 79n.

Albert, Bishop of Prussia, on the problem of common liturgical services, **(4)** 20

Albert the Great, marital doctrine of, **(5)** 99

Alcántara, P. on diocesan collegiality, **(8)** 19n.; on the function of the bishop, **(8)** 25n.

Alexander V, Pope, election of, **(7)** 42

Alexandria, Church of, **(8)** 65–80

Alivizatos, H., objections against the Oriental Code, **(8)** 132; on Uniat Churches, **(8)** 132

Alt, Albrecht, on the decalogue, (5) 67; on genuine Israelite law in the Old Testament, (5) 69; on the origins of the Israelite law, (5) 58ff.

Altar, (2) 91–97; architectural problems of the, (2) 67

Ambo, (2) 89–91

Amenemope, teaching of, (5) 72

America, the Catholic Church in, (9) 114–115

Americanism, (6) 43

Americanization, process of, (1) 104–105

Amery, Carl, on German Catholicism, (3) 118

Anabaptists, (6) 148

Analogia Fidei, (9) 19–23

Analogy, between the covenant and the decalogue in the ancient East, (5) 68ff.; Thomist principle of, (6) 89–90

Anamnesis, (6) 53

Anastasius the librarian, comparison of the five patriarchs by, (8) 75; on the ecumenical character of the Fourth Council of Constantinople, (8) 77

Anatolius of Constantinople, (8) 79

Anatta, Buddhist principle of, (9) 89

Anciaux, Paul, on the priestly image, (2) 189

Anderson, C., on natural law in St. Thomas, (5) 45n.

Angelism, effect of, (9) 54

Anglican Church, (6) 144–148; eucharistic liturgy in the, (4) 84; preservation of Catholic structure and tradition in the, (4) 75

Anglican Communion, see Anglican Church

"Anonymous" Christians, new concept of, (3) 150

Anthropisms, meaning of, (9) 81

Anthropology, (6) 33, 99–102; Christian, (6) 16; philosophical, (6) 34, 90–91; transcendental and evolutionary, (6) 36; Western philosophical, (9) 82

Antioch, Apostolic Constitutions at, (2) 54; Church of, (8) 65–80; Patriarchs of, (8) 140–142

Antiquity, rationalistic civilization of pagan, (9) 54

Antonelli, Cardinal, on the propositions of the Syllabus, (7) 102

Apocalypse, apocalyptic dualism of the, (7) 111

Apocalypticism, Jewish, (6) 89

Apocrypha, (1) 36

Apologetics, former prevalence of, in theology manuals, (4) 67; the justification of, (3) 150; need for, (9) 103; role of, (6) 79–80

Apostasy, as grounds for deposing a pope, (7) 40

Apostles, collegiality of the, (1) 39–73; "collegium" of the, (3) 16; concept of "the Twelve", (1) 13, 39–40; place of, in St. Paul's ordering of the hierarchy, (4) 55; twofold office of, (1) 51f.; witness of, (1) 65

Apostolate, American, (9) 116–120; eschatological and incarnational aspects of, (9) 126; lay, importance of, (9) 67; ministerial grace of, (8) 9; rediscovery of, (9) 27; theology of, (9) 100–101

Apostolic activity, coordination of, (6) 178; integration of all fields of, (3) 33–34; need for reexamination of, (3) 25; relation between Church aid and, (3) 44

Apostolic age, preservation of the spirit of the, (4) 92

Apostolic centers, ecumenical work of, (4) 127

Apostolic episcopate, in the Eastern Churches, (4) 74

Apostolic heritage, preservation of, in the Eastern Churches, (4) 84

Apostolic nihilism, the danger of, (3) 45

Apostolic See, juridical power of, (2) 48–49

Apostolic succession, relation between the episcopal tradition and, (4) 180f.; solution of the problem of, in the New Testament, (4) 61

Apostolic tradition, bishops as the guarantee of, (4) 180

Aquinas, see Thomas Aquinas

Architecture in the Church, (2) 72, 76

Areopagus, Paul's address at the, (6) 24–31

Aristotelianism, (9) 11–12

Aristotle, (1) 62; "action" spirituality of, (9) 10, 12; intellectualism of, (5) 46; view of science of, (5) 44

Arles, Vicariate of, (7) 24

Armenia, non-Catholics in, (4) 30

Arnaldich, L., on the collegial function of the *Rabbim*, (8) 22n.

Arnauld of Brescia, spirituality of, (9) 49

Arntz, Joseph, O.P., (5) 182

Art, commission on, in the Church, (2) 39; representation of Christ in Christian, (1) 53

Artigas, J. Tena, on the religious mentality of Spanish youth, (3) 127

Arts, advancement of the, in a Christian spirit, (4) 126

Asceticism, methodological effort of, (9) 84–85; individual and collective situation of, (9) 56–57

Ashram, Christukula, Hindu notion of, (9) 143–156

Asia, changes effected by the independence of countries in, (4) 7; heresies as impediments to the evangelization of, (4) 6; Northern and Central, cultural traditions of, (9) 81–82; religions in, (3) 158–160

Assembly, faith of the, (2) 90; pastoral and theological exposition of the mystery of the, (9) 41; theology of the, (2) 74

Assumptionist Fathers and Eucharistic Congresses, (1) 157ff.

Atheism, (6) 27, 76–77; Marxist logic inspired by, (3) 85; problem of, (6) 15; (9) 134–135

Athenagoras, Patriarch of Constantinople, meeting of Paul VI with, (4) 39, 142

Aubert, Roger, (1) 154; on the pontificate of Pius IX, (7) 97

Audet, J. P., on religion, (9) 97

Augsburg, law of discord at, (7) 138

Augustine, St., (1) 135; on Church music, (2) 122; on community prayer, (2) 62; *Contra Epistolam Manichaei*, (9) 140; on eucharistic communion, (4) 133; on freedom of error, (7) 91; on his search for God, (1) 108; on the Holy Spirit, (1) 33; interpretation of prologue to St. John's gospel by, (5) 42; on knowledge of God, (6) 29; on marriage, (5) 122; on papal authority, (7) 7; on the relationship of Neoplatonism to Christianity, (3) 175; on the right of legitimate collective defense, (5) 89; on the unity of the Church, (5) 167

Augustinians, apostolate of, in the diocese of Groningen, (4) 127

Austria, pastoral sociology in, (3) 111–119

Authority, and liberty in the Church, (4) 17

Avatara, as a periodic manifestation of God in Hinduism, (3) 176

Aznar, Severino, on priestly vocations in Spain, (3) 126; on sociology in Spain, (3) 124

Bainton, R. H., on the early Church and war, (7) 108

Balmes Institute of Sociology, in Spain, (3) 130

Baltzer, K., on the draft of a covenant, (5) 66, 68

Baptism, of children in mixed marriages, (4) 121; Christian mystique of, (9) 85; ecclesial milieu of, (1) 89; as the element of Christian unity, (4) 10; entrance into the People of God through, (1) 15; and the eucharist, (2) 99–102; Japanese idea of, (9) 99; meaning of, (1) 118f.; and membership in the Church, (1) 139–141; (4) 144; necessity of, (1) 137; regulation of rite of, (2) 40; salvation of children without, (1) 150; validity outside the Church of, (1) 133

Baptist Churches, (6) 148–151

Baptistry, architectural problems of the, (2) 67; place and furnishing of the, (2) 86, 100–101

Barberena, Tomas Garcia, (8) 183

Barcelona, sociological and socio-religious analysis in, (3) 130

Barion, J., on ideology, (6) 113

Baroque architecture, symbolism of, (2) 71

Baroque Christianity, (7) 137–145

Barrida y Vida, Dominican sociographic center in Spain, (3) 130

Barth, Karl, Catholic dialogue with, (4) 158–159; on Catholicism and Neo-Protestant Modernism, (4) 88; on Christian metaphysics, (6) 28; on dogma, (3) 151; on the meaning of ideology, (6) 108–109; on philosophy, (6) 97; on Vatican Council II, (4) 99

Baruch, Apocalypse of, (10) 36

Basilicas, liturgical arrangement of space in ancient, (2) 72

Basler, Hans Rudolf, on Church music, (2) 123

Batazole, B., on diocesan collegiality, (8) 19n.

Baudoux, Maurice, on need for an adequate foundation for ecumenical dialogue, (4) 63f.

Baum, Gregory, O.S.A., (4) 213; on the danger of isolation in the ecumenical movement, (4) 154

Bäumer, R., on the Constance decrees, (7) 61, 67–68

Baumont, J. C., on de-christianization, (7) 150n.

Bavaria, pastoral ordinances on mixed marriages in, (4) 113

Bea, Augustine Cardinal, address to the W.C.C., (6) 174–176; on ecumenical dialogue, (4) 151; work of, (3) 156

Beauduin, Dom Lambert, on concelebration, (2) 137–138; on pastoral liturgical renewal, (2) 68

Beautiful, Japanese idea of the, (9) 95

Beck, H.-G., on the Byzantine Church, (4) 149

Beemer, T., on sterilization, (5) 116

Beguiristiain, Santos, study of, combining religious sociology and pastoral theology, (3) 129

Behan, Brendan, (1) 108

Being, analogy of, (6) 31; investigation of, (6) 102–104

Bekkers, Bishop Wilhelmus M., on the importance of communication between bishop and people, (4) 195–196; on the sufficiency of general confession, (4) 197

Belgium, intensity of eucharistic devotion in, (1) 157; religious sociology in, (3) 120–123

Belief, as a gift of grace, (6) 63; interpretation of, (6) 67n.; the real sense of, (4) 46

Believing subject, ontological unity of the, (6) 67; self-understanding of the, (6) 65

Bellido, José Dammert, criticism of the Codex, (8) 107

Benedict II, Pope, on common liturgical services, (4) 22

Benedict XIII, Pope, heretical conduct of, (7) 39

Benedict XIV, Pope, on the administration of sacraments, (4) 37; on common liturgical services, (4) 35; on mixed marriages in Central Europe, (4) 109; on statutes of diocesan synods, (8) 112–113

Benedict XV, Pope, on the heritage of the Eastern Churches, (5) 166; on the principal duty of bishops, (8) 85; resumption of eucharistic congresses by, (1) 161f.

Benedict Labre, school of spirituality of, (9) 48

Benedict of Teano, on the problem of common liturgical services, (4) 34

Benedictine office, structure of public worship in, (2) 57

Benz, E., on the spirit and life of the Eastern Churches, (4) 148

Benzo, Miguel, on the religious mentality at Madrid University, (3) 133

Berdyaev, N., on Communism, (6) 124; on poverty, (6) 166

Bergson, on Christianity, (9) 103; on movement within psychology, (9) 11–12; on the open religion of the heroes, (9) 50–51

Berkouwer, C., on justification, (5) 178

Beumer, J., post-Tridentine theology on Scripture and Tradition, (4) 168–169

Bhagavad Gita, (9) 148

Bhaktiyoga, Indian, (9) 86

Bhatki, Hindu notion of, (9) 147

Bhave, Acharaya Vinoba, land-reform work of, in India, (3) 184

Bible, as the book of the People of God, (10) 2–4, 25–38; as a development of God's Plan, (1) 14; and the Hindus, (3) 172; as a means of reviving theology, (3) 147; messianic suffering in the, (1) 78; misuse of, (9) 36; monarchical ideology in the, (10) 59–61; need for a catechism oriented on the, (4) 201; structure of morality in the, (5) 2; revealed truth in the, (10) 19–22; use in ecumenical dialogue of the, (4) 125; as the Word of God, (3) 177; services, (2) 38, 89, 104

Biblical interpretation, primary norm of, (10) 8–9

Biblical theology, renewal of, (4) 153
Bigotry, as infidelity to truth, (3) 164
Birth control, (5) 97–129
Birthrate, limitation of the, (10) 144; recent decline of, (3) 99
Bisegger, Ronald, on Church music, (2) 115, 126
Bishops, authority of the, (2) 9, 42; collegiality and, (8) 81–91; as collegium, ordo, corpus, and fraternitas, (1) 47; conferences of, (1) 63ff.; difference between patriarchs and, (8) 37; function of the, (2) 10; as the guarantors of the apostolic tradition and ecclesiastical faith and discipline, (4) 180–181; as high priests of the flock, (2) 7, 20–22; as the image of the Father, (2) 26; imposition of hands by, (4) 179; juridical obligations of, (8) 82; juridical power of, (2) 33–49; legislative power of, (2) 25; the liturgy and, (2) 7–24, 51–58; magisterium of, (8) 83; necessity for an advisory board of, (3) 20; office of, (1) 56; ordination of, (3) 17f.; plurality of, (1) 48; powers of, (3) 18; relation between priests and, (2) 25–31, 190; as shepherds of the Church, (3) 21; and the structure of the Church, (1) 44–45; as successors of the apostles, (3) 16; (4) 178
Bkerke, synod of, (8) 62
Blaj, Council of, (8) 60
Blessed Sacrament, (1) 160; Corpus Christi devotion to Christ in the, (2) 97
Blessings, reservation of, (2) 40
Blinzler, J., on the Passion, (9) 101
Blomjous, Archbishop, on the mission of the Church, (3) 64; on religious pluralism in India, (3) 62
Blondel, M., on the inner life of God, (6) 103; on the role of Tradition, (4) 170
Böckle, Franz, (4) 214; and the Societas Ethica, (5) 181
Body of Christ, and the Catholic Church, (4) 69–70; concept of, (1) 13, 24; eucharistic and mystical, (1) 57–62; idea of, (1) 29–37; manifestation in the local congregation of the, (4) 77; Pauline concept of, (1) 36, 118ff.
Bodzenta, Erich, on the social and religious situation in Austria, (3) 114f.
Bologna, center of socio-religious research at, (3) 136
Bombay, Eucharistic Congress at, as a stimulant for Hindu-Christian dialogue, (3) 186
Bomm, Urbanus, on Church music, (2) 128
Bonaventure, St., marital doctrine of, (5) 99
Bonet, Manuel, (8) 183
Bonhoeffer, D., on the problem of present-day Christianity, (9) 137n.; on religion, (6) 13
Boniface I, Pope, on the primacy of Rome, (7) 20
Boniface VIII, Pope, (1) 135; conflict with Philip the Fair, (7) 13; on papal primacy, (7) 47
Bonze, Buddhist, (9) 102
Book of Concord, (6) 136
Bornkamm, G., on the importance of the historical Jesus, (3) 146
Bossuet, on the baroque cult of rulers, (7) 144; on the eucharist, (6) 101; Variations of, (7) 166
Botte, Bernard, (4) 214; on concelebration, (2) 139n., 142; on diocesan collegiality, (8) 19n.
Botterweck, Gerhard Johannes, (5) 182
Bouillard, Henri, S.J., (6) 183
Boulard, Canon, on decentralization of pastoral work, (3) 33; influence in Spain of, (3) 130; on pastoral care, (3) 25f.; on pastoral sociology, (3) 117; on religious sociology, (7) 151n.
Bouscaren, T., on canon law, (8) 100n.
Bouyer, L., on the People of God, (1) 36; on spirituality, (9) 45n., 51n., 134n.
Brahman, four stages of, (9) 145n.
Bratsiotis, P., on the spirit and life of the Eastern Churches, (4) 147
Brazil, pastoral work in, (3) 28, 35, 37; problem of secondary education in, (3) 38
Brendenburg, A., on Luther, (4) 162, 165
Brien, A., on faith, (9) 130n.
Britto, J., on Hindu and Christian spirituality, (9) 153–154

Brockmüller, Klemens, on the Church and social change, (3) 118

Brugger, Walter, on the ends of marriage, (5) 128

Bruno, Giordano, on man's limitations, (9) 13

Brunschvicg, Léon, on de-christianization, (4) 13

Buber, Martin, on the structure of *eros*, (9) 12

Buddha, statues of, (9) 104

Buddhism, cultural studies of, (1) 175; morality of, (5) 83–84; notion of spirituality in, (9) 7; origin of, (9) 145

Buisson, L., on the principle of papal immunity, (7) 41

Bultmann, R., on Catholicism, (5) 179; on demythologizing, (6) 13; *God's Word in the Old Testament*, (10) 81; influence of Luther on, (4) 162; on kerygma, (3) 146, 148; on mystical phenomena, (9) 85

Bureaucracy, the role of, (2) 177

Burials, official recognition of, in the Ottoman Empire, (4) 25

Burundi, Africa, pastoral project in, (3) 38

Caglio, Ernesto Moneto, on Church music, (2) 111, 116–117, 119, 130

Cairo, synod of, (8) 63

Callahan, D., on the American Catholic layman, (9) 114n.

Calvary, anthropological connection of death and, (6) 101

Calvin, John, (6) 140, 143

Calvinism, Orthodox, on mysticism, (9) 85

Calvinists, Geneva Confession of the, (6) 135

Camps, Arnulf, (8) 184

Candelabra, location of the, (2) 93

Canonists, task of, (8) 118–122; work and study of, (8) 3

Canon law, codification of, (2) 44; codification of, in the Eastern Catholic Churches, (4) 141; and heresy, (7) 57; historical development of, (8) 2–4; inspiration of, (3) 18; and mixed marriages, (4) 112–113; Oriental Code of, (8) 63; Oriental, reforms in, (8) 45–46; Oriental, survey of recent developments in, (8) 129–152; reform of, (8) 95–128; and theology, (2) 33f.

Canons of Hippolytus, on military service, (7) 110

Canons of Windesheim, (9) 48–49

Cantors, function of, at a solemn celebration, (2) 113, 125

Capitalism, (2) 168, 177

Capital punishment, Christian view of, (5) 18

Cardijn, Canon Joseph, (9) 111

Carey, William, (6) 150–151

Carmel, reformed communities of, (9) 39–40

Caste system, in India, (3) 59–60, 170

Casuistry, objections to, in moral theology, (5) 10f.

Catechesis, in Africa, (4) 199–207

Catechetical work, ecumenical approach to, (4) 14

Catechetics, (3) 147

Cathedral, dedication of a, (2) 21

Cathedral Chapter, diocesan council and, (8) 45–46; origin of, (8) 25

Catherine of Siena, St., on the election of Urban VI, (7) 38; "famiglia" of, (9) 39

Catholic Action, (1) 14–15; bibliography on, (3) 105; forms of, (9) 59; spirituality of, (9) 50

Catholic Bishops' Conference of India, work of the, (3) 69

Catholic Church, as a dogmatic religion, (3) 157; and the ecumenical movement, (4) 107–108; concept of, as the one true Church of Christ, (4) 30; danger of using, as the only norm in dialogue, (4) 87; *institutional* perfection of, (4) 72; Luther's charge of fanaticism against, (4) 87f.; need of constant reform and purification in, (4) 72; in religious dialogue, (3) 165

Catholic communities, break-up of old, (1) 110

Catholic Congress of Stuttgart, motto of the, (4) 109

Catholic ecclesiology, aspects of, (4) 75

Catholic education, different situations confronting, (4) 184–192; and mixed marriages, (4) 112, 119

Catholic hospitals, number of, in India, (3) 65–66

Catholic missions, factors influencing the ecumenical awareness of, **(4)** 7

Catholic Social Ecclesiastical Institute (KSKI), work of, **(3)** 97

Catholic theology, failure of traditional, **(4)** 1

Catholicism, **(6)** 134; American, **(9)** 111–112; in developing countries, **(3)** 85; need for cultural openness in, **(4)** 140

Causality, efficient, **(1)** 145; sacramental, **(1)** 144

CELADE, Latin-American Demographic Center of Santiago, Chile, **(10)** 150

CELAM, episcopal conference of, **(3)** 52

Celebrant, function of the, **(2)** 80–83; oneness of the, **(2)** 149

Celibacy, **(2)** 189–190

Center for Social Development in Latin America (DESAL), **(9)** 163

Center for Social Research of the diocese of Linz, in Austria, **(3)** 113

Center for Socio-Religious Research, in Brussels, **(3)** 121

Center for Statistics and Socio-Religious Research (CELAM), **(9)** 162

Center for Studies in Applied Sociology, in Spain, **(3)** 131

Central Committee of the World Council of Churches, **(6)** 171–172

Cerfaux, Canon L., **(1)** 15–16; on the People of God, **(1)** 36, 120

Cesarius, St., **(7)** 24

Chalice, theological riches of the, **(2)** 156–158

Chant, Gregorian and Plain, **(2)** 118–120, 124

Charfeh, synod of, **(8)** 63

Charisma, basic, **(9)** 20

Charismata, **(9)** 20–21; in the Church, **(4)** 41–61; new emphasis on, **(4)** 83

Charisms, variety of, **(1)** 23; diverse and complementary, **(9)** 42

Charity, the Church's mission of, **(6)** 16; St. Paul's description of, **(4)** 52; in the separated Churches, **(4)** 73

Charleroi (Belgium), survey of Sunday mass attendance in, **(3)** 98; study of religious practice in, **(3)** 121–122

Chelini, J., on vocabulary of de-christianization, **(7)** 151

Chenchiah, P., on the notion of ashram, **(9)** 145n.

Chethimattan, J. Britto, **(3)** 156

Chile, apostolic activity in, **(3)** 36; pastoral projects in, **(3)** 28, 35

Chiliasm, **(6)** 43

China, the Church in, **(2)** 51; ideological conflict between the U.S.S.R. and, **(3)** 87

Choir, liturgical function of the, **(2)** 82–83, 116–117; the true function of the, **(2)** 62–65

Christ, as the Alpha and Omega of history, **(1)** 75; coming of, **(1)** 89; commandment of, **(9)** 76–77; communion in, **(9)** 41; conversion of Hindus to, **(9)** 145–146; death and resurrection of, **(1)** 65, 88; encounter with, **(1)** 134; as our fellowman, **(1)** 73f.; as High Priest, **(2)** 88; human existence of, **(1)** 81f.; humanity of, **(6)** 100; *kenôsis* and *hypsôsis* of, **(1)** 90; layman's way to, **(9)** 65; life of, **(9)** 38; as "Logos" and "Shepherd", **(1)** 53; messianic community of, **(1)** 89; mystery of, **(1)** 92; mysteries of, **(9)** 50; the person of, **(2)** 71; redemptive work of, **(1)** 94; Second Coming of, **(1)** 133; service of, **(1)** 148; Spirit of, **(9)** 20; and spirituality, **(9)** 15–17

Christa Prema Seva Sangna, Anglican ashram, **(9)** 151; Christian ashram, **(9)** 151–152

Christarakhjshia, **(9)** 150

Christa Sishya Sangnam, Christian ashram, **(9)** 151–152

Christian, the model for every, **(9)** 53; position in the modern world of the, **(5)** 1; task of a, **(9)** 33; witness of the, **(1)** 101

Christian belief, the problem of ideology and, **(6)** 107–129

Christian casuistry, instances of, in St. Paul, **(5)** 14

Christian Churches, ecclesial character of, **(1)** 143

Christian colloquies on Hinduism, **(3)** 172

Christian communities, corporate structure of, **(7)** 5; ecclesial character of, **(4)** 65; ecclesial reality of, **(4)** 81–86; headship of, **(2)** 80; unity of, **(4)** 10–11

Christian conversion, in India, **(3)** 62

Christian cooperation, necessity of, in social matters, (4) 126
Christian Corridors to Japan: a case-study on pre-evangelization, (8) 175–182
Christian dialogue, and non-believers, (4) 14
Christian dogmatics, (6) 34–35
Christian education, the Catholic school and, (4) 184–192
Christian effectiveness, the problem of, (3) 55
Christian eschatology, and the WCC, (4) 96
Christian experience, ecclesial milieu of, (9) 36; purification of, (9) 27
Christian faith, (4) 89–90
Christian Family Movement (CFM), (9) 112–113
Christian life, evangelical foundation of, (9) 3; expressions of, (1) 85
Christian love, pastoral theology and, (3) 9
Christian message, (3) 167, 173; relation of culture to the, (1) 173f.
Christian mystery, contemplative dimension of the, (9) 32
Christian pacifism, (5) 84–85
Christian practice, existential possibilities of, (5) 10ff.
Christian reality, incarnational view of, (4) 158
Christian revelation, great themes of, (2) 57
Christian Scientists, (6) 158
Christian secular activity, bibliography on, (3) 109–110
Christian spirituality, one or more, (9) 8
Christian unity, demanded by Jesus Christ, (4) 123; interrelationship of mission and, (4) 6ff.; a Protestant view of the WCC and, (4) 100–108; renewal of Churches as an essential part of, (4) 86; and sacrifice, (4) 99; as a spiritual concern, (4) 155–156; theology of, (5) 159
Christian worship, (2) 59, 71
Christianity, the absolute reality in, (3) 175; characteristics of, (9) 85; communitarian values of, (9) 40; failure of, (3) 83, 85; (9) 2–3; and Hinduism, (3) 165–169, 175; and ideology, (1) 69f.; (6) 41–58; and Marxism, (7) 171; modern culture

and, (9) 102; mysticism of Eastern, (9) 82; power of, (9) 103; as the principle of life, (6) 91; and Stoicism, (5) 41–42; task of, (9) 104–105; Western form of, (9) 138
Christians, Communist accusations against, (3) 86; dialogue between, (5) 157; interrelationship among, (1) 56–57; and military service in the early Church, (7) 107–119; pastoral mission of, (3) 90
Christology, (5) 179; (6) 34–35; centrality of, in Luther's theology, (4) 161–162
Church, activities of the, (1) 87, 90; (3) 21; (4) 88–91; as the agent of human salvation, (1) 177; apostolic tradition in the, (10) 22–24; aspects of the, (1) 17, 95; bibliography on the general organization of the, (3) 104; canonical practice in the, (3) 18; catholicity of the, (1) 145; (5) 169; charismata in the, (4) 58; as the communion of the faithful, (4) 81; as a community, (1) 71; composition of the, (1) 22; concept of the, (9) 62; concepts of "I" and "We" in the, (1) 53–57; conditions of incorporation into the, (4) 82–83; democracy in the, (9) 106; dialogue between contemporary cultures and the, (1) 169–177; dogmatic tradition of the, (9) 57; dualistic view of the, (1) 138f.; ecclesial brotherhood of the, (1) 78; ecclesiastical structures of the, (1) 109; and education in India, (3) 71–74; episcopal nature of the, (3) 23; episcopal power in the, (2) 33; eschatological vision of the, (2) 164; essence of the, (3) 23; fellowship in the, (1) 71, 95–98; freedom within the, (1) 103–113; government of the, (1) 45f.; government of the, in the Middle Ages, (7) 123–136; growth in India of the, (3) 182; heavenly existence of the, (1) 15; as the herald of Word-revelation, (1) 82; hierarchical character of the, (1) 95; hierarchical function of the, (1) 81, 94; hierarchical organization of, (1) 12–13, 18; historicity of the, (6) 18; holiness of the, (1) 98–101; immanence of Jesus in the, (1) 87; infallibility of the, (1) 29, 33; juridi-

cal concept of the foundation of, (1) 14; juridical and social organization of the, (1) 145; "kerygma" of the, (3) 149; and laity, (9) 2-3, 61, 117, 130; law in the, (3) 18; liturgy in the, (1) 166; (2) 16; magisterium of the, (4) 171-172; and mankind, (1) 69-101; and marriage, (4) 111; and Mary, (8) 156; mediatory role of the, (1) 147; membership in the, (4) 144; (9) 55; mission of the, (3) 64; (4) 8; missions in the, (9) 22; and modern man, (4) 14; musical tradition of the, (2) 61; mystery of the, (1) 12-13, 21; (5) 158; nature of the, (1) 15f., 177; (3) 6; (6) 7ff.; need for reform in the, (1) 23-24; Newman's capsule history of the, (3) 168-169; ontology of communion and collegial structures in the, (8) 7-17; Pauline notion of the, (1) 35n.; as the People of God, (1) 117-129, 146; (2) 69-88; powers of the, (2) 16; proportionality within the, (9) 19; realities in the modern, (1) 112-113; reality of the, (3) 23; realization of the, (2) 13; renewal in the, (1) 177; (9) 35; responsibility of bishops with regard to the universal, (8) 83-86; as the "sacrament of unity", (2) 11, 69-88; sacramental communion of the, (8) 9-10; and salvation history, (1) 21; salvific mission of, (9) 67-68; as the saving revelation, (1) 88; and society, (3) 117; as the source of grace, (1) 80; as the source of redemption, (1) 87; spirituality of the, (1) 35; (9) 7-23, 45; structure of the, (1) 43-45; (3) 16-17, 21; (4) 119; (8) 3, 51; synods of the early, (8) 55-56; teaching ministry of the, (6) 55; theology in the, (3) 1; unity of the, (2) 12; (5) 158; (7) 127; vitality of the, (9) 44; vocation of the, (1) 148; and the Word of God, (4) 87-93; and the world, (1) 169f.
Church aid, and developing countries, (3) 43-55
Church and State, conflict in the Middle Ages of, (7) 12-14; principle of, and the educational system, (4) 189; separation in India of, (3) 60
Church building, liturgical arrangement of, (2) 67-107

Church discipline, character of, (4) 114
Church division, (4) 12, 14, 116
Church growth, disparities in, (4) 15-17
Church marriage, not binding for the validity of the sacrament, (4) 121
Church membership, conference on psychological and social aspects of, (3) 100
Church of Christ, (4) 70-72, 82-83; in China, (6) 156; in Japan, (6) 156-157
Church of Constantinople, (8) 65-80
Church of South India, (6) 157
Church provinces, (3) 19
Church structure, danger of overemphasis on, (4) 76
Church unity, connection between mission and, (4) 154-155
Church Unity Week, and conversion, (4) 14
Cicero, on the spirituality of duty, (9) 54
Civil law, (8) 112, 114-115
Civil marriage, (4) 110, 113
CLAR, the federation of national associations of higher superiors, (3) 52
Class distinction, program in Spain for the abolishment of, (4) 212
Claudel, Paul, on Hinduism, (3) 159
Clement VII, election of, (7) 35
Clement Hofbauer, St., on the German Reformation, (6) 138
Clement of Rome, St., exhortation to the Corinthians of, (2) 79; on collegiality, (8) 20
Clergy, catechetics and the, (3) 147; canonical office of the, (2) 51; collegial authority of the, (7) 5; in developing countries, (3) 85; distribution of the, (3) 97; ecumenical training of the, (4) 123; incardination and excardination of the, (8) 86; pastoral training of the, (3) 40; sociological training of the, (3) 93; spirituality of the, (9) 2-3; theological training for the, (4) 127
Clerical domination, danger in the Church of, (4) 61
Clericalism, in the Church, (1) 55; danger in developing countries of, (3) 53; explanation of, (4) 47

Cleri sanctitati, (8) 83, 85, 87–88, 90, 135, 143

Coates, J. B., humanist manifesto of, (5) 26

Cochläus, influence of, on Catholic biographers of Luther, (4) 159–160

Code, commission for the revision of, (8) 96; development of, (8) 103–106; task of reforming, (8) 51; updating of, (8) 99–100

Codex juris canonici, aggiornamento of, (8) 27–28, 95, 100–119, 123–128

Cognet, L., on spiritualities in the Church, (9) 45n.

Colegio de Artes y Teologia, importance of, (7) 139

College, canonical term of, (8) 15

"Colleges," synodal activity of, in the ancient Church, (1) 63

Collegiality, episcopal, pastoral implications of, (1) 39–67; pastoral work and, (3) 28–29; patriarchal rights of, (4) 135f.; and the Roman Curia, (4) 182

Collegiality, presbyteral, evolution of, (8) 19–32

Collegium, apostles defined as a, (1) 42; as a designation for all bishops, (1) 47

Colonialism, as a cause of expansion, (2) 162; missionary undertakings of, (3) 169

Commission for Liturgical Reform, (8) 51

Common Law, principles of justice in, (8) 110

Common liturgical services, (4) 18–40

Common prayer, as a prerequisite in ecumenical meetings, (4) 124, 126, 153

Communicatio in sacris, (4) 18–40, 145f.; (5) 172–174; (8) 149

Communio, holy eucharist signified as, (1) 59

Communion, (8) 7, 12–15; of bishops, (2) 9

Communion of saints, (1) 71–75, 90

Communism, (1) 108; (6) 43, 122; appeal to developing countries, (3) 76–87

Community, emphasis in the early Church on, (2) 71; essence of the, (3) 22, 26; place of the layman in, (9) 61; relation between individual and, (1) 174

Comte, on ideology, (6) 113

Concelebration, altar specifications for, (2) 92–93; bibliographical survey on, (2) 135–151; and the bishop, (2) 39–40; without a bishop, (2) 29; and communion of the Churches, (4) 84; in the early Church, (2) 28; and presbyteral collegiality, (8) 25; restoration of, (2) 34, 39f.

Conciliar commission for seminary training, (2) 186

Conciliar concept, development from Constance to Vatican I, (7) 32–33, 65

Conciliarism, downfall of, (7) 14; of Constance and the decrees *Haec sancta* and *Frequens,* (7) 45–61

Concupiscence, (6) 68–70

Confession, negative, (5) 73–74; pastoral discussions on, (4) 195–198

Confession of Augsburg, (6) 136

Confession of Westminster, (6) 141

Confessionals, (2) 102–103

Confirmation, administration of, (2) 30; in Africa, (4) 205; renewal of baptismal vows before, (2) 101; and the People of God, (1) 15, 18

Confucianism, (9) 94

Congar, Yves, (1) 10, 131; on the Constance decrees, (7) 32; on the Church as an historical reality, (7) 2; on ecclesiology (8) 7n., 16; on ecumenism, (4) 152; on the Great Schism, (7) 124; on the laity, (9) 127; on Luther's Christology, (4) 161; on mission, (10) 164–165; on Scripture, (4) 173; on Tradition, (4) 169f.

Congo, pastoral work in the, (3) 28, 35–36

Congregation, constitution of the, (2) 63; location of the, (2) 84–86

Congregation of Rites, instruction of the, (2) 52

Congregationalist Churches, (6) 151–153

Conjugal morality, position of the Church on, (10) 152–162

Conscience, conflicts of, (5) 9–12, 17, 19, 25–26; discussions on, (4) 196f.; individual, (1) 95, 113; as the means of obtaining grace, (3) 177; and mixed marriages, (4) 117; and morality, (5) 35; objectivity of, (5) 25;

as the ultimate norm for all Christians, (4) 125
Consciousness, epistemology of, (6) 111
Consecration to God, idea of, (1) 19
Conservatism, (3) 83
Constitution on the Church, (1) 11–14, 25; (2) 10, 16, 42, 44, 69f.; (3) 15ff., 20, 183; (4) 41ff., 52–54, 62, 64, 66–72, 78; (5) 168; (7) 15–16, 137; (8) 17, 29, 49, 81, 83–84, 86, 155–172; (9) 55, 63, 66–67, 71, 79, 114
Constitution on the Sacred Liturgy, (2) 3, 8, 10, 13–14, 20–23, 25–31, 33–49, 53, 62–65, 67–107, 111–131, 151, 153–158; (4) 79; (5) 156, 168; (8) 48, 53
Constitutiones Apostolorum, (2) 79
Contemplative life, intensification of, (9) 22
Contemporary history and the Church, (3) 11
Contemporary situation, meaning of the, (5) 36
Contemporary society, (3) 10, 14, 117f.
Contemporary spirituality, (9) 25–44
Contemporary world, demands of the, (2) 106; relation of the Church to the, (6) 41; situation of the, (3) 12
Continence, periodic, (5) 104
Contraception, (5) 124, 142–154; (10) 158–159; in India, (3) 61
Contraceptives, the problem of, (5) 18–21
Conversion, ascetical effort of, (9) 57; definition of, (3) 167
Cooperation, international and economic, (6) 166
Cooperatives, formation in India of, (3) 65
Coptic priests, secret conversion of, (4) 36
Copts, reunion of the, (4) 32
Cosmos, man's position in the, (6) 38; the world as a, (5) 41
Coste, René, (5) 182
Cottier, Georges, O.P., (3) 76
Council of Basle, (7) 61, 67
Council of Brest-Litovsk, (8) 59
Council of Chalcedon, (4) 19, 31, 161; (8) 9, 17, 58, 79
Council of Constance, (7) 29–68

Council of Constantinople, (7) 40; (8) 67, 77–78
Council of Florence, (1) 135; (4) 27, 138, 142, 145; (5) 171–172; (7) 164; on biblical inspiration, (10) 7
Council of Jerusalem, (1) 126; (8) 55–56
Council of Lyons, (4) 138
Council of Nicaea, (4) 136, 179; (7) 19, 26; (8) 115
Council of Pisa, (7) 39, 42–43, 52
Council of Quiersy, (6) 100
Council of Soissons, (7) 25
Council of Trent, (2) 88–89, 155f.; (4) 27, 110, 118, 163, 167; (5) 176–179; (6) 69–70; (7) 69–87; (8) 27, 85; on Scripture and tradition, (10) 14–15
Councils, the Church's co-responsibility at, (7) 60; diocesan, (8) 35, 37–45; ecumenical character of, (8) 76; history of, (7) 31n.; juridical power of, (2) 45; plenary, (8) 90; provincial, (8) 47; topical, (8) 57
Counsels, the three evangelical, (9) 71–79
Counter-Reformation, (4) 23–31
Covenant, the decalogue and the, (5) 67; dispensation of the, (1) 21, 30–31, 34; dispositio of the, (1) 81; idea of, (1) 19; and the liturgy, (5) 77; norm of, (9) 14; rite of the, (5) 66f.
Cozza, Lorenzo, on rigorism in common liturgical services, (4) 33
Creation, (1) 84, 92; (5) 2–3; (6) 32; (9) 87
Credo, (2) 64, 80
Creeds, integration within multiplicity of, (4) 92
Cronin, Vincent, Life of Robert de Nobili, (9) 151n.
Cross, prominence in the Church of the, (2) 78, 93
Crottogini, J., on vocations to the priesthood, (3) 116f.
Cuernavaca, restored cathedral of, (2) 78
Cullmann, O., on the Church's recourse to violence, (7) 111
Culture, evangelization and, (4) 7; history of, (1) 169–177; relation to Christianity of Greek, (9) 92
Curia, Roman, (3) 20, 29
Cushing, Cardinal, letter from Holy Office to, (1) 137

Cuttat, J.-A., on Eastern spirituality, (9) 147n.

Cyprian, St., on the episcopate, (4) 181

Cyprus, problem of common liturgical services in, in the Middle Ages, (4) 20

D'Ailly, Pierre, on conciliar ideas, (7) 45; De Materia Concilii Generalis, (7) 51

Dalmais, I. H., O.P., on Eastern liturgy, (4) 149

Daniélou, Jean, on Christian hospitality, (1) 57; on Tertullian, (7) 110

Danneels, Godfried, (2) 152; on concelebration, (2) 145, 149

Darshan, Hindu notion of, (9) 144

David, J., S.J., on sexual intercourse, (5) 126–127

Davis, H., on early Christian attitude toward war, (7) 107n.

Davis, Kingsley, (10) 147–151

Deacon, place of the, (1) 44; (2) 26f.; singing of the Gospel by the, (2) 64

Dead, Book of the, (5) 73; judgment of the, (5) 74

Deanery, establishment within some dioceses of, (3) 34

Death, Latin-American concept of, (10) 145; Pauline concept of, (10) 103–104

De Beata Virgine, conciliar text, (8) 157–159

De Brauwere, Y. Nolet, on the Latin patriarchate of Jerusalem, (8) 142

Decalogue, (5) 41–42, 45, 58–79; cultic and moral dimensions of the, (10) 63–66

Decentralization, pattern for, (4) 78

De Chardin, Teilhard, conclusions of, (9) 139; The Divine Milieu, (9) 129; on the human spirit, (6) 26; spiritual writings of, (9) 128

De-christianization, and evangelization, (4) 7; necessity in the modern world for, (4) 13–14; problem of, (7) 149–157

Decree on Catholic Oriental Churches, (8) 45, 63–64, 129, 138

Decree on Ecumenism, (4) 62f., 64f., 73–106, 108, 123; (5) 156–174; (6) 168, 171–176; (8) 7n., 10, 15–16, 63–64, 114n., 145; (9) 55

Decree on Justification of 1546, (7) 74

Decretals, principal points of law in, (7) 21–22

Decretists, (7) 6–9

Decretum Gratiani, contact with Christian antiquity through, (7) 81

De Divina Revelatione, on the unity of the two Testaments, (10) 9; on Scripture and tradition, (10) 15

De Ecclesia, see Constitution on the Church

De Echevarrìa, L., on diocesan synods, (8) 28–29

Defense, legitimate, principle of, (5) 80f., 92; right to a, (5) 82, 90

De Foucauld, Charles, 20th-century prophet, (9) 59

De Gaulle, Charles, (1) 108

De Guibert, J., on spiritualities in the Church, (9) 45n.

Deiss, Lucien, on sung readings, (2) 129

Dejaifve, Fr., on mission, (10) 166

De la Potterie, Fr., on faith and baptism, (10) 166

De Legarde, G., on the Middle Ages, (7) 126n.

Deleury, P., on Eastern spirituality, (9) 147n.

Delièvre, J., on concelebration, (2) 140–141n.

Dellepoort, J. J., on the pastoral situation in Austria, (3) 117

Delphi, Pythian priestess at, (4) 50

De Lubac, Henri, on the ecumenical movement, (4) 155; on the Mystical Body, (7) 130n.; on Teilhard de Chardin, (9) 129; on the unbeliever, (6) 75

De Meester, Dom Placidus, on concelebration, (2) 137

De Mende, Durand, sermons on the priesthood by, (4) 178

Democracy, definition of, (3) 78; product of Christianity, (9) 103

De Montfort, Grignon, on the Blessed Virgin, (8) 164n.

Denominational politics, danger of, (3) 45

Denys of Corinth, on extradiocesan solidarity, (8) 56

De pastorali Episcoporum munere, (8) 48–50, 89

De Populo Dei, (1) 11–13, 26

De Reynold, G., on absolutism, (7) 144–145

DESAL, a technical advice service, (3) 52

Deschamps, Cardinal, of Belgium, (1) 157

Deschanet, Fr., on Hatha-Yoga, (9) 89

Desqueyrat, H. P., on the effectiveness of the Church, (3) 118

Deuteronomic code, (1) 122

Deuteronomy, great commandment of, (9) 75; institutions in, (10) 69–70

Devanandan, Dr., on Hinduism, (3) 170

Developing countries, appeal of communism to, (3) 76–87; Christian purpose in, (3) 70–71; Church aid for, (3) 43–55; the Church's attitude toward, (3) 32; the Church's contributions to, (3) 2; evangelization of, (3) 25; social change in, (3) 28

Development, the organic concept of, (2) 166

De Vooght, Paul, on the Constance decrees, (7) 31, 45, 67–68

Devotio moderna, (9) 39, 48–49

Devotions, dignity of, (2) 38; and the eucharist, (2) 103–105; and the liturgy, (2) 51–58

De Vries, Wilhelm, S.J., (4) 213; (8) 183; on the authority of patriarchs, (8) 65n.; on the changing Churches, (3) 103; on the Eastern patriarchates, (4) 136–137; on the Orthodox Churches, (4) 143f.; on the patriarchate, (7) 27–28; on the rights of patriarchs, (8) 139

De Witte, Egidius, on the Church, (7) 161–163, 166

Diaconate, restoration of the, (2) 83f.

Dialectics, Marxist law of, (3) 80

Dialogue, attitude of the Church toward, (4) 195; beginning of, (6) 15; and the Christian message, (3) 167; ecumenical, (1) 142; and faith, (1) 177; (9) 42; need for, (4) 196; and unity, (4) 102; validity for the Catholic Church of, (4) 87ff.

Dibelius, M., on the kerygma of the New Testament, (3) 146

Didache, on collegiality, (8) 20

Didascalia apostolorum, on the function of presbyters, (8) 23

Diekmann, Godfrey, O.S.B., (2) 66

Dingemans, L., O.P., on pastoral work, (3) 31, 89f.

Diocesan liturgical commission, (2) 39

Diocesan organization in developing countries, (3) 28

Dioceses, apostolic potential of, (6) 177; autonomy of, (4) 135; contact between, (6) 178; as ecclesiastical structures, (1) 109; ecumenism in, (4) 123; feudal concept of, (8) 28; liturgical life of, (2) 7f.; reunion in, (4) 123–128; significance of, (3) 21; size of, (3) 20

Dionysius the Areopagite, on knowledge of God, (6) 29

Dionysius of Corinth, St., letters of, (1) 46, 63

Disunited communities, permanent presence of, (4) 9

Divarkar, Parmananda, S.J., on the liturgy in India, (3) 180–181

Divine cult, diocesan legislation concerning, (2) 40

Divine office, (2) 19, 41, 46

Divine providence, (3) 168

Divine truth, (4) 89

Divino afflante Spiritu, on biblical inspiration, (10) 8–9

Divorce, (4) 113

Doctors of the Church, spiritualities effected by the, (9) 21

Doctrine of Dordrecht, five points of the, (6) 141

Dodecalogue, (5) 77–78

Doepfner, Cardinal, directive at Munich Congress of, (1) 165

Dogma, definition of, (3) 145; and faith, (4) 90; and kerygma, (3) 145–153; on mixed marriage, (4) 118; and moral theology, (5) 1; purpose of studying, (1) 5–7; summary of Christian, (1) 82

Dogmatic theology, (3) 13, 152

Dombois, Hans, (4) 214

Dominic, St., evangelism of, (9) 39; school of spirituality of, (9) 48

Dominican Thomists, position on justification of, (5) 177

Donatist controversy, (9) 62

Don Bosco, school of spirituality of, (9) 48

Dondeyne, A., on Church aid for developing countries, (3) 48; on the importance of mission, (10) 166–167

Dostoyevski, Fyodor, on freedom, **(1)** 106

Doubting believers, question of, **(9)** 37–38

Dournes, J., case-study on pre-evangelization, **(8)** 176

Droulers, P., on de-christianization, **(7)** 152n.

Dualism, dialectical opposition between monism and, **(9)** 82

Dumont, C., on the rights of the patriarchs, **(8)** 138; on the sin of separation, **(8)** 148

Dumont, J. C., O.P., **(4)** 142

Duocastella, Rogelio, **(3)** 124

Dupanloup, Bishop, commentary on the *Syllabus*, **(7)** 103–104

Dupont, Jacques, O.S.B., **(1)** 116

Dupront, A., on the Council of Trent, **(7)** 78

Dupuy, M., on religious experience, **(9)** 34n.

Dutch Church, Rome's influence on, **(7)** 163

Duty, spirituality of, **(9)** 54

Dynastic theology, **(10)** 59

East, dialogue with the, **(5)** 174; Uniat Churches of the, **(8)** 59–64

Easter, **(1)** 37

Easter liturgy, **(2)** 100–101

Eastern Churches, **(1)** 160; **(4)** 6, 74, 115, 136–142, 147–149; **(5)** 159–171

Ebeling, G., on importance of the historical Jesus, **(3)** 46; interpretation of Luther by, **(4)** 162

Ecclesia, **(1)** 44; **(2)** 71, 73, 77, 86–88, 105

Ecclesial infallibility, **(4)** 44

Ecclesial mission, **(4)** 6

Ecclesial missionary organizations, **(4)** 8

Ecclesial pluralism, **(4)** 6

Ecclesial reality, of the separated Churches, **(4)** 62–86; of the Orthodox Churches, **(4)** 143–146

Ecclesiam Suam, **(1)** 169ff., 177; **(5)** 157

Ecclesiastes, **(10)** 133–135

Ecclesiastical decisions, and the laity, **(3)** 45

Ecclesiastical institutions, **(7)** 156

Ecclesiastical jurisdiction, **(2)** 43

Ecclesiastical life, **(4)** 106

Ecclesiastical office, **(1)** 43–50

Ecclesiology, **(6)** 34–35; Catholic, **(5)** 160–161; controversies between Luther and Catholicism on, **(4)** 161; medieval writings on, **(7)** 5–14; neglect of charismata in, **(4)** 49; and the New Testament, **(4)** 47; ontological aspect of, **(2)** 14; pastoral theology and, **(3)** 8; patristic, **(1)** 22n.; problems of, **(9)** 62; social and universal, **(8)** 7; study of, **(1)** 117

Eckhardt, Master, spirituality of, **(9)** 46

Economic expansion, evolution of, **(2)** 161–180

Economic progress in India, **(3)** 57–64

Economics, and pastoral activity, **(3)** 90

Ecuador, pastoral project in, **(3)** 38

Ecumenical Councils, the first seven, **(5)** 167

Ecumenical movement, **(4)** 1–2, 40, 63f., 85–86, 94–95, 100–108, 124, 154–159, 170; **(6)** 161–163, 169–170

Ecumenism, Decree on, see Decree on Ecumenism

Ecumenism, and the charismatic structure of the Church, **(4)** 49; conceptions of, **(6)** 168; definition of, **(4)** 150–156; development of, **(4)** 99; and the diocese, **(4)** 123; mission of, **(4)** 5–17; and the modern world, **(3)** 71; the nature of, **(4)** 107–108; and pastoral activity in India, **(3)** 70–71

Education, in Africa, **(4)** 200; aid for, **(3)** 47; freedom of choice in, **(4)** 190–191; in India, **(3)** 71; nature of, **(4)** 185; for the priesthood, **(2)** 186–191

Educational institutions in India, **(3)** 60

Educational systems, **(4)** 184ff.

Egotism, **(5)** 12

Eirênê, holy eucharist signified by, **(1)** 59

El Escorial 1563–1963, importance of, **(7)** 138

Emge, C. A., on ideology, **(6)** 118–123

Empiricism, **(6)** 31

Engels, on progressivism, **(3)** 84

England, Catholics in, **(1)** 103

English Reformation, Puritan sector of, (6) 151

Eparchy, meaning of, (8) 33–36

Episcopacy, observations on the, (3) 15–23

Episcopal authority, (2) 40

Episcopal collegiality, see Collegiality, episcopal

Episcopal conferences, (2) 40, 44; (3) 17, 19, 28–29, 51, 139; (8) 47–54, 88–91

Episcopal consecration, (1) 58

Episcopal office, (1) 47, 57ff., 62; (3) 19

Episcopal power and canon law, (2) 35, 41

Episcopate, collegial character of the, (4) 177–183

Ermecke, G., on birth control, (5) 120n.

Erni, R., objections against Oriental Code, (8) 132

Eschatology, (5) 14–16; and the Church, (1) 82; and ecumenism, (4) 157–158; meaning of, (1) 20; movement toward, (1) 28; rediscovery of, (1) 14

Eternal law, (5) 42–43

Ethics, Christian, (5) 1, 9, 27, 73, 75

Ethnocentrism in the West, (2) 177

Ethos, man's relationship to the, (5) 55

Eucharist, (1) 57–59, 61; celebration of the, (2) 27, 58, 153f.; (3) 148; (4) 19, 39, 67, 78–79, 198; (5) 163–164; centrality of the, (2) 88–105; definition of the, (2) 149; ecclesial milieu of the, (1) 89; mystery of Christ in the, (4) 9; reunion of men in the, (2) 13; role of bishop in the, (2) 40; as the "sacrament of unity", (2) 11; as a sacred banquet, (6) 101–102; as the source of grace, (2) 19; table of the, (1) 97; theology of the, (5) 158

Eucharistic action, (2) 75, 94

Eucharistic Body of Christ, (1) 52–57

Eucharistic community, (3) 22

Eucharistic Congresses, from Leo XIII to Paul VI, (1) 155–167

Eucharistic ecclesiology, (4) 131–133

Eucharistic liturgy, (1) 60f.; (2) 89–91; (3) 181; (4) 84

Eucharistic piety, (2) 97; in India, (3) 182

Eucharistic sacrament, nature of the, (2) 147

Eucharistic unity, (2) 27

Eucharistic worship, (2) 93

Europe, bibliography on pastoral sociology in, (3) 143–144

European Congress of Protestant Sociology, (3) 102

Eusebius, on synods, (8) 56

Eustathius, Patriarch, message to Pope John XIX, (8) 80

Eutychius, Patriarch, on the Second Council of Constantinople, (8) 76

Evangelical Churches, (3) 21; (4) 113

Evangelical experience, spirituality of, (9) 33–39

Evangelical life, practice of, (9) 41–42

Evangelical poverty, (6) 19

Evangelism, resurgence of, (9) 36–37

Evangelization, the Church and, (3) 49; definition of, (8) 180; new needs of, (3) 42; and pastoral projects, (3) 39; the problem of, (3) 34; work of, (4) 7–8

Evdokimov, P., on the Eastern Churches, (4) 147; on spirituality, (9) 134n.

Evening services, (2) 52, 54

Evolution, historicity implied in, (5) 1

Exaltation, Christology of, (10) 44

Excommunication, and civil marriage, (4) 113

Exegesis, Catholic and Protestant, (1) 41–42

Exhortation, as a charisma of the Holy Spirit, (4) 51

Existence, influence of faith on, (9) 38; as a messianic prophecy, (1) 92; mystery of, (1) 82; search for the truth of, (9) 8–9

Existential experience, (1) 5

Existential faith, (4) 165

Existential theology, (4) 164–165

Existentialism, (6) 122; dialogue with, (9) 126; and revelation, (3) 147

Exorcism, (4) 50

Ezekiel, mission-vision of, (10) 88–89

Faber suiipsus, man represented as, (1) 6

Faith, adherence to, (1) 70f.; as a charisma of the Holy Spirit, (4) 51; of the Church, teachings of the magisterium on the, (10) 6–10; and conversion, (3) 149; in developing countries, (3) 54; doctrine of, (6) 63–72; ecclesial milieu of, (1) 89; early formulas of, (10) 43–45; gift of, (4) 73; human approaches to, (3) 150; and moral awareness, (5) 21; mysteries of, (1) 165; and philosophy, (6) 95–104; as a presupposition for the sacraments, (2) 13; renewal of, (4) 9; sacraments of, (2) 17; (8) 10; source of, (4) 88

Faith and Order Conference, (4) 106; (6) 147, 161–162

Faithful, call to action by the, (2) 85; common priesthood of the, (9) 63; communions of the, (8) 12; function of the, (2) 63; relation of ministers to the, (2) 79f.; unity of all the, (9) 63

Familia, sacrificial meal of the, (2) 75

Family life, pastoral administration of, (10) 161–162; principles governing, (6) 20

Family planning, in present-day Latin America, (10) 142–162

Famine, Christian cooperation in the removal of, (4) 126

Fanaticism, (6) 57

Fascism, ideology of, (3) 82

Fathers of the Church, ecclesiological thought of, (1) 22; on eucharistic communion, (4) 133; on the People of God, (1) 117f.; on the Petrine office, (4) 134; on reform, (1) 24; on unity of the Bible, (1) 52

Fenélon, on "pure love", (9) 10

FERES, pastoral work of, (3) 35, 101, 112, 134

Ferin, J., on anti-ovulation pills, (5) 114

Fermentum, a host consecrated by the pope, (2) 27–28

Fertility, surveys in Latin America of, (10) 151

Festingière, A., on pagan antiquity, (9) 54

Feuerbach, Ludwig, on the idea of God, (6) 37; on the structure of eros, (9) 12

Fichte, on the absolute value of the spirit, (9) 10; on the structure of eros, (9) 12

Fichter, Joseph, on the urban parish, (3) 114

Final judgment, doctrine of, (6) 37

Fink, K.A., on the Council of Pisa, (7) 42–43; on the election of Urban VI, (7) 36

Finke, Heinrich, on the Council of Constance, (7) 29

Flahiff, George, on the ecumenical movement, (4) 85–86

Flavian, St., and the Antiochian schism, (4) 146

Floristán, Casiano, on religious sociology, (3) 133–134

Florovsky, Georges, on the People of God, (1) 36

Fomento Social, Jesuit sociological review in Spain, (3) 126

Fonseca, Aloysius, S.J., (3) 56

Fontaine, Jacques Fernand, (7) 178

France, pastoral sociology in, (3) 143–144; problem of priest-workers in, (4) 178; split among Catholics in, (9) 128

Francis of Assisi, St., evangelism of, (9) 39; school of spirituality of, (9) 48

Francis of Salem, and the reunion of the Copts, (4) 32

Francis Xavier, St., appeal of, (9) 91; motto of, (7) 141

Franciscans, apostolate of, (4) 127; and common liturgical services, (4) 25

Fraternitas, as a designation for bishops, (1) 47, 49

Free Catholic Church, (6) 158

Free will, Luther's doctrine of, (4) 163

Freedom, American, (1) 103; communism and, (3) 81; and humanity, (5) 25–26; psychological limitations of, (5) 8ff.

Frequens, conciliar theory of, (7) 64; on councils, (7) 59

Freyer, H., on the role of ideologies in modern society, (6) 123

Fries, Heinrich, on ecumenical theology, (4) 155

Frisque, Fr., on the laity in the mission field, (10) 167

Fuchs, Josef, on marital morality, (5) 111–112

Fulfillment, scriptural meaning of, (10) 83–84

Fullness of God, penetration of, (9) 30–31

Functional theology, (6) 181

Fundamental atheism, challenge of, (9) 42–43

Fundamental theology, aim of, (6) 1f.; function of, (6) 83; meaning of, (6) 79–83; starting point for, (6) 84–86

Gallicanism, problems connected with, (7) 160

Gandhi, Mahatma, (5) 88; (9) 146

Garaudy, R., on the dialogue between Christians and Marxists, (7) 171

Gardet, L., on mystical phenomena, (9) 82–83

Gautier, J., on spiritualities in the Church, (9) 45n.

Gâyatri, Hindu prayer for unity, (3) 178

Geday, M., on the mission of Uniat Churches, (8) 131

Geiger, T. on ideology, (6) 111–112; on progress, (6) 123

Geiselmann, J.R., on Scripture and Tradition, (4) 166–167

Gelasius, on the primacy of Rome, (7) 20

Gelineau, Joseph, S.J., (2) 58; on Church music, (2) 111ff., 118, 120–121, 125–126, 129–130

Gemeinschaft, structure of social action in the, (1) 104

Geneva Catechism, (6) 141

Genicot, L., on spiritualities in the Church, (9) 45n.

Gentiles, (1) 79; God's Word to the, (1) 42; St. Paul as witness for the, (1) 41

German Sociological Association, study on religious sociology of the, (3) 113

Germany, cultural evolution of, (1) 105; pastoral sociology in, (3) 111–119; resignation of mystics in, (9) 10; Salve devotions in, (2) 56; seminarians in, (2) 188

Gerson, John, on conciliar ideas, (7) 45; on election of 1378, (7) 39; on structure of Church government, (7) 14

Gerstenberger, on statutory law, (5) 75; on treaties, (5) 69

Geschehenlassen, spirituality of, (9) 12

Gewirth, A., on philosophy, (7) 133n.

Ghetto-Christianity, (1) 70

"Ghetto" mentality, need for extinguishing, (4) 124

Giblet, Canon, on the scriptural foundation of mission, (10) 164

Gilson, on philosophy, (6) 96

Gloria, function of the, (2) 126; importance of the choir at the, (2) 64; in a mass, (2) 80

Glossolalia ("speaking with tongues"), (4) 50

Gnosticism, apologists' attack on, (2) 70; danger of, (3) 173; modern representatives of, (9) 88–89; movement of, (9) 82

God, Arian concept of, (1) 54; creative act of, (1) 150; encounter with, (6) 39; grace of, (5) 178; (6) 57; glory of, (6) 36–37; idea of, (3) 150; immanence of, (6) 24, 33; knowledge of, (6) 38; love of, (5) 38; man's relation to, (6) 73; as the Moral Governor of the world, (3) 168; pagans' knowledge of, (6) 24; problem of, (6) 102–104; redeeming presence of, (2) 59; supernatural authority of, (6) 126n.; transcendence of, (4) 88–89; (6) 32; trinitarian life of, (6) 102–103; truth of, (4) 88–89; union with, (9) 57; will of, (1) 74f., 145

Golomb, Egon, (3) 97, 112, 114

Gommenginger, A., on Church membership, (4) 144–145

Good Friday, adoration of the cross on, (2) 98; Christian ritual of, (10) 121

"Good News", Jesus as the, (3) 148; meaning of, (9) 37; spreading of the, (2) 15

Good Samaritan, parable of the, (1) 96; (3) 46

Gordillo, M., S.J., on Eastern Orthodoxy, (4) 148

Görres-Gesellschaft, scholars of, (7) 71; collection of Tridentine sources, (7) 79

Gospel, distinct character of the, (10) 31–32; continuation of the, (9) 35; and ecumenical dialogue, (4) 93; historicity of the, (9) 101; human reaction to the, (9) 57; inner meaning of the, (9) 17–18, 53; message of the, (2) 131; and morality, (5) 7–21; need for deeper understanding of the, (4) 86, 89; oneness of the, (9) 2; proclamation of the, (4) 93; realization of the, (9) 37; and renewal, (4) 91; in separated Churches, (4) 101; simplicity of the, (1) 49; spirituality of the, (9) 17; spreading of the, (1) 149; witness to the, (9) 136

Gozzer, Giovanni, (4) 215

Grace, absence of the source of, (1) 79; activity of, (5) 177–179; applications of, (9) 21; call to, (1) 149–151; controversy between Luther and Catholicism, (4) 161; distribution of, (4) 84; effect of, (9) 53–54; efficacy of, (6) 37; gift of, (1) 93; and the incarnation, (1) 148–149; life of, (1) 82; (4) 73; man as object of, (1) 86; means of, (9) 56; sacramental power of, (1) 97; source of, (2) 18–19; trinitarian character of, (1) 92

Gracias, Valerian Cardinal, on hunger and disease, (3) 66

Gradual, form of the, (2) 120; singing of the, (2) 63, 118

Graduale Romanum, new critical edition of the, (2) 119

Graham, Billy, (6) 150

Grail, movement of the, (9) 119

Grasso, D., on pre-evangelization, (8) 175

Gratian, on ecclesiology, (7) 6–14; on the heresy clause, (7) 40

Gravrand, H., case-study on pre-evangelization, (8) 176

Great Britain, bibliography on pastoral sociology in, (3) 144

Great Schism of 1378, (7) 11

Greece, philosophy and Christianity in, (3) 174, 184; "unwritten law" in, (5) 40; view of the world in, (5) 40

Greene, Graham, (1) 108

Gregorian reform, history of, (1) 35

Gregory I (the Great), (4) 135; (7) 8–9, 67–68; (8) 67; (9) 92

Gregory XII, heretical conduct of, (7) 39

Gregory XV, founder of the Congregation for the Propagation of the Faith, (7) 142

Gregory XVI, (7) 91–95

Gregory of Nyssa, St., on the brotherliness of Christians, (1) 50n.; on

mysticism, (3) 175; on the Spirit, (9) 11

Greinacher, Norbert, (3) 111; on Germany, (3) 103, 114–116, 118

Griffiths, Bede, on Christianity in India, (3) 184

Grisar, H., biography of Luther by, (4) 160

Grond, Linus, O.F.M., on the pastoral situation in Austria, (3) 117; on seminary training, (2) 187

Groot, Jan, (4) 214

Groote, Gerard, on Devotio Moderna, (9) 48

Grotz, H., S.J., on Eastern Orthodoxy, (4) 148

Growth, idea of, (2) 162; methods of, (2) 174; man's responsibility in, (2) 170; structural changes in, (2) 167

Guénon, René, traditionalist doctrine of, (9) 81

Guerra, M., on collegiality, (8) 22n.

Guillet, J., on the mysteries of Christ, (9) 131

Günthör, Anselm, on marriage, (5) 100

Habachi, R., on benefits of schisms, (4) 11

Hackin, Joseph, on Indian religions, (3) 160

Hadrian II, and the heresy clause, (7) 40

Haec sancta, theological significance of, (7) 57, 59–63, 66

Hajjar, Joseph, (8) 183; on Eastern Orthodoxy, (4) 148; on the Patriarchate of Constantinople, (8) 79; on permanent synods, (8) 59n.

Hameline, Jean-Yves, on sung readings, (2) 129

Hamer, J., on ecclesiology, (8) 7n.

Hammurabi, Code of, (10) 58

Hanssens, J.M., on concelebration, (2) 139, 146

Häring, Bernard, on the Church and society, (3) 119; on conjugal morality, (10) 153–154; The Law of Christ, (10) 146n.; on mixed marriages, (4) 109f.; on ovulation, (5) 119–120

Harvard University, (1) 137

Hatha-Yoga, methods of, (9) 89

Havemann, Robert, on ideology, (6) 115–116

Hegel, (1) 20; on nature, (5) 48; on the spirit, (9) 9; on truth, (5) 54

Heidegger, on Christian metaphysics, (6) 28; influence of, (3) 146; on the mystery of reality, (5) 33; on science and reflection, (6) 114; on the spirit, (9) 9–10; on truth, (5) 34

Heidelberg Catechism, (6) 141

Heinemann, on negative commands, (5) 69

Hellenism, mysticism of, (4) 50

Hengsbach, Franz, (6) 178

Heraclitus, on man's limitations, (9) 13

Heresy, (1) 146

Heretics, (4) 23ff., 27–29

Herman, E., on the primacy of Constantinople, (8) 79

Hernegger, R., on ideology, (6) 126–127

Hersch, Jeanne, on ideology, (6) 124–125

Herskovits, M.J., on culture, (1) 171

Hertling, L., on ecclesiology, (4) 133; (8) 7n.; on eucharistic celebration, (4) 19

Hierarchical structure in the Church, (4) 49, 73, 144

Hierarchical unity and concelebration, (2) 138, 143

Hierarchy, and the apostolate, (9) 69; collegial structure of, (9) 41; in De Ecclesia, (1) 12–13; pastoral responsibility of the, (3) 90; and the People of God, (2) 10; and St. Paul, (4) 55; and unity, (2) 12

Hilton, Walter, (9) 48

Hindu-Christian dialogue, (3) 156–178, 183–186

Hinduism, and hierarchy, (3) 60; pearl of, (9) 145, 154

Hippolytus, apostolic tradition of, (2) 26, 51

Hirsch, on conciliar ideas, (7) 46

History, and Christianity, (9) 101, 127–140; and the Church, (6) 12ff.; and ecumenism, (4) 5–8, 152; Hegel's philosophy of, (6) 109; and humanity, (5) 29–31, 33–34, 53

Hochhuth, R., The Deputy, (9) 136–137

Hocking, W.E., on religion, (3) 159, 161

Höffner, Joseph, on German Catholicism, (3) 115–116

Hollnsteiner, J., on Haec sancta, (7) 62

Holy communion, (2) 96–99, 153ff.

Holy orders, (4) 178ff.; hierarchical division of, (1) 18; People of God and, (1) 15

Holy See, and the liturgy, (2) 54; (4) 27f.

Holy Spirit, and charismata, (4) 43, 60; doctrine of the, (1) 33; first fruits of the, (9) 37; and holy orders, (4) 178; Old Testament meaning of the, (10) 104–105; Pauline theology of the, (10) 105; and the People of God, (4) 42; response of the Churches to the, (6) 163; role of the, (3) 148; sending of the, (1) 80; signing with the, (10) 104–106; universal manifestation of the, (4) 51

Homily, restoration of the, (2) 89, 91

Homiletics, nature of, (10) 51

Homo oeconomicus, attitude of the, (2) 167

Homosexuality, (5) 123

Honorius, Pope, condemnation of, (7) 40

Hope, as the basic attitude of the Christian, (1) 66–67; as present in the separated Churches, (4) 73

Hopkins, Gerard Manley, on lay spirituality, (9) 121

Horkeimer, on knowledge, (6) 114

Hormisdas, Pope, on provincial councils, (7) 23

Hornus, J.M., on religion, (7) 115, 116n.

Houtart, François, (3) 24; on African Catholicism, (4) 200; on American Catholicism, (7) 155n.; on the Church in Latin America, (9) 159n., 162; on de-christianization, (7) 154n.; on diocesan collegiality, (8) 19n.; on parishes, (3) 120–122

Hucke, Helmut, (2) 110

Hugh of St. Victor, on marriage, (5) 98, 100; theological treatise De Sacramentis, (7) 5–6

Huguccio, on the pope, (7) 8–10

Huguenots, destruction of the, (7) 142

Huizing, Petrus, (8) 184

Hulsbosch, A., on hermeneutics, (5) 179

Human activity, (3) 49

Human compromise, (5) 7–21

Human disciplines, (6) 27–28
Human existence, (5) 16, 28–31
Human experience, (2) 165; (6) 79–91
Human person, (1) 176; (2) 188; (4) 126; (5) 17, 36–37
Human race, (6) 21
Human reason, (5) 48
Human relations, (9) 29
Human respect, (5) 52–54
Human sexuality, (5) 121–122
Human spirituality, (9) 8–13, 17
Human understanding, (4) 88–89
Human values, (9) 31
Human work, (9) 27
Humani Generis, encyclical of Pius XII, (1) 136; (4) 68
Humanity, growth of, (5) 33; spirituality of, (9) 22
Humbert of Silva Candida, Cardinal, formulation of the heresy clause by, (7) 40; ghost-writer to Pope Leo IX, (8) 73
Humility, (3) 164
Hundred Years' War, conflicts of the, (9) 49
Hürth, influence on Pius XII of, (2) 141; on concelebration (2) 146
Husband and wife, sexual relationship between, (10) 156–157
Huss, John, execution of, (7) 29
Hussites, opposition to Rome of the, (2) 154f.
Huxley, Aldous, syncretist attitude of, (3) 160
Huybers, Bernard, on hymnody, (2) 130
Hymns, role of the choir in singing, (2) 130
Hypostatic union, definition of, (1) 82

Idealism, absolute, (5) 31; in St. Thomas Aquinas, (5) 49
Ideology, absolutizations of, (6) 58; and Christianity, (6) 41; (9) 2; definition of, (6) 42–43; nature of, (6) 54–55; the problem of, (6) 107–129; and social dynamics, (3) 82
Idolatry, prohibition of, (5) 64
Ignatius of Antioch, St., (1) 43–46; on bishops, (2) 26; canon law of, (2) 31; on collegiality, (8) 21; on the episcopate, (4) 180; on extra-diocesan solidarity, (8) 56; letters of, (2) 91f.; terminology of, (2) 14;

on the Trinity, (5) 168; on unity, (2) 12
Ignatius of Loyola, St., motto of, (7) 141; on salvation, (6) 29; spirituality of, (9) 46
Immanence, ideology of, (6) 42–58
Immortality, Old Testament doctrine of, (10) 137–140
Imperialism, (2) 164; ecclesiastical, (6) 19
Incardination, (8) 13–14
Incarnate Word, (1) 17
Incarnation, (1) 37; affirmation of the, (1) 82–83; effect of the, (1) 145; and grace, (1) 149; means of the, (2) 12; and the reality of creation, (5) 2; universal significance of the, (1) 144
India, society and the Church in, (3) 56–75, 170–171, 180–186
Indifferentism, (4) 7
Individual, the community and the, (1) 105, 174; (3) 122; latent anxiety of the, (9) 40
Individual rights, and the Catholic school, (4) 188
Individual Christian, and charismata, (4) 57; and the Holy Spirit, (4) 42–43; and pastoral theology, (3) 8
Individual nationalities, (3) 92
Individual parishes, (3) 26
Indefectibility of the Church, (1) 33
Industrialization, (2) 163; in Africa, (4) 100; in Germany, (3) 112; in India, (3) 57–60, 184
Industrial revolution, (3) 116
Industrial society, (3) 123
Infallibility of the Church, (1) 29, 33
Infant mortality, decline in, (5) 103
Infrastructure, Marxist theory of, (3) 80
Innocent I, Pope, (2) 27; (7) 20; (8) 25, 69
Innocent III, Pope, (2) 28; (4) 20; (7) 11, 47
Inspiration and revelation, (10) 6–24
Institutionalism, (3) 28
Institutionalization, (3) 52
Integration, (3) 92
Intercourse, contraceptive intervention in the act of, (5) 112, 116–119
Interdependent world, (6) 165–166
International assistance, (6) 166
International Catholic Auxiliaries, movement of, (9) 119

International conflicts, (5) 89
International Congregational Council, (6) 153
International Federation of Institutes for Socio-Religious Research (FERES), (3) 100–101; (9) 159
International Missionary Council, (4) 96, 103; (6) 161
International problems, (6) 173
International proletariat, (3) 82
Intersubjectivity, (6) 73n.
Introit, function of the, (2) 126; importance of choir at the, (2) 64
Irenaeus, St., on the episcopate, (4) 180; theology of, (1) 51
Isaiah, Apocalypse of, (10) 114
Isambert, F., on de-christianization, (7) 152n.
Islam, in Africa, (4) 15; the Church and, (3) 169; in the Middle East, (4) 14
Israel, continuity of the Church with, (1) 14; faith of, (5) 75; history of, (1) 75; monarchial ideology in, (10) 59–61; "mystery" of, (1) 21; as the People of God, (1) 15; rejection of, (1) 125–126; restoration of the twelve tribes of, (1) 40; wisdom movement in, (10) 128–130; Yahweh's presence in, (1) 122
Italy, sociology and pastoral theology in, (3) 135–140
Izard, Raymond, on seminary training, (2) 187

Jacobites, (4) 22
James of Viterbo, (7) 124
Jansenism, formation of, (7) 163; prevalence in the 18th century of, (4) 33; severity of, (1) 155
Janssens, Louis, on St. Augustine's interpretation of the doctrine of marriage, (10) 159–160; on marriage, (5) 99–100; on ovulation, (5) 113–114, 120; on procreation, (5) 119; on sexual intercourse, (5) 128–129
Japan, Christianity in, (9) 91–107; religion in, (8) 177–181
Jaspers, on philosophy, (6) 114
Jedin, Hubert, on the Constance decrees, (7) 31–32, 61, 65–66; on the Council of Trent, (7) 69n., 72–74
Jehovah's Witnesses, (6) 158
Jerome, St., on the role of the presbyterate, (8) 24

Jerusalem, the Church in, (8) 65–80; the community in, (9) 41–42; the Latin Patriarch of, (8) 142–143; oracle of, (10) 116; temple of, (10) 117
Jesuits, and common liturgical services, (4) 31; in India, (3) 172; in Germany, (4) 127; and probabilism, (4) 33
Jesus Christ, acknowledgment of, (4) 101; Bible spirituality and, (9) 14–17; and Christian unity, (4) 123; dominion of God in, (5) 79; and ecumenism, (4) 75; encounter with God in, (9) 134; eucharistic mystery of, (4) 9–11; as the "Good News", (3) 148; and history, (6) 51–52; as the ideal of morality, (5) 38; love of, (5) 84; the message of, (9) 37; presence of, (4) 80, 101; selflessness of, (9) 23; as God's first and last Word, (10) 75–95
Jewish race, destruction of the, (9) 136–137
Jewish synagogue, in the Palestinian Church, (4) 61
Jews, blindness of the, (10) 47
Jiménez-Urresti, Teodoro, (8) 11n., 15n., 114n., 183
Joachim of Flora, spirituality of, (9) 49
Job, (10) 131–133
John I, Pope, on Church unity, (5) 167
John VIII, Pope, on the pallium, (7) 25; on Photius, (8) 72–73
John XXII, Pope, on the beatific vision, (7) 11; on common liturgical services, (4) 21
John XXIII (antipope), (7) 30, 42
John XXIII, Pope, (1) 4; Ad Petri Cathedram, (8) 95n.; aggiornamento of, (2) 78; on atomic war, (5) 90; on Christianity in the modern world, (9) 105; on Church aid, (3) 55; comparison of Pius XII with, (1) 108; on ecumenical dialogue, (4) 151; and episcopal collegiality, (4) 183; establishment of the Secretariat for Christian Unity by, (3) 156; on the lay apostolate, (9) 112; Mater et Magistra, (9) 112; on pastoral projects, (3) 28; Questa festiva ricorrenza, (8) 95; on unity, (6) 176

John, St., faith in Jesus of, **(10)** 95; *new* commandment of, **(9)** 75–76; prologue to the Gospel of, **(2)** 129; **(5)** 42; spread of the Christian message by, **(3)** 167

John Chrysostom, St., and the Antiochian schism, **(4)** 146; on the eucharist, **(6)** 101; on marriage, **(5)** 122

John of the Cross, St., mystical teaching of, **(9)** 86; spirituality of, **(9)** 46

John the Deacon, on Church unity, **(5)** 167

Joris, J., on Church music, **(2)** 122–123

Joseph II, Pope, reform measures of, **(7)** 165

Joseph, St., devotions to, **(2)** 52–53

Journet, Charles Cardinal, on Church spirituality, **(1)** 35; on nuclear weapons, **(7)** 119

Jung, C. G., on the Spirit, **(9)** 11

Jungmann, Joseph A., S.J., **(2)** 50

Juridical institutions, **(2)** 180

Juridical power, and the Church, **(2)** 14; **(4)** 133; and the episcopate, **(2)** 33–49; **(4)** 179

Juridical structure, capability of change in, **(4)** 182

Justification, the doctrine of, **(4)** 162; and moral obligation, **(5)** 9; Tridentine decree on, **(5)** 176–179

Justinian, canonical legislation of, **(8)** 57; Decree of, **(8)** 16

Jyotiniketan, Christian ashram, **(9)** 149–150

Kagame, A., case-study on pre-evangelization, **(8)** 176

Kähler, M., on "kerygma", **(3)** 146

Kalapesi, M., on spirituality, **(9)** 153–154

Kant, Emmanuel, on the absolute value of the spirit, **(9)** 9–10; differences between St. Thomas Aquinas and, **(5)** 49; on the metaphysical perception of God, **(6)** 26–27; on philosophical ethics, **(6)** 33; on the synthesis of truth and reality, **(5)** 56

Kantorowicz, E., on theology, **(7)** 130n., 131

Kappel, K., on *communicatio in sacris,* **(8)** 146

Karkafe, synod of, **(8)** 61

Karpp, H., on the early Church, **(7)** 112–114, 119

Kasper, Walter, **(4)** 213

Kelsen, H., on ideology, **(6)** 119

Kemmeren, C., on the structure of the Church, **(8)** 8n.

Kéramé, Orest, on schism, **(4)** 146

Kerkhofs, Jan, S.J., **(3)** 43; on Belgian religious practice, **(3)** 121

Kerygma, and dogma, **(3)** 145–153; essential part of, **(6)** 37; summary of, **(1)** 82

Keyserling, Count, on Asiatic religions, **(3)** 158–159

Kierkegaard, Soren, influence of, **(3)** 146; on the morality of the *plebs,* **(5)** 24

King, W. L., on dialogue between spiritualities, **(9)** 87–89

Kingdom of God, advent of the, **(1)** 85; **(9)** 47; the Church and the, **(1)** 18; as the dominant idea of Christ's teaching, **(1)** 119; humanity and the, **(9)** 32; life of the, **(9)** 37; matter and form of the, **(9)** 30

Knowledge, innate, **(5)** 44; sociological theory of, **(6)** 111

Knuth, W., on ideology, **(6)** 122

Koinonía, **(1)** 46, 59, 61, 72, 78, 88, 96

Kolakowski, L., on ideology, **(6)** 116–117; on knowledge, **(6)** 114

Kolmel, W., on papal immunity, **(7)** 41

Kolryn, synod of, **(8)** 60

Kornfeld, W., on exhortations and warnings in Proverbs, **(5)** 70

Koster, M. D., on the People of God, **(1)** 18, 36, 118

Kösters, Reinhard, on justification, **(5)** 178

Kraemer, Hendrik, on Christian "faith" and non-Christian "religions", **(9)** 88; on Hinduism, **(3)** 159

Kraus, H. J., on the People of God, **(1)** 122

Kruse, L., on the sacraments, **(8)** 10n.

Kühn, U., on the dialogue between Luther and St. Thomas, **(4)** 164

Küng, Hans, **(4)** 213; on Church structures, **(7)** 31; on conciliar elements in canon law, **(7)** 45–46; on the Constance decrees, **(7)** 31, 65, 67; dialogue with Karl Barth, **(4)** 158–159

Kuttner, S., on medieval canonists, **(7)** 128

Kyriale, choir's function in the, **(2)** 65

Labat, R., on the monarchy, **(10)** 57

Labbens, J., on religious practice, **(7)** 156n.

Lacombe, O., on mystical phenomena, **(9)** 82–83

Lacroix, Jean, on the problem of unbelief, **(6)** 61

Lafont, Dom G., on the eucharist, **(4)** 8–9; on the People of God, **(9)** 129n.

Laissez faire, **(1)** 107

Laity, activity of the, **(9)** 22; American Catholic, **(9)** 111–126; apostolic mission of the, **(9)** 68–69; Catholic Action among the, **(9)** 41; the chalice and the, **(2)** 153f.; collaboration between clergy and the, **(2)** 190–191; **(9)** 61–70; definition of the, **(9)** 121n.; dialogue with the, **(3)** 53–54; ecumenical training of the, **(4)** 124ff.; eucharistic devotion among the, **(9)** 125; function of the, **(4)** 195; instability of the, **(9)** 2–3; passive, **(9)** 115; pastoral activity in India of the, **(3)** 67–70; task of the, **(3)** 32; theology of the, **(1)** 18

Lambert, B., on the ecumenical problem, **(4)** 156–157

Lamennais, first prophet of Catholic liberalism, **(7)** 90

Last Supper, **(1)** 160; **(2)** 157

Lateran, basilica of the, **(2)** 27

Lateran Council IV, **(1)** 135; **(7)** 26–28

Latin America, cultural evolution in, **(1)** 105; demographic problems of, **(10)** 142–162; expectations of the Church in, **(9)** 161–164; pastoral sociology in, **(3)** 142; pastoral work in, **(3)** 32, 34f., 40

Latin American Episcopal Conference (CELAM), **(3)** 27; **(9)** 161

Latin American Institute of Pastoral Activity, **(3)** 40

Latin patriarchates in the East, **(4)** 138

Latin rite, canon of the, **(2)** 127

Latinization, **(4)** 140

Latter Day Saints, **(6)** 158

Laurentin, René, **(8)** 184; on the Blessed Virgin, **(8)** 157n.

Lausanne Faith and Order Conference, **(6)** 162

L'Avenir, **(7)** 90, 93

La Vie Spirituelle, on the mystery of Christ in the Church, **(9)** 130–131

Law, ecclesiastical, **(8)** 95; international, **(5)** 75; Israelite, **(5)** 58ff.; natural, **(9)** 76; Oriental, **(8)** 63; Roman, **(9)** 92; St. Thomas' treatise on, **(5)** 43f.; in Stoicism, **(5)** 40

Lay Retreat Movement, **(9)** 125

Leadership, charismata connected with, **(4)** 53

Leclercq, J., on papal authority, **(7)** 13n.; on the schism of Utrecht, **(7)** 159n.

Lectern, place of the, **(2)** 81

Lectors, function of, **(2)** 113

Legalism, in the Church, **(2)** 35; **(4)** 47

Legality of the popes and the Council of Constance, **(7)** 34–35

Léger, Cardinal, on the ends of marriage, **(10)** 154–155; on marriage, **(5)** 126n.

Le Guillou, Marie-Joseph, O.P., **(4)** 213; on Church unity, **(4)** 154; on the Eastern Churches, **(4)** 148; on missionary spirituality, **(10)** 165

Leibniz, **(4)** 13; **(6)** 95

Leisure, spirituality of, **(9)** 29

Le Monde, on liberalism, **(7)** 103

Lenhart, L., influence in Germany of, **(7)** 144

Lenk, K., on ideology, **(6)** 107n.

Lennerz, H., on Scripture and Tradition, **(4)** 168

Lenski, G., on membership in religious groups, **(3)** 95

Lent, **(4)** 205

Leo IX, Pope, letter to Emperor Michael, **(8)** 73; letter to Patriarch Peter of Antioch, **(8)** 69

Leo X, Pope, on common liturgical services, **(4)** 27; on Luther, **(4)** 165

Leo XIII, Pope, **(1)** 135; on common liturgical services, **(4)** 30; on the Eastern Churches, **(4)** 141; **(5)** 166; **(8)** 62; and Eucharistic Congresses, **(1)** 156ff.; on the laity, **(9)** 127; *Orientalium dignitas*, **(8)** 143–144

Leo the Great, **(8)** 68–70

Leonhard, W., on Marxism-Leninism, **(6)** 116

Leonine Sacramentary, on the ministry of the apostles, **(4)** 178

Lercaro, Giacomo Cardinal, on the Mystical Body of Christ, (4) 69; (5) 182

Lescrauwaet, Josephus Franciscus, (6) 183

Levi, Sylvain, on Asiatic religions, (3) 158

Lewis the Bavarian, appeals to the council of, (7) 48

Liberalism, in developing countries, (3) 48

Liege, P. A., on atheism, (9) 137n.

Life, Christian, (9) 56, 130; intensity of, (9) 33–34; religious, (9) 78; social, (9) 163; spiritual, (9) 134

Litany, in public worship, (2) 127; of the Saints, (2) 104

Literature, Japanese, (9) 106; spiritual, (9) 140

Litterae synodales, (8) 70

Littré, atheistic philosophy of, (7) 97

Liturgical assembly, (2) 59; authority, (2) 33f.; catechumenate, (2) 40f.; celebrations, (2) 8, 11–12, 17f., 20; education, (2) 47; movement, (1) 14–15, 164–165; (2) 2–3, 68, 73, 100; reforms, (2) 1–3, 23, 35, 42, 89, 126; rites, (2) 39ff.; (4) 30; seasons, (2) 57; services, (2) 8, 36, 69; worship, (2) 67–107; year, (2) 47, 52

Liturgy, in Africa, (4) 204; and the bishops, (2) 7–24, 38–43; and the catechism, (4) 201; and the choir, (2) 65; and the Church, (2) 34–35; (4) 80; and Church music, (2) 47, 112–115, 125; commitment of the, (2) 2; and the community of the faithful, (1) 22; for the dead, (1) 32; and devotions, (2) 51–58; distribution of roles in the, (2) 78–86; and the Eastern tradition, (4) 136; in ecumenical dialogue, (4) 125; and heretical patriarchs, (4) 28; in India, (3) 180–186; introduction of the vernacular into the, (2) 47; lack of appeal of the, (1) 108; and the laity, (4) 195; language in the, (2) 113; misuse of the, (9) 36; nature of the, (2) 15, 69; and the ordination of a priest, (2) 30; pastoral approach of the, (2) 73; and pastoral theology, (3) 8; and the People of God, (1) 117; (2) 75; purpose of the, (2) 84; reality of the, (2) 73; sacramental, (1) 100; and sociology,

(3) 100; (9) 41; uniformity of the, (1) 108; of the Word, as the first part of the mass, (2) 89–91

Local assembly, (2) 74, 103

Local Churches, (4) 132; not self-sufficient, (4) 179; problem of, (6) 177

Logos, (5) 40–41; (9) 10, 23

Lohfink, N., on the decalogue, (5) 77

Lortz, J., on Luther, (4) 160

Louis XIV, (7) 165

Love, and charisma, (4) 51, 60; of Christ, (1) 147; Christian, (1) 100; in the Church, (1) 96f.; Eastern mystiques of, (9) 86; and personalist morality, (5) 38; ways of expressing, (5) 107

Loyola, St. Ignatius, spirituality of, (9) 46

Ludovisi, Ludovico, on Eastern rites, (4) 27

Lukesch, A., on pre-evangelization, (8) 176

Luther, Martin, (1) 121; on the Church, (4) 87f.; on divorce, (4) 113; on faith, (6) 143; on the just sinner, (5) 178; the new Catholic view of, (4) 159–166; theology of, (4) 92

Lutheran Churches, (6) 136–140

Lutheran theology, (4) 158

Lwow, synod of, (8) 60

Lyons, pastoral work in the diocese of, (3) 34

Maccarone, M., on medieval canonists, (7) 128

Mackey, J. P., on Tradition and the Church, (4) 171

MacMullen, R., on the Roman Empire, (7) 119n.

Madrid, pastoral programs in, (4) 211–212

Magnificat, Luther's commentary on the, (4) 165

Maitland, on medieval jurisprudence, (7) 6

Malabar, Mar Thoma Church of, (9) 152

Malinowski, on functionalism, (1) 172

Malthus, on consumption, (2) 178–179

Man, and atheism, (6) 13ff.; Christian approach to, (6) 35–36; and death, (6) 99–100; definition of, (5) 28–29; and existence, (5) 2; (9) 51; and faith, (1) 150; and grace, (1) 86;

(5) 178; the just, (5) 78; nature of, (5) 47, 55–56; as a member of the People of God, (10) 101–104; relationship to God, (9) 14; relationship to nature, (5) 50–51; solidarity of, (9) 40; as a source of harmony, (1) 109; transcendentality of, (6) 52–53; vocation of, (6) 18; and the world, (6) 26

Manders, Hendrik, C.SS.R., (2) 134

Mankind, the Church and, (1) 69–101

Mannheim, K., on ideology, (6) 110–111

Manpower, exploitation of, (2) 162

Mariology, (6) 34–35; the Church and, (9) 20–21; controversies on, (4) 161; development of, (8) 155–156; questions on, (1) 128; and theology, (6) 100

Maritain, Thomism of, (9) 82–83

Mark, St., literary style of, (10) 87–90

Maronites, (4) 24

Marot, Hilaire, O.S.B., (7) 177

Marriage, advances in the understanding of, (10) 159–162; casuistic approach toward, (5) 112–120; Catholic teaching on, (5) 110; and the Church, (4) 111–120; ends of, (5) 122–123; indissolubility of, (6) 21; institution of, (5) 132; intercourse in, (5) 104–107, 109–112; and Japanese morality, (9) 93–94; love in, (5) 99; and the love of Christ, (6) 20; and morality, (5) 7, 97, 124; nature and purpose of, (5) 133–137; the permanence of, (5) 14; physical and psychological problems in, (5) 98; rights and obligations in, (5) 101; sacrament of, (8) 12; sacramental grace of, (9) 72; salvation aspect of, (5) 20; sex in, (5) 19; spirituality of, (9) 21–22, 29; stability of, (5) 103

Marsilio of Padua, on conciliarism, (7) 46, 48, 50, 54

Martelet, G., on Christian unity, (4) 10–11; on progress, (9) 139n.

Martin V, Pope, approval of the Constance decrees by, (7) 124; on common liturgical services, (4) 23, 36

Martyrs, (9) 103

Marx, Karl, (1) 20; (2) 168, 178–179; (3) 94; (6) 109–110; (9) 12

Marxism, (1) 105; (3) 48, 80, 82–83; (6) 122, 126; (9) 126

Mary, devotions in honor of, (2) 53; humanity of, (6) 100; mercy of, (8) 164; mission of, (9) 20; mysteries of, (8) 164–165; present-day interest in, (8) 155–156; Protestant approach to, (8) 162–163; as the prototype of the worshiping Church, (2) 104

Mary Magdalene, (1) 22

Mass, baptism and the, (2) 102; Catholic conception of the, (4) 163; celebration of the, (2) 22, 140; and communal character of the, (2) 140; and the consecration, (2) 79; eucharistic piety in the, (2) 97; ordinary of the, (2) 114; participation in the, (9) 67; twofold division of the, (2) 89–91; and Vatican II, (7) 175

Masson, Fr., on the means of salvation, (10) 165

Masturbation, (5) 123

Mateos, J., S.J., on Eastern Orthodoxy, (4) 148

Materialism, (3) 177; (6) 43

Matins, regulation of, (2) 55

Mauriac, F., on faith, (9) 133

Maximos IV, Patriarch, (4) 130, 142; (5) 100; (8) 134–135, 146–147; on conjugal morality, (10) 155

McCarthy, D. J., on the Old Testament, (5) 68

McDonagh, Enda, (5) 183

McManus, Frederick R., (2) 32

Medawar, Archbishop Petrus, (4) 141; (8) 130, 135–136

Mediator Dei, encyclical of Pope Pius XII, (2) 36, 53, 70–71, 74, 86, 93

Mediatorship, the notion of, (1) 73; varieties of, (10) 93–94

Medical Mission Sisters, in India, (3) 66

Medieval theology, view of episcopal consecration in, (1) 58

Meinhold, Peter, (6) 134, 137–138

Mekhitarists, foundation of the, (4) 37

Melchite Church, affairs of the, (4) 34; patriarchal synods of the, (8) 60; problems of reunion with the, (4) 140–142

Melitios, St., and the Antiochian schism, (4) 146

Melkite Church: see Melchite Church

Menges, Walter, (3) 111, 115

Mennonites, (6) 149–151

Mensching, C., on religious phenomenology, (3) 95
Meritum de congruo, (5) 176
Merleau-Ponty, M., (5) 35, 51
Merovingians, (7) 22
Mersch, E., on the Mystical Body, (7) 130n.
Merton, R. K., on religious sociology, (3) 94
Mesnard, P., on theology, (6) 97–98
Message-dialogue, the content of, (6) 18–22
Messe communautaire, problems created by the, (2) 141–142
Messiah, figure of the coming of the, (1) 73; fulfillment of promises in the, (1) 66
Messianic prophecy, literature on, (10) 117n.
Metaphysics, (6) 28, 44, 47–49
Methodist Churches, (6) 153–156
Metrophanes of Smyrna, on the five patriarchs, (8) 75–76
Metropolitan, function of the, (8) 22–23
Metropolitan system, restoration of the, (7) 23–28
Metz, Johannes, (6) 183
Mexican Institute of Social Studies (IMES), (9) 162
Meyer, S., on canon law, (8) 100n.
Meyjes, P., on conciliarism, (7) 50, 52
Microphones, location in a church of, (2) 94
Middle Ages, collegiality in the, (7) 5–14; power of the bishop in the, (8) 26; teachings in the, (7) 166; vespers in the, (2) 55
Migration, as a pastoral problem, (3) 116
Milton, John, (6) 150
Mind, ontological dynamism of the, (6) 102
Ministers, and the faithful, (2) 79f.; and modern society, (3) 117
Miracles, (4) 50; (6) 86–87
Mirari vos, doctrinal significance of, (7) 89–105
Misereor, (3) 48, 65–66, 69
Missiology, (6) 180
Mission, and Church unity, (4) 154–155; and ecumenism, (4) 5–17; primary function of, (10) 168; scriptural foundation of, (10) 164–165; union of liturgy and, (2) 24
Missionaries, attitude toward Protestants of, (4) 5f.; charismatic initiative of, (3) 12; and common liturgical services, (4) 22ff., 28, 34; formation of, (10) 168; in India, (3) 63; objective of, (6) 21; and the plan of salvation, (4) 9
Missionary activity, (2) 23; (4) 96, 103, 111
Missionary institutes, (4) 15
Missions, aggiornamento in the, (10) 164–168; and the catechism, (4) 201; regional, (3) 26, 111; sociology and the, (3) 109
Mixed marriages, (3) 97; (4) 35, 109–122
Modern catechesis, (4) 201
Modern Christian, true aims of the, (9) 34
Modern exegesis, (4) 153
Modern idealism, (6) 32
Modern Protestantism, history of, (4) 6
Modern world, Christians in the, (6) 24; de-christianizing factors in the, (3) 91; interdependence of the, (6) 165; socializing tendencies of the, (9) 40
Modernism and natural theology, (9) 83
Modernist Crisis, (9) 81
Modesty, necessity for, (2) 106
Möller, Joseph, on seminary training, (2) 187
Monarchy, limitations in the Torah of the, (10) 59–61
Monchanin, Jules, (9) 153; on Eastern spirituality, (9) 147n.
Monism, Oriental, (9) 84
Monnerot, J., on Communism, (6) 124
Monophysites, (4) 6, 19–20; (6) 53; (8) 55, 80
Montalembert, (7) 103
Montesquieu, (1) 20
Moral choice, (1) 104
Moral judgment, (3) 99
Morality, (5) 7–38; (6) 19; Japanese idea of, (9) 95; and marriage, (5) 130–154; norms of, (9) 55; positivistic, (5) 46; and religion, (5) 74–75; and salvation (5) 2
Moret, A., on the sacred function of the pharaoh, (10) 57
Morisi, Anna, on war, (7) 116–117
Mormons, (6) 158
Morning service, decline of the, (2) 55

Mörsdorf, K., on canon law, (8) 100n.; on the People of God, (1) 18

Mortal sin, (4) 197

Moses, mediation of, as the condition of salvation in the Torah, (10) 61–70; message of, (10) 52–53; representative function of, (1) 73

Moss, C. B., on the schism of Utrecht, (7) 159n.

Mott, Dr. John R., (6) 156, 161–163

Motte, Father, O.F.M., on pastoral care, (3) 25f.

Motu Proprio, (2) 37, 48, 63, 68

Mounier, Emmanuel, on sentimental pacifism, (5) 87

Mount Lebanon, synod of, (8) 61

Mount Sinai, covenant at, (2) 157

Mouroux, J., on Christian experience, (9) 34n.

Movement, biblical, (9) 59; ecumenical, (9) 56, 59; Gandhian, (9) 147; liturgical, (9) 59, 67

Mowinckel, S., on the decalogue, (5) 67

Moynihan, J. M., on papal immunity, (7) 41, 125n.

Mozart, mass written by, (2) 116

Mozaz, J. M., on methodological principles, (3) 131

Mulago, V., case-study on pre-evangelization, (8) 176

Müller, Michael, on marriage, (5) 100

Munshi, Sri K.M., on Hindu-Christian dialogue, (3) 156

Music, Church, (2) 111–131; commission on, (2) 39; sacred, (2) 59–65

Muslims, population of, in India, (3) 62

Myrdal, G., on economic expansion, (2) 174

Mystical Body, biological concept of the, (1) 28; and the Church, (1) 23; doctrine of the, (4) 67–68; (6) 21; (9) 41; and the eucharist, (1) 57–62; in St. Paul, (1) 15

Mystici Corporis Christi, encyclical of Pius XII, (1) 33, 118, 136–138; (4) 66–68

Mysticism, (9) 56–57, 81–85, 89

Napoleon, on atheism, (6) 109

Nationalism, (2) 164; (6) 43; (9) 107; in India, (3) 62; in Japan, (9) 106–107; and neo-Marxism, (3) 82; the rise of, (2) 175

National Socialism, (6) 122

Natural law, and contraception, (5) 148n.; history of, (5) 39–57; principles of, (5) 86; revision of the concept of, (10) 155–156

Natural resources, adequate distribution of, (10) 144

Natural sciences, realm of, (6) 45–46

Nature, definition of, (5) 29; and morality, (5) 123–124; order of, (5) 41–42; relationship between man and, (5) 50, 55; Stoic view of, (5) 40f.; transcendental Christian, (6) 56

Nave and the sanctuary, (2) 79, 82f.

Nebrada, A. M., on pre-evangelization in Japan, (8) 175

Nédoncelle, Maurice, (6) 183

Nehru, Pandit, on social change in India, (3) 184

Neill, S., on the Ashram Movement, (9) 152n.

Neo-Marxism, (3) 82

Neo-Platonism, (9) 82

Neo-Protestant modernism, (4) 88

Neo-Pythagorism, (9) 82

Nestorian Churches, (8) 55, 80; in areas under Latin rule, (4) 20

Nestorian heresy, (4) 6

Nestorius, excommunication of, (8) 68

Netherlands, pastoral sociology in the, (3) 144

Netherlands Reformed Church, (3) 103

Netherlands Society of Humanists, (5) 26

Neuner, Father, on Indian spirituality, (9) 89

Newbigin, L., on the People of God, (1) 123

New Covenant, God in the, (6) 29; spiritual understanding of the, (4) 90

New Dispensation, (1) 121; God's dwelling place in the, (1) 32; people in the, (1) 118; the temple of true worship in the, (2) 70f.

Newman, Cardinal, on the history of the Church, (3) 168–169; on a personalist morality, (5) 36

Newman clubs, (1) 111

New nations, emergence of, (6) 165

New Testament, and apostolic succession, (4) 61; and charismata, (4) 47; ecclesiastical offices in the, (1) 43; emphasis on "service" in the, (4) 57;

evidence in the, **(4)** 65; existential interpretation of the, **(3)** 146; growth of books in the, **(10)** 30–32; inheritance of eternal life in the, **(1)** 32; kerygmatic approach to the, **(3)** 146; lack of "abstract" values in the, **(1)** 72; language of the, **(6)** 89; and the People of God, **(1)** 123–124; preaching in the, **(10)** 39–41; and the Spirit of God, **(1)** 31

Nicholas I, Pope, **(7)** 25; **(8)** 66–67, 71, 74

Nicholas of Cusa, **(6)** 26, 29; **(7)** 134–136

Nichomachean Ethics, **(5)** 36

Nicolau, M., on concelebration, **(2)** 146, 147n., 148n.

Nierman, Peter, **(4)** 214

Nietzsche, Friedrich, **(3)** 160; **(5)** 33

Noah, representative function of, **(1)** 73

Nominalism, **(5)** 176–177; **(6)** 27, 31, 133

Non-violence, **(5)** 83, 88–89, 91

Norris, Frank B., on the People of God, **(1)** 17

North America, pastoral sociology in, **(3)** 142

Nothomb, D., case-study on pre-evangelization, **(8)** 176

Novak, Michael, **(1)** 102; on the American Catholic layman, **(9)** 115n.; on structures of the Church, **(7)** 16n.

Novatian, schism of, **(4)** 181

Novenas, not essential to liturgy, **(2)** 52

Nuclear arms, **(6)** 21

Obedience, **(1)** 77f.

Oberman, Heiko A., on justification, **(5)** 176

Office, nature of the spiritual, **(9)** 61; theology of, **(4)** 48, 96

Ogino-Knous, on the rhythm method, **(10)** 146–147

Oi, K., on the absolute, **(9)** 106

Oldham, J. H., on Christian unity, **(4)** 99

Old Law, people of Israel in the, **(1)** 118

Old Testament, **(1)** 5; divine choice in the, **(1)** 73; God's Word in the, **(5)** 42; **(9)** 14; growth of writings in the, **(10)** 28–30; inheritance of life in the, **(1)** 31–32; lack of "ab-

stract" values in the, **(1)** 72; law in the, **(5)** 58–63; prophets of the, **(1)** 41; relation of the Church to the, **(1)** 19; spirituality in the, **(9)** 14; wisdom literature of the, **(5)** 70; **(10)** 126–140; works on the, **(1)** 122–123

Olympic Games, liturgy of the, **(9)** 102

Onasch, K., on the Eastern Churches, **(4)** 148

Onclin, Willy, **(8)** 183

O'Neill, C., on the membership of the Church, **(7)** 134n.

Onory, F. Mochi, on medieval canonists, **(7)** 128

Ontology, **(6)** 24–25, 98

Ophir, legend of the gold in, **(3)** 183

Orders, sacrament of, **(4)** 179f.

Ordination, character of, **(9)** 64; and charismata, **(4)** 47–48; diocesan, **(2)** 21; power of, **(1)** 57–58; rites of, **(4)** 179

Ordo, **(3)** 19

Ordo Lectionum, purpose of the, **(10)** 42

Ordo Missae, reformation of the, **(2)** 90

Organ, in church music, **(2)** 121–122

Origen, anti-militaristic statements of, **(7)** 110; on the Canticle of Canticles, **(9)** 86; on the perfection of the Church, **(1)** 94; on the service of bishops, **(1)** 46; on the shedding of blood, **(7)** 110

Oriental Code of Canon Law, **(8)** 129–134, 139

Oriental Rite, **(8)** 131–132

Original sin, the doctrine of, **(5)** 16

Orphic-Pythagorean movement, **(9)** 82

Orthodox Churches, **(1)** 51; **(5)** 159; and common liturgical services, **(4)** 18–40; dialogue with the, **(4)** 131–149; the local congregation in the, **(4)** 84; similarity to Catholicism of the, **(4)** 63; and Vatican Council II, **(4)** 15–16

Orthodoxy, **(6)** 134; and Eastern Catholicism, **(4)** 146–147; growing importance of, **(4)** 98

Otto, R., on Eastern spirituality, **(9)** 83

Ottoman Empire, **(4)** 24–25

Our Father, universal outlook of the, **(3)** 178

Ourliac, P., on the Council of Basle, **(7)** 130n.

Ovid, on the golden age of Greece, (5) 23
Ovulation, (5) 101, 113, 115
Oxford Conference on Church, Community and State, (6) 165

Pacem in Terris, (6) 21
Pacifism, (5) 80–94
Paideia, relation to mysticism of the, (9) 87
Palestrina, mass written by, (2) 116
Pallium, importance of the, (7) 25
Pan-African Catechetical Study Week, (4) 201–207
Papal primacy, (1) 47, 50–52; (4) 139; (7) 47
Parenthood, (5) 140–142; new developments in regard to, (10) 156–162
Paris, university seminary at, (2) 187
Parishes, (2) 75–77; bibliography on, (3) 104; as ecclesiastical structures, (1) 109; in India, (3) 59, 74; liturgical life of, (2) 22, 34f.; sociological functions of, (3) 114–115
Parochial sociology, survey of, (3) 114
Parousia, (1) 34; (2) 86–88
Pascal, Blaise, (5) 10, 33; (9) 10
Paschal banquet, (2) 87
Paschal candle, (2) 87
Paschal mystery, (1) 166–167; (2) 86–88
Pascher, Joseph, (2) 24; (8) 25n.
Parenthood, (5) 140–142
Pastoral activity, (3) 1–2, 25, 39, 42, 90f., 108–109; (4) 14–15
Pastoral discussion, on confession, (4) 195–198
Pastoral letters, (3) 50; (4) 48–49
Pastoral ministry, (4) 84
Pastoral office, revitalization of the, (9) 27
Pastoral perspectives, in India, (3) 56–75
Pastoral problems, (3) 24–42, 96–98, 116; and the Reformers, (4) 165
Pastoral projects, (3) 25–28, 35, 37, 40
Pastoral sociology, (3) 33, 104, 111–119, 135–144; in Spain, (4) 209–210
Pastoral theology, (3) 1–14, 17, 124–140; (6) 180; (9) 27
Pastoral work, (3) 27–30, 33–35, 41–42; and kerygma, (3) 151; the liturgy and, (2) 23; new basis of, (2) 2; and sociology, (3) 89–110, 127–128

Pastors, the duties of, (2) 18; in India, (3) 70
Patriarchates and the Church, (3) 17–19; (4) 135–139; (7) 26–27
Patriarchs, the twelve, (1) 73, 77; (4) 137, 142, 145; (8) 134–140
Patristic literature, (1) 143
Patristic sources, authentic character of, (2) 34; (7) 1
Patristic theology, (1) 54
Paul V, prohibition of common liturgical services by, (4) 36
Paul VI, Pope, (1) 4; advocation of curial reform by, (3) 20; allocution of, (1) 11; (2) 116; on birth control, (10) 152–153; Constitution on the Sacred Liturgy, (2) 37; on ecumenical dialogue, (4) 151; on episcopal conferences, (3) 139; establishment of a Vatican Secretariat for Non-Christian Religions by, (3) 156; on eucharistic celebration of separated Christians, (4) 39; on Hinduism, (9) 144; on the liturgy, (2) 45; on Mary, (8) 164–165; Mater Ecclesiae, (8) 159–164; meeting of, with Patriarch Athenagoras, (4) 39, 142, 147; (8) 148; on the nature of man, (6) 82; on the purpose of the Vatican Council, (2) 3
Paul, St., on the apostolate, (2) 24; (9) 100–101; on the Areopagus, (1) 134; on the Body of Christ, (1) 16, 36; (2) 77; charismata in the theology of, (4) 47–50, 53; on charity, (4) 52; on Christian life, (1) 83; on Christian unity, (9) 57; on Church administration, (4) 56–57; on conjugal love, (10) 160–161; on conversion, (3) 166; on eucharistic celebration, (2) 79; on the hierarchy, (1) 13; (4) 55; on justification, (1) 16n.; on lay spirituality, (9) 121; letters of, (2) 71; (4) 48; (5) 42; on liberty, (9) 102; on the local community, (4) 77; mission of, (2) 23; on mixed marriage, (4) 111; on the Mystical Body, (4) 67; preaching of, (3) 174; (9) 115; on salvation, (1) 134; on spiritual movements, (9) 44; spread of the Christian message by, (3) 167; on temporal possessions, (9) 126; on temptation, (6) 69; theology of the Church in, (1) 120; on turning to Christ, (10) 46–50; on the "visible" and "invisible", (1) 91

Pauline privilege, (5) 14, 17
Pelagianism, (5) 177
Penance, (2) 102; administration of, to non-Catholics, (4) 24; during Lent, (2) 47; liturgical forms of, (4) 197
Pentateuch, Elohist traditions of the, (10) 29–30
Pentecost, (1) 33–34, 37, 39, 42
Pentecostal movement, (6) 158
People of God, the bishop and the, (2) 34–35; the charismata of the, (4) 41ff.; the Church as the, (1) 117–129, 145–147; (7) 137; concept of the, (1) 5–37; devotions of the, (2) 56; divine worship in the, (2) 2; and the eucharist, (2) 71; function of service in the, (1) 97; and the hierarchy, (2) 10; history of the, (2) 77; Israel as the, (1) 66; the local congregation and the, (4) 77, 82; mankind as the, (1) 72; mission of the, (10) 103; New Testament theology of the, (10) 108–109; origin of the, (10) 97–100; primary function of the, (10) 106; salvation and the, (1) 93; spiritual blessings of the, (10) 98–99; witness of the, (4) 42
Perichoresis, (1) 54, 64
Pericope and preaching, (10) 39–51
Personalism, Christian, (5) 26ff.; (6) 73n., 122; (9) 89, 126
Peter, St., basilica of, (2) 94; letters of, (2) 71; mission-vision of, (10) 88–89
Petrine office, (1) 62; (4) 134
Pfiffner, Ernst, on Church music, (2) 114–115, 117–118
Pfürtner, S., on Luther's doctrine of the certainty of salvation, (4) 163
Phenomena, mystical, (9) 82
Phenomenology, (3) 95; (9) 126
Philips, Gérard, (6) 183; on collaboration between clergy and laity, (9) 66–67
Philosophy, common ground of, (9) 11–13; contemporary, (3) 147; (5) 28; limitation of, (6) 31, 33; mystic, (9) 84; pluralism in, (6) 49; syntheses of, (6) 38; and theology, (6) 93–104
Pia exercitia, (2) 36, 103
Picard, François, on Church music, (2) 115–116, 118

Piety, Confucian, (9) 106; eucharistic, (1) 155f.; lay, (9) 65; Marian, (8) 170–172
Pilgrimages, revived interest in, (1) 156
Pills, control of fertility by, (5) 114, 116
Pius IV, Pope, implementation of Tridentine decrees by, (7) 75–76
Pius V, Pope, missal of, (2) 80
Piux IX, Pope, (1) 135; on liberal forms of government, (7) 95–98; *Maxima quidem*, (7) 98; on non-Byzantine Uniat Churches, (8) 61–62
Piux X, St., (1) 135; on Catholic Action, (9) 111–112; on common liturgical services, (4) 39; and Eucharistic Congresses, (1) 161ff.; *Motu Proprio* of, (2) 63, 68
Pius XI, Pope, on concelebration, (2) 137; condemnation of contraception by, (10) 152; on the Eastern Churches, (1) 141; (5) 166; on the lay apostolate, (9) 112; on marriage, (5) 122
Pius XII, Pope, *Christus Dominus,* (8) 116–117; comparison of John XXIII with, (1) 108; on concelebration, (2) 141, 148n.; condemnation of contraception by, (10) 152; on developing countries, (3) 25; and episcopal collegiality, (4) 183; on faith, (4) 90; on international conflicts, (5) 90–91; and the liturgical movement, (2) 3, 70; *Mediator Dei,* (2) 36, 53, 73; and the Melchite hierarchy, (4) 141; on the Mystical Body, (4) 67; (9) 41, 63; on pacifism, (5) 87; on pastoral work, (3) 28, 36, 132; on procreation, (5) 101–102, 104–105; on the Queenship of Mary, (8) 160; on the separated Churches, (4) 66
Plato, (1) 62; (5) 40; (6) 33; (9) 9–11
Platonism, (6) 32; (9) 11–12
Plessner, H., on the sociology of knowledge, (6) 114, 125–127
Plotinus, (6) 26; (9) 11
Pluralism, Eastern, (7) 26–28; philosophical, (6) 1, 49; regional, (7) 16–19
Pluralistic community, (3) 49
Pneumatology, (5) 179
Politics and religion, (3) 169

Polman, Pontien, O.F.M., (7) 179; on the schism of Utrecht, (7) 162n.

Polycarp of Smyrna, St., episcopal views of, (8) 21–22; on extra-diocesan solidarity, (8) 56

Pontifical, collegiality of the, (8) 27–28

Pontifical Commission for Latin America, (6) 178

Pontifical documents, (2) 36

Pontifical Preparatory Liturgical Commission, (2) 48, 68

Popes, and the bishops, (3) 19; and common liturgical services, (4) 20; legitimacy of the, (7) 30, 44; primacy of the, (2) 9; (7) 5; and reunion, (4) 143; supreme authority of the, (3) 16

Population explosion, (6) 20–21

Postconciliar Liturgical Commission, (2) 69, 95

Poverty, (2) 106; (4) 126; (6) 165

Prayer, (1) 99; (2) 56, 62; (3) 177; (4) 100–101, 126; (9) 57

Preachers, scriptural training of, (10) 51

Preaching, (2) 23; (3) 151–152; (4) 53; Johannine theology of, (10) 93–94; New Testament theology of, (10) 92–93

Predella, (2) 93

Predestination, (1) 19; (6) 37

Pre-evangelization, meanings of, (8) 175

Presbyterate, collegiality of the, (8) 19–32

Presbyterian World Alliance, (6) 144

Presbyters, (1) 44, 55; (3) 25; (8) 23–24

Priesthood, in Africa, (4) 200, 203; celibacy of the, (2) 189; collegiality of the, (2) 191; (4) 177–183; function of the, (3) 5f.; (4) 195; (9) 61; guidance as a function of the, (9) 69; image of the, (2) 188; and the laity, (2) 190–191; ministerial nature of the, (2) 80; (9) 63; and the People of God, (2) 69f.; problems of the, (2) 191; relation between the bishop and the, (2) 25–31, 190; repercussions on the, (9) 2–3; representative function of the, (2) 25–26; role of the, (3) 32, 123; sacramental function of the, (2) 147; service of the, (2) 80; shepherd function of

the, (3) 21; spirituality of the, (2) 141; theology of the, (2) 189

Primacy, dialogue with the Orthodox on the question of, (4) 131ff.; doctrine of papal, (2) 9; in the early Church, (7) 15–28; of 5th-century Rome, (7) 14–28

Primitive Church, faith of the, (9) 34

Problematic, post-Kantian, (9) 82

Processional songs, (2) 127, 130

Processions, eschatological significance of, (2) 87

Procreation, (5) 105, 107–108

Prodigal Son, parable of the, (1) 126; ecumenical significance of the, (4) 157

Production, economic, new methods of, (2) 171–172, 174, 178

Progestogene, use of, (10) 158–159

Prolegomena, (6) 80

Proletariat, in Marxism, (3) 83; the notion and mission of the, (3) 79

Propaganda, and common liturgical services, (4) 27–28

Prophetic inspiration, (10) 122–125

Prophetical messianism, (10) 117–118

Prophets, the Church and the, (4) 42; and the covenant, (10) 118–122; the hierarchy and the, (4) 55; and Israel's worship, (10) 113–118

Protestantism, (4) 64–65; (6) 134; and the Bible, (9) 59; and capitalism, (3) 94; and collegiality, (1) 55; in developing countries, (3) 46; dialogue with, (1) 28–29; (4) 150–173; eucharistic liturgy in, (4) 84; mysticism of, (9) 88; and religious sociology, (3) 102–103

Proverbs, commentaries on, (10) 130–131

Providentissimus, on biblical inspiration, (10) 8

Provincial conferences, (2) 45

Przywara, E., on Luther's theologia crucis, (4) 162

Psalmody, (2) 127, 130

Psalms, cantor's singing of, (2) 64; royal messianism of the, (10) 117–118

Pseudo-Dionysius, on the power of the bishop, (8) 25

Psychology, (6) 33; catechetics and, (3) 147; evangelization and, (4) 7; sociology and, (3) 89–90

Putz, Louis, C.S.C., on the modern

apostle, (9) 117n.; on the YCS in the United States, (9) 111

Quakers, (6) 161
Quanta cura, (7) 98–101, 104
Quietism, (6) 43, 56; (9) 84
Quru, Hindu notion of, (9) 144

Race, ideologies of, (6) 43
Radio, and religious education in Africa, (4) 207; transmission of sacred rites on, (2) 38
Rahner, Hugo, on St. Francis Xavier, (7) 141; on St. Ignatius of Loyola, (7) 140
Rahner, Karl, S.J., (3) 15; (6) 183; on baptism, (9) 116n.; on belief in the unbeliever, (6) 75; on diocesan collegiality, (8) 19n.; on existential concepts, (3) 147; on ideology, (6) 128; on the liturgy, (2) 2; on the People of God, (1) 92–93; on religious sociology, (3) 119; on spiritual theology, (9) 132n.; *The Church and the Sacraments*, (8) 8n.; on theology, (2) 183f.
Ramdas, Swami, teachings of, (9) 148
Randulf, Andreas, on conciliar ideas, (7) 46
Rationality, as the true nature of man, (5) 55
Rationalization, modern movement toward, (3) 42
Ratzinger, Joseph, (1) 38; on episcopal collegiality, (8) 17n.; on ideology, (6) 127–128; on the People of God, (1) 36
Rayan, Samuel, S.J., on India, (3) 184–185
Reality, meaning of, (6) 83–84; and truth, (5) 55
Real Presence, in the eucharist, (2) 74; mystery of the, (1) 160; theology of the, (2) 154
Reason, authority of, (6) 126n.; eschatological dimension of, (3) 78; and law, (5) 43–44; man's consciousness of, (5) 50; Marxist appeal to, (3) 80; Stoic view of, (5) 40f.
Redemption, anthropological conception of, (1) 86; grace of, (1) 88; and the People of God, (3) 6; the purpose of, (4) 85; source of, (1) 87
Reform, desire for, (4) 87; need of, (4) 72

Reformation, change in the goals of the, (4) 7; eschatology and the, (4) 157–158; influence on the Western Church of the, (4) 6; justification and the, (5) 176; reaction against the, (9) 58–59
Reformed Churches, (6) 133–158
Regatillo, E., on canon law, (8) 100n.
Relativism, (3) 171, 173–174; (6) 43, 48
Relics, authenticity of, (2) 103
Religion, communist controversy with, (3) 84f.; functions of, (3) 96; Hegelian interpretation of, (3) 158; Japanese notion of, (9) 96–97; Marx's analysis of, (3) 94; as personal intercourse with God, (1) 100; politics and, (3) 169; power of, (4) 122; public vows of, (9) 72–73; realization of, (3) 163; society and, (3) 33; sociological research in, (3) 94–98
Religions, comparative study of, (9) 96–97; dialogical approach to, (3) 166; *ersatz*, (9) 57
Religionsgeschichtliche Schule, works of, (9) 85
Religious, evangelical counsels of, (9) 2–3; holiness of, (9) 120; pastoral work of, (3) 106
Religious belief, (3) 173; ideology and, (6) 108–129
Religious communities, (3) 85
Religious dialogue, (3) 162–163, 174
Religious divisions, (3) 177
Religious experience, (9) 34–36
Religious individualism, (4) 65, 157
Religious liberty, (7) 89–105; ecumenism and, (4) 15; the problem of, (3) 12
Religious orders, (6) 178
Religious sociology, (3) 89–144
Religious superiors, authority of, (2) 42
Religious syncretism, (3) 160
Religious vocations, (4) 185
Rémond, René, (7) 178; on de-christianization, (7) 150n.
Remy, Jean, (3) 120
Renan, (7) 97; (9) 101
Renewal, ecclesial, (6) 22; ecumenism and, (4) 154; necessity of, (4) 125; obligatory norm of, (1) 65f.
Research, socio-religious, in Latin America, (9) 159–164

Restoration, political philosophy of the, (7) 91

Resurrection, effect of the, (3) 148; redemptive role of the, (2) 86; result of the, (1) 51; significance of the, (1) 80

Reuss, J.M., on ovulation, (5) 116–118; on procreation, (5) 119; on sexual intercourse, (5) 128–129

Revelation, (1) 14, 65; (3) 147; (4) 16, 89–91; (6) 36–38; (9) 82; and the Bible, (10) 18–24

Rexach, Modesto, on vocations in Spain, (3) 133

Rhythm method, (5) 113–114

Ricardo, on consumption, (2) 178

Richtlinien, of the German bishops, (2) 76, 88

Ricoeur, Paul, on belief, (6) 88

Riedlinger, Helmut, on the Council of Constance, (7) 34

Robert Bellarmine, St., on separated Eastern Christians, (4) 31; on the soul and the body of the Church, (1) 139

Robinson, John A. T., on existential knowledge, (3) 146

Rock, Dr. John, on anti-ovulation pills, (5) 114

Rodriguez, Christopher, on separated Christians, (4) 32

Rogers, C. Murray, on Hinduism and Christian unity, (9) 156n.

Rolle, Richard, works of, (9) 48

Roman Church, and the Eastern patriarchates, (4) 137; spiritual renewal in the, (6) 167

Roman Curia, Eastern patriarchates and the, (4) 138; and episcopal collegiality, (4) 182

Romanesque architecture, symbolism of, (2) 71

Romanus, Aegidius, papalism of, (7) 124; on the power of the pope, (7) 147

Rome, Church of, (8) 65–80; and the Reformed Churches, (6) 171–176

Rosary, as a private devotion, (2) 56

Rota, role of the, (8) 125

Rotterdam, pastoral organization in, (3) 34

Rouquette, P., on the Melchites, (8) 130

Rousseau, O., on the diocesan presbytery, (8) 29; on nature, (5) 23

Roustang, F., on spirituality, (9) 134n.

Rowley, H. H., The Old Testament and Modern Study, (10) 126n.; The Relevance of Apocalyptic, (10) 120n.; The Unity of the Bible, (10) 114n.

Rubrics, rules for the celebrant in the, (2) 80

Rulers, baroque cult of, (7) 144

Rural class, spirituality of the, (9) 50

Rüschemeyer, D., on ideology, (6) 117–119

Ruysbroeck, John, spirituality of, (9) 46

Ryan, E. A., on military service and the early Church, (7) 109

Saccidananda, mysticizing currents of, (9) 85–86; Roman Catholic ashram of, (9) 152–153

Sacerdotal institutions, varieties of, (10) 55–56

Sacra exercitia, introduction of the, (2) 103

Sacramental grace, (2) 154

Sacramental life, (4) 74, 133

Sacramental sign, (2) 157

Sacramental theology, (2) 88ff., 143

Sacramental understanding, and ecumenism, (4) 10–11

Sacramentals, (2) 40–41; relation to the eucharist of, (2) 19

Sacramentaries, (4) 178

Sacraments, celebration of the, (2) 13; charismata and the, (4) 52f.; ecclesial nature of the, (2) 102; ecclesial role of the, (2) 105; and episcopal authority, (2) 40; as an expression of unity, (2) 12; and faith, (2) 13, 89; as juridical signs, (1) 15; as an offshoot of anthropology, (6) 100–102; as a part of the Church, (1) 82; as symbols of grace, (1) 15; validity outside the Church of the, (1) 133; the vernacular in the, (2) 46

Sacred Congregation of Religious, (6) 178

Sacred Congregation of Rites, (2) 68, 95

Sacred Heart, devotions to the, (2) 53

Sacristy, place of the, (2) 82

Saints, existence of, (9) 18–19; veneration of, (2) 52

Salvation, acceptance of, (1) 77; aim

of, (5) 14; biblical notion of, (10) 53–54; collective, (10) 17; and common liturgical services, (4) 40; discrepancy between life and, (5) 21; through the divine choice of the king, (10) 54–61; the economy of, (9) 73; eschatological, (1) 95; and eucharistic liturgy, (3) 181; God's ratification of, (1) 73; and Luther, (4) 162–163; mission of, (8) 12; necessity of Church membership for, (9) 61; the pagan and, (1) 143; realization of, (5) 12; relation between goodness and, (5) 14; and the separated Churches, (4) 74

Salvation Army, (6) 155

Salvation history, the Church's significance in, (1) 144; the People of God in, (1) 17; perspective of, (5) 78; theology centered on, (1) 12; two phases of, (1) 81; the world and, (9) 31–32

Samâdhi, state of, (9) 83

Samkya, origin of, (9) 145

Sanctification, law of, (5) 77; means of, (9) 71

Sanctity, (1) 101; (5) 12–13

Sanctuary, (2) 79–83

Sanctus, singing of the, (2) 112, 117

Sankarâcharya, (3) 161

Sannyasis, (9) 153

Sartory, Thomas, on Christian unity, (4) 155–156; on Protestant theology, (4) 164–165

Sartre, Jean Paul, (5) 24, 54n.; (7) 33–34

Savior-King, in the ancient East, (10) 57–59

Scandal, and common liturgical services, (4) 34

Scarpati, Rosario, (2) 160; (3) 135

Scharper, P., on American Catholicism, (9) 119n.

Schasching, J., on the Church, (3) 114, 118

Schauf, H., on Scripture and Tradition, (4) 168

Schelsky, Helmut, on the Church, (3) 117

Schick, Bishop Edward, on the local congregation, (4) 78

Schillebeeckx, Edward, O.P., (1) 68; (5) 183; on contraception, (5) 124; on the norms of morality, (5) 122; on "physicism", (5) 123; on the purpose of culture, (1) 172; on sexual intercourse, (5) 125–127

Schiller, on the baroque cult of rulers, (7) 144

Schism, (4) 1, 11, 20–21, 27, 32, 144–145

Schlette, Heinz Robert, (6) 183

Schmaus, M., (1) 23; on the People of God, (1) 17, 35, 119

Schmemann, Alexander, on eucharistic ecclesiology, (4) 131f.

Schmidt, Hermann, on community singing, (2) 117; on concelebration, (2) 143, 145

Schnackenburg, Rudolph, (1) 116; on the People of God, (1) 35, 122

Schneider, R., Winter in Wien, (9) 132–133

Scholasticism, (4) 179

School systems, (4) 184–188

Schools, Catholic, bibliography on, (3) 109–110

Schumpeter, J., (2) 168–170, 172

Schuster, Heinz, (3) 4

Scripture, (4) 10, 91–93, 124, 152, 172–173; human reality of, (10) 1–2; personal reading of, (10) 37–38; two extremes in, (10) 4; and Tradition, (4) 96, 166–173

Second Coming of Christ, (1) 66, 76

Secretariat for Christian Unity, establishment of the, (3) 156; (4) 99

Secret marriages, the Council of Trent on, (4) 110

Sectarianism, (1) 76

Secularism, the age of, (2) 78

Secularization, in India, (3) 61–62

Sedile, (2) 81

Self-defense, (5) 10, 14; natural right to, (5) 88

Self-sacrifice, messianic act of, (1) 96; use of, (5) 13

Self-sufficiency, (1) 147

Seminary training, reform of, (2) 38, 186–191; (3) 40

Semmelroth, O., on the Mystical Body, (9) 61–62; on the structure of the Church, (8) 8n.

Sensus fidei, (4) 43, 45

Sensus fidelium, (4) 45

Separated Churches, ecclesial reality of the, (4) 62–86; new relationship between Catholicism and, (4) 128; responsibility for the existence of, (4) 143

Sermon, nature and purpose of a, (10) 40–41

Sermon on the Mount, (5) 8–13, 84–85, 109; theme of the, (10) 41–43

Service, (6) 22; as a charisma of the Holy Spirit, (4) 51; function in the Church of, (3) 16

Sex, (5) 97–129

Shamanism, (9) 81–82, 85

Shankara, (9) 84

Sicard, Claude, on common liturgical services, (4) 34

Siefer, Gregor, on worker priests, (3) 116

Sigmund, P., on Nicholas of Cusa, (7) 135

Simon, Richard, on missionaries as an obstacle to unity, (4) 5

Simplicius, Pope, letter to Acacius of Constantinople, (8) 69–70

Sin, changing views on, (4) 196f.; concept of, (1) 108; disintegration of man through, (5) 1–2

Sincerity, necessity for, (2) 106

Sirach, (10) 135–136

Sixtus V, Pope, on the primacy of Rome, (7) 26

Skepticism, (6) 48, 56

Slavery, (5) 14

Smith, Adam, influence of, (2) 173; on consumption, (2) 178–179

Smith, Huston, on religious syncretism, (3) 161

Smulders, P., on the sacraments, (8) 10n.

Social change, (3) 110; in developing countries, (3) 28

Social life, the effects of the religious phenomenon on, (3) 94

Social problems, (6) 165, 173

Social work, spirituality of, (9) 50

Socialism, (6) 43; in Africa, (1) 174

Socialization, (6) 21

Societas Ethica, (5) 180–181

Societas Liturgica, (7) 173–175

Societas Neo-Testamentica, (5) 180

Society, development of, (6) 20; ideological concept of, (3) 49; laicization of, (9) 32; Marxist concept of, (3) 81; religion and, (3) 3; structural forms in, (2) 163

Society of Jesus, (7) 165

Sociology, (6) 33; bibliographical survey on pastoral work and, (3) 89–110; empirical, (6) 126; problems

of, (3) 10–11; spirituality of, (9) 40; and theology, (3) 124–140

Socrates, (3) 150

Sodality of Our Lady, (9) 118

Söderblom, Nathan, (6) 161–163

Solesmes, abbey of, (2) 119; foundation of, (2) 1

Solidarity, secret of, (6) 166

Sorel, George, on Neo-Marxism, (3) 82

Soul, conduct of the, (9) 51; rational psychology of the, (9) 56–57

Spae, Joseph, Christian Corridors to Japan, (8) 175–182

Spain, sociology in, (3) 124–134; (4) 208–212

Spiessens, C., on the Patriarchs of Antioch, (8) 140–141

Spirit, dominance of the, (9) 9–10; transcendency of the, (9) 11–12

Spiritual renewal, and the eucharist, (2) 88; risks of, (9) 35–36; signs of, (6) 167–169

Spiritualities, characteristics of, (9) 50; Christian, (9) 59–60; Christian and non-Christian, (9) 81–90; differences between, (9) 56–57; multiplicity of, (9) 2–3, 45, 47; spirituality and, (9) 20, 45–60

Spirituality, and asceticism, (9) 52; Catholic, (5) 177; (9) 56; charisma of, (9) 1; Christian, (9) 16–17, 52–58, 122, 129; definition of, (9) 7–8, 52; desire for authentic, (9) 25–26; dialogue of, (9) 13; difficulties of, (9) 2; and eros, (9) 9; and evangelical brotherhood, (9) 39–44; forms of, (9) 2–3, 12, 23, 25, 34, 48; fundamental dilemma of, (9) 28–29; and gnosticism, (9) 28–29; Hindu, (9) 153; history of, (9) 26, 34, 41, 52, 58; and idealism, (9) 28–29; lay, (9) 120–122; and life, (9) 29–32; Marian, (9) 20; and mysticism, (9) 52; need for, (9) 27–29; non-believing systems of, (9) 30; norm of Christian, (9) 16–17; notion of, (9) 7–10; object of, (9) 51; Orthodox, (9) 55–56; pantheism of, (9) 13; post-conciliar, (9) 26; present-day, (9) 33, 58–60; Protestant, (9) 55–56; schools of, (9) 47–49, 51–60; sources of, (9) 19, 36; synthesis of, (9) 25–26; the, (9) 51–60; and

theology, (9) 7–8, 51–52; traditional, (9) 42
Spiritus Paraclitus, on biblical inspiration, (10) 8
Stanculescu, I., on Oriental archbishops, (8) 140
State, duties of the, (9) 76; Hegel's philosophy of the, (6) 109
Statio Orbis, idea of, (1) 166
Statutory law, (5) 59–70
Stele of Beki, on negative confessions, (5) 74
Sterilization, (5) 103, 114–115; in India, (3) 61
Steroid drugs, use of, (10) 158–159
Stoa, apatheia of, (9) 23; spirituality of, (9) 10
Stoicism, (6) 32; and natural law, (5) 39–42, 47; and philosophical ethics, (6) 33; spirituality of, (9) 13; syncretist element of, (9) 11
Structured institutions, salvation and life in, (10) 54–56
Structures, Church, (1) 103–113; collegial, (8) 14–17
Stutz, U., on canon law, (8) 100n.
Subdeacon, rite of ordination of, (2) 92
Subjective belief, (6) 71
Suenens, Cardinal, (6) 5; on the charismatic dimension of the Church, (4) 41; on procreation, (5) 102
Sufi spirituality, notion of, (9) 7
Suicide, (3) 99
Sunday, significance in Western Europe of, (2) 184
Supernaturalism, (6) 43
Superstructures, Marxist theory of, (3) 80
Supply and demand, (2) 178
Suso, Henry, spirituality of, (9) 46
Sweden, cultural evolution of, (1) 105
Sybils, ecstatic mysticism of the, (4) 50
Syllabus, (7) 95–105; doctrinal significance of the, (7) 89
Symphonía, holy eucharist signified by, (1) 59
Syncretism, and Hinduism, (3) 171
Synod of Jamnia, on the canonicity of biblical books, (10) 33–34
Synodicon, (8) 56
Synodos endemousa, (8) 79–80
Synods, (8) 28; bishops', (1) 47; con-

celebration at, (2) 40; diocesan, (8) 32; Maronite, (8) 61; regional, (8) 55–58

Tabernacle, and altar, (2) 95–97; architectural problems of the, (2) 67
Tantum Ergo, (2) 117
Tapas, Hindu notion of, (9) 144–145
Tauler, John, spirituality of, (9) 46
Teaching, as a charisma of the Holy Spirit, (4) 51; dialogue implied in, (3) 166
Technological revolution, (2) 162, 179; in India, (3) 64
Technological society, influence of, (1) 170, 174; religion in a, (3) 95, 170
Television, transmission of sacred rites on, (2) 38
Temptation, (6) 70
Teresa of Avila, spirituality of, (9) 46; Ways of Perfection, (7) 143
Tertullian, (2) 70; (3) 174–175; (5) 110, 113, 162, 167
Theodore of Studios, on the ecumenical character of a council, (8) 75–78
Theology, Christian, (6) 36–37; and the Church, (2) 183f.; comparative mystical, (9) 81; contemporary, (6) 1; dogmatic, (1) 7; (9) 51; function of, (3) 1; fundamental, (3) 150; generic imperatives of, (8) 3–4; as an ideology, (6) 117; in Japan, (8) 181; and the laity, (9) 122; and mariage, (5) 131–132; medieval, (1) 59; and mission activity, (4) 8–12; moral, (5) 1–2, 11–12, 18; movement of, (8) 2; and pastoral work, (3) 31; and philosophy, (6) 31, 93–104; present-day, (1) 1–2; (4) 1; sources of, (6) 80; systematic, (5) 42; teaching of, (6) 97; trinitarian, (6) 103
Theophanes, on common liturgical services, (4) 28
Theophany, accounts of the, (5) 66
Theosophic Movement, (6) 158
Thils, G., on apostolic succession, (1) 142; on non-Christian religions, (10) 165; on spiritualities in the Church, (9) 45n.
Third Pan-Orthodox Conference, (6) 175
Third-World, people of the, (6) 11
Thomas Aquinas, St., and Aristotelian

intellectualism, (5) 46; on communion, (2) 154; on concelebration,
(2) 28f., 136; dialogue with Martin
Luther, (4) 163-164; on the essence
of a counsel, (9) 75; on the eternal
law, (5) 43; on the eucharist, (1)
59; (2) 19, 87; on freedom, (5) 23;
on grace, (1) 71, 80, 149; (5) 179;
idealism in, (5) 49; and the immac-
ulate conception, (4) 146; on man,
(5) 47; merits and limitations of,
(4) 92f.; on the Mystical Body, (1)
136; on natural law, (5) 42-47; on
the New Testament, (5) 109-110;
ontological basis in, (4) 164; on the
People of God, (1) 25n.; on pru-
dence, (9) 112; realism of, (5) 48;
spirit of prayer of, (3) 177
Thomists, (4) 89
Tierney, Brian, (7) 177; on the community, (7) 128-130; on conciliar
ideas, (7) 45-46; on medieval canonists, (7) 128n.; on papal immunity, (7) 41
Tihon, on concelebration, (2) 150n.
Tillich, Paul, on knowledge, (6) 114;
on supernaturalism, (6) 13
Time, definition of, (2) 166-167
Topitsch, E., on ideology, (6) 119-121
Torah, (5) 58, 78; of Moses and
Christ as Savior, (10) 52-74
Tractarian Movement, (6) 147
Trade-Unionism, (6) 115-116
Tradition, and apostolic succession,
(4) 180f.; the modern community
and, (1) 174-175; the problem of,
(10) 14-17; and Sacred Scripture,
(4) 166-173; significance of, (4) 18
Traditionalism, danger of, (3) 167
Transcendence, ideology of, (6) 42-
58; principle of, (2) 94
Transmanence, ideology of, (6) 42-58
Transmigration of souls, (3) 186
Transubstantiation, (2) 146n.
Treaty of Perpignan, (7) 45
Tresmontant, M., on philosophy, (6)
95-96
Tridentine Decree on Justification, (5)
176-179; (7) 83
Tridentine historiography, (7) 69-87
Trinity, difference in teachings on the,
(4) 93; mystery of the, (6) 34
Triumphalism, ecclesiastical, (6) 22;
rejection of, (2) 106
Triumphus, Augustinus, on the

Church, (7) 132; on the papacy, (7)
47, 134; radical papalism of, (7)
124
Triune God, mystery of the, (1) 54;
revelation of the, (9) 16
Truth, Japanese idea of, (9) 95-96;
and morality, (5) 27-35; and reality, (5) 55-56
Tüchle, Hermann, (7) 178

Ullmann, Walter, on Church government, (7) 125; on the Great Schism,
(7) 123-128; on the double election
of 1378, (7) 35; on hierocratic prin-
ciples of government, (7) 127; on
medieval canonists, (7) 127n.; on
papal immunity, (7) 41
Ulpian, on natural law, (5) 41, 46, 98;
on sexual relationships, (5) 123
Ultramontanists, (7) 167
Unbelief, nature of, (6) 82-83; theo-
logical problem of, (6) 59-77
Unbelievers, question of, (9) 37-38;
spirituality of, (9) 30
Underdeveloped countries, (1) 96,
175; (2) 170-176
UNESCO, (1) 91
UNIAPAC, (3) 53; (6) 179
Uniat Churches, (7) 28; (8) 55, 60
Unions of Baptists, (6) 148
Unitarians, (6) 158
United Brethren in Christ, (6) 156
United Church of Canada, (6) 156
United Churches, (6) 156-157
United Nations, economic aid and
the, (3) 44
United States, the Catholic layman
in the, (9) 113-126; the Church in
the, (1) 110f.
Unity, in the Church, (4) 98-99, 102
Universalism, (6) 21
Universalists of the United States, (6)
158
University of Paris, and common li-
turgical services, (4) 23
Unknowing child, baptism of the, (9)
18
Unselfishness, (5) 35
Untouchables, in the caste system in
India, (3) 59
Upanishad, (3) 170, 177-178; (9) 145
Urban II, Pope, reunion conferences
of, (4) 145
Urban V, Pope, on common liturgical
services, (4) 21ff.

Urban VI, Pope, sanity of, (7) 36-39
Urban VIII, Pope, on common liturgical services, (4) 26; profession of faith of, (4) 32; *Sacrosanctum apostolatus officium*, (8) 59
Urban environment, (5) 102
Urbanization, in Africa, (4) 200
Useros, M., on the sacraments, (8), 10n.
U.S.S.R., ideological conflict between China and the, (3) 87
Utilitarianism, (1) 107
Utopianism, forms of, (6) 43
Utraquists, (2) 154f.
Utrecht, Schism of, (7) 160-167

Vaccari, F. A., on the interpretation of prophecy, (10) 122n.
Vagaggini, Cipriano, O.S.B., (2) 6
Valdes, John, spirituality of, (9) 49
Van der Marck, W., O.P., on conception, (5) 115-116
Van Erkel, J. C., on the Christian Churches, (7) 161-166
Van Kets, Raphael, O.P., (1) 168
Van Ouwerkerk, Coenraad A. J., C.SS.R., (5) 182
Vatican Council I, on biblical inspiration, (10) 7-8; ecclesiology of, (2) 10, 23; on invincible ignorance, (1) 135; Oriental commission of, (8) 62; papal authority at, (3) 16; on reason and faith, (6) 88; role of the bishop after, (2) 11
Vatican Council II, on the apostles as a *collegium*, (1) 42-43; on charismata, (4) 41ff.; on the Church in the world, (3) 103; on collegiality, (1) 39, 50; (2) 43; (8) 47; on common liturgical services, (4) 18; on *concelebration*, (2) 29f., 135f., 143f.; conflict between conservative and progressive views at, (3) 147; Coordinating Commission of, (1) 11; *De Ecclesia*, (2) 10; on the Eastern Churches, (4) 115; ecclesiology of, (2) 16; (5) 171; on ecumenical dialogue, (4) 107-108; the episcopacy in light of, (3) 15-23; on equality of patriarchs, (8) 142; on juridical power of the bishop, (2) 37; on the liturgy, (2) 63; on the dignity of marriage, (10) 154-163; message of, (2) 24; on mixed marriages, (4) 114; *Motu Proprio*, (2) 63; new image

created by, (4) 195; on the Orthodox Churches, (4) 15-16, 147; pastoral preoccupation of, (2) 62; on the permanent office of bishops, (8) 30; on preaching of the gospel, (1) 1; purpose of, (2) 3; on separated Churches, (4) 63-65; on the spirit of renewal, (8) 50-51; as a supplement to the Council of Trent, (5) 178; theological perspective at, (4) 1; on witness to the gospel, (9) 2
Vatican Secretariat for Non-Christian Religions, (3) 156
Vedas, age of, (9) 144
Vernacular, in the liturgy, (2) 46; music in the, (2) 114, 124, 127-130
Versailles, dictatorial peace of, (5) 82
Versteeg, Montanus, O.F.M., (6) 177-181
Vespers, (2) 54-55, 58
Vestigia Ecclesiae, (1) 141-143
Vestments, (2) 47
Victor, Pope, on the Easter question, (8) 56
Vincent Ferrer, St., on Clement VII, (7) 38
Vincent of Gallicano, on common liturgical services, (4) 26
Vincke, J., on the Council of Pisa, (7) 42
Virginity, state of, (9) 72
Virton, Pol, on sociology and the parish priest, (3) 117
Virtues, theological, (9) 57
Vischer, Lukas, (4) 214; on Rome and the WCC, (4) 94, 98; on Vatican Council II, (6) 172-173
Visser 't Hooft, W. A., (6) 143, 172; on the WCC, (4) 94-95, 97
Vocations, bibliography on, (3) 106; the problem of, (3) 97
Vogel, C., on the organization of the Church, (8) 22n.
Voltaire, (4) 13
Von Balthasar, Hans Urs, (6) 183; on Christian life, (9) 134-135; dialogue with Karl Barth, (4) 158-159; on proportionality within the Church, (9) 19n; on spirituality, (9) 3
Von Geinhausen, Konrad, on conciliar ideas, (7) 45; *Epistola concordiae*, (7) 50
Von Harnack, Adolf, on undogmatic Christianity, (3) 146

Vonier, Dom Anscar, on the People of God, (1) 33; on reform, (1) 23f.; on reservation of the sacrament, (2) 95

Von Langenstein, Heinrich, on conciliar ideas, (7) 45

Von Niem, Dietrich, on conciliar ideas, (7) 45; on the election of Urban VI, (7) 36

Von Rad, G., on the People of God, (1) 122; on the Sinai pericope, (5) 68

Votum ecclesiae, (1) 146f.

Wach, J., on religious phenomenology, (3) 95

Wagner, Johannes, on Church music, (2) 124

Wahner, Gotthard, on improvement of the Code, (8) 102

Walgrave, Jan Henricus, O.P., (5) 182

War, casuistic approach to, (5) 14; contradictory attitudes toward, (5) 80; irrationality of, (5) 86; just, (5) 10, 18

Warnach, V., on the People of God, (1) 122

Watanabe, M., on Nicholas of Cusa, (7) 135

Watts, Alan W., on Hindu-Christian dialogue, (3) 159

Way of the Cross, devotion of the, (2) 53, 56

Wealth, unequal distribution of, (4) 126

Weber, G., on concelebration, (2) 150, 150n.; on salvation and pastoral care, (3) 147

Weigel, Gustave, S.J., on Protestant theology, (4) 153

Weiler, Anton Gerard, (7) 178

Weise, George, on the Escorial, (7) 140

Wenck, on conciliar ideas, (7) 46

Wesley, John, (6) 155

Westemeyer, Dietmar, O.F.M., (6) 179

Westminster Confession, (6) 152

Wetter, G. A., on Marxism-Leninism, (6) 116

Whitehead, N.A., on the definition of religion, (3) 162

Wiesel, Elsie, *La Nuit*, (9) 133

Wildberger, H., on the People of God, (1) 122

Wilks, M.J., on papal immunity, (7) 41; on philosophy, (7) 133; on sovereignty, (7) 131n.

Willems, Boniface, (1) 130

William of Auxerre, on moral sense and speculative reason, (5) 42–43

William of Ockham, on conciliarism, (7) 46; *Dialogus*, (7) 50–51; ecclesiology of, (7) 13–14

Wisdom, book of, (10) 136–137; Buddha's rules of, (9) 53; as a charisma of the Holy Spirit, (4) 51; international and Israelite, (10) 127–128; and theology, (10) 137–140; writings, (10) 130–137

Witness, (6) 22; kinds of, (10) 94–95

Wölber, H.O., on social classes, (3) 115

Word, importance of the, (2) 89–90; mystery of the incarnate, (8) 8; preaching of the, (3) 8; theology of the, (4) 163

Word of God, (10) 77–84, 92–93; the Church under the, (4) 87–93; and conversion, (3) 149; inexhaustibility of the, (4) 173

Work, Christian concept of, (3) 70; spirituality of, (9) 29

Working class, spirituality of the, (9) 50; vocations from the, (2) 188

World, the apostolate in the, (9) 106; Christianity in the, (9) 103, 136; the Church in the, (6) 5–22, 163; (7) 137; (9) 43; evangelical fidelity in the, (9) 43; God and the, (6) 15–18, 23–39; (9) 17–18; peace of the, (3) 12; (6) 21; responsibility of the laity and priests for the, (9) 65–67

World Conference of Christian Youth, (6) 162

World Conference on Church and Society, (6) 165

World Convention of the Churches of Christ, (6) 151

World Council of Churches, (6) 139, 147, 161–170, 174–176; Catholic view of the, (4) 94–99; Protestant view of the, (4) 100–108; study of religious sociology by the, (3) 102; Toronto statement of the, (1) 142

World Methodist Council, (6) 155

World Missionary Conference, (6) 151

Worship, authority over, (2) 37–38; discussion of, (2) 3; essentials of,

(2) 73; as part of the Church, (1) 82; public, regulation of, (2) 43; public, singing in, (2) 111ff., 126; public, structure of, (2) 57

Wright, G. E., on wisdom literature, (10) 138

Yahweh, as the heritage of the just, (1) 31–32; covenant of, (1) 73; the power and glory of, (5) 69; the will and majesty of, (5) 74–76

Y Gasset, Ortega, on man, (5) 29

Yoga, form of asceticism, (9) 82; origin of, (9) 145

Young Christian Students (YCS), (9) 111–112

Young Christian Workers (YCW), (9) 112–113

Young people, bibliography on the religious attitude of, (3) 116

Youssef, Patriarch Gregory, (8) 62

Ysturiz, Ramon Echarren, (4) 208

Zabarella, Francesco Cardinal, on conciliar ideas, (7) 46; on *Haec sancta*, (7) 58; on the structure of Church government, (7) 14; teaching of, (7) 125n.

Zamosc, synod of, (8) 60

Zen, *apatheia* of, (9) 10

Zimmerli, W., on God's self-presentation, (5) 64; on wisdom literature, (10) 138–139

Zimmermann, H., on canonical principles, (7) 39–40; on conciliar thought, (7) 46–47; on the trial of John XXIII, (7) 43

Zoghby, E., on the problem of precedence, (8) 135

Zosimus, on the primacy of Rome, (7) 20

Zuñiga, E. Vargas, on the religious problem in Spain, (3) 124

Zužek, Ivan, S.J., (8) 184; on Eastern Orthodoxy, (4) 148

Zwingli, Huldrych, (6) 140

International Publishers of CONCILIUM

ENGLISH EDITION
Paulist Press
Glen Rock, N. J., U.S.A.

Burns & Oates Ltd.
25 Ashley Place
London, S.W.1

DUTCH EDITION
Uitgeverij Paul Brand, N. V.
Hilversum, Netherlands

FRENCH EDITION
Maison Mame
Tours/Paris, France

GERMAN EDITION
Verlagsanstalt Benziger & Co., A.G.
Einsiedeln, Switzerland

Matthias Grunewald-Verlag
Mainz, W. Germany

SPANISH EDITION
Ediciones Guadarrama
Madrid, Spain

PORTUGUESE EDITION
Livraria Morais Editora, Ltda.
Lisbon, Portugal

ITALIAN EDITION
Editrice Queriniana
Brescia, Italy